The Spirit–filled Believer's Daily Devotional

The Spirit–filled Believer's Daily Devotional

BY DICK MILLS
"Student of the Word Series"

Harrison House
Tulsa, OK

4th Printing

The Spirit–filled Believer's Daily Devotional
Revised Copyright © 1995 by Dick Mills
ISBN 0–89274–844–3
Copyright © 1990 by Dick Mills
P. O. Box 520
San Jacinto, California 92581

Published by Harrison House, Inc.
P. O. Box 35035
Tulsa, Oklahoma 74153

This inspirational devotional will take you through a full year of Bible study complete with Greek and Hebrew word studies. Here is what others are saying about Dick Mills and *The Spirit–filled Believer's Daily Devotional:*

The essence of Bible study, and, thereby, spiritual growth, is to grasp and receive the *spirit of the word.*

Every study resource that assists the penetration of the spirit *behind* the words which comprise the Holy Scriptures is worthy of communication and use. And on the grounds of study alone, I heartily encourage your pursuit of searching God's Word — the Bible — aided by this product of the scholarship of Dick Mills.

For my part, Dick Mills' character, ministry in the Word of God and prophetic gift continue to define the ministry of a prophet to the Body of Christ.

His Scripturally centered style and his submissiveness of spirit are the fountainhead of the authority with which he ministers.

Jack W. Hayford
Senior Pastor
The Church On The Way
Van Nuys, California

**From the beginning of the year to
the very end of the year.
Deuteronomy 11:12 NKJ**

This verse, which ended the old year, is also ideal for starting out a new year with eyes of faith. The whole passage assures God's people that He cares for their setting, surroundings, and situation in a fatherly way. He cares for their land. His eyes lovingly and with protective purpose are on them from the first day of the year to the last day of the year.

This is a verse for us. It assures that God's watchful care can be depended upon from January 1 right through until December 31, year in and year out. The Lord is telling us today just what He told the children of Israel in their day: "He who keeps you neither slumbers nor sleeps." (Ps. 121:4.) Our heavenly Father does not take days off, vacations, sick days or leaves of absence. His eyes are ever upon us. He cares for us just as much as He cared for the children of Israel. Our land is in His focus just as much as the land promised to the descendants of Abraham. Our Lord is concerned for our homes, our families, our transportation, our jobs, our places of worship, and our safety. None of these things escapes His sight.

You and I may have a tendency to rate certain days above others. You may have already marked out your calendar and circled all the special events during the coming year. This promise reassures us that as believers we are special to God; He keeps us in special consideration every day: "...from the beginning of the year to the very end of the year."

Be strong and of a good courage...
Joshua 1:9

Joshua 1:9 provides us with two words for looking ahead to the new year: **strength** and **courage.** The Lord issued this statement as a command to Joshua. Often we think of God's commandments as being strictly prohibitive ("thou shalt *not*"). Here the command is quite affirmative. The Bible tells us that the commandments of the Lord are not **grievous** (or cumbersome) (1 John 5:3).

The thing to remember is that each commandment given us by the Lord carries with it the enablement of its own fulfillment. That is, each command comes with an assurance that you and I are able to perform it. God, in His infinite love and mercy, would never issue an order we are not capable of carrying out.

Strength and courage are the two qualities the Lord demands of us as we face the unknown future. Strength and courage are ideal characteristics for making progress into the new year.

Courage is found in the inner man, and strength is shown in bodily action. This command coincides with Philippians 2:13 in which the Apostle Paul declares that it is the Lord who works in us both to will and to do of His good pleasure. Courage and strength are placed into our frame by the Lord. Courage motivates our will, and strength accompanies effort.

It is incongruous to say, "I have a lot of courage, but no strength," or, "I am a powerhouse of energy, but am afraid." The best confession is: "The Lord is my strength for this year. The Lord is my source of courage for this year."

The Lord will perfect that which concerns me ....
Psalm 138:8 NKJ

In English there are two words which are spelled **perfect**. Each has a different pronunciation and definition. *PER-fect* is an adjective referring to flawlessness or sinlessness. *Per-FECT* is a verb whose Biblical definition is "completion" or "termination."

This second word is the one which is used in this verse. The Lord will *per-FECT* that which concerns us. That is, the Lord will complete or terminate it.

Every area of our life is in a state of development. All of life is a learning process. The Lord is bringing us along by a timetable which has a divine design to it. None of us is standing still. Contrary to possible appearances, we are not spinning our wheels or merely treading water; we are making progress.

Our faith is growing. Our understanding of God's purposes is unfolding. Our knowledge of God's attributes is expanding. Our priority lists are constantly changing as we evaluate what is important to us and what is not.

Besides all the daily growth in our life of faith, we have a glorious destiny. The Lord is perfecting or completing us so we will be ready for His Second Coming. All our growth, development, and maturing is pointing to a grand and glorious consummation. The anticipation of the future meeting of the Lord Jesus Christ with His Church makes us patient during this perfecting process. The Lord has begun a good work in us, and we can be assured that He will bring it to completion. (Phil.1:6.) He has brought us thus far; He will take us onward. We can be confident that God loves us too much to leave us the way we are.

....As your days, so shall be your strength be.
Deuteronomy 33:25 NKJ

You and I are equal to any demands put upon us. Life presents many trying situations which can drain our resources and leave us depleted. This promise assures us that life will not leave us like an empty reservoir or a dry well. As the demands of each day, so shall our inner resources of strength be to make us equal to any situation.

Some days would leave us physically drained, but we draw on the Lord's inexhaustible supply of divine strength. Some days would place great financial strain on our budget, but the Lord's riches in glory are ours. Some days would leave us spiritually fatigued, but as our days so shall be our spiritual energy be. Mental fatigue is replaced by mental strength. Emotional strain is met with emotional strength.

Instead of the depressing prospect of becoming an empty reservoir drained dry of all resources, we now have a promise of a superabundance of everything we need for victorious Christian living. Instead of functioning solely on raw nerve power, we can now live each day in the realm of full supply. Say it out loud: "I'm equal to any demands put upon me." It's important to verbalize it: "As the day's requirements, so is the day's supply." Proclaim it gladly: "The need is met. I can face today with the assurance that my strength is more than sufficient for the demand of this day."

**"The year of My redeemed has come.
Isaiah 63:4 NKJ**

It is great to start the new year with hopes, aspirations, and dreams. We are highly motivated at the beginning of each new year thinking that perhaps this is the year "our ship will come in." Solomon expressed it this way: **Hope deferred makes the heart sick, but when the desire comes, it is a tree of life** (Prov. 13:12 NKJ).

In the verse above from Isaiah, the Lord is saying to us in so many words: "You have waited a long time for this, and now the time has arrived. It is here. This is your year. You are not going to have to wait any longer."

I believe that as you read these words a new hope will spring up inside you. I pray you will be quickened and energized by the Holy Spirit to believe for yourself that this is *your* year. *Your* time to go center stage has arrived. The seemingly endless period of waiting is over. The long dark night of walking by faith will soon be replaced by the dawning of *your* day of deliverance.

You have kept hope alive. You have held on to your dreams. You have believed in the vision the Lord gave you. You have stood upon the promise. Now this glorious assurance from the Lord breaks in on the scene: "The year of My redeemed has finally arrived." Victory at last!

I can do all things through Christ who strengthens me.
Philippians 4:13 NKJ

This statement of faith by the Apostle Paul carries with it an assurance of "in-strengthening" for every child of God.

The Greek word translated **strengthens** in this verse is *endunamoo (en–doo'–nam–o–o)*. It is made of up of two Greek words, *en* and *dunamoo*, which is derived from the root word *dunamis (doo'–nam–is)*. *En* is defined as "within," or "positioned as the instrument of action." *Dunamis* is the power resident within each individual believer because of the presence of the indwelling Holy Spirit.

Thus Paul's word to you and me is: "The Holy Spirit dwells within me. His dynamic power is not inactive or inoperative. He 'in-strengthens' me with such power and releases such force that I am made able to accomplish anything in accordance with God's will.

This is true of any Christian. Exploits can be done by any empowered and "in-strengthened" believer. Demons flee before the anointed saint of God. Fear vanishes, weaknesses are removed, poverty is banished, infirmities are overcome, obstacles disintegrated, and impossibilities obliterated.

Say it out loud: "I can do all things through Christ who 'in–strengthens' me." Say it often. Say it enthusiastically. Say it confidently: "I am going to make it, because God is *with* me, *for* me, and *in* me!"

For we are His workmanship....
Ephesians 2:10 NKJ

The original Greek word translated **workmanship** in this verse is *poiema (poy'–ay–mah)*, from which we derive our English word *poem*. Thus, in a sense, this verse tells us that we Christians are God's "poetry."

As believers, we have a new existence now that we knew nothing about when we were living in our sins. People's lives are either B.C. ("before conversion") or A.D. ("after deliverance"). B.C., our lives didn't make any sense. There was no rhyme or reason to them at all. Because of the sin in our hearts, we only lived for self-gratification. Our lives were in disharmony, discord and disarray. A.D., things took on a new symmetry. The Lord began bringing harmony where there had been disharmony. Gradually we became concordant instead of discordant. Bit by bit we were fashioned into God's *poiema*, His work of art, His "poem."

As people observe us they can see the work of God's grace in us. Because our lives are resonant, they "ring a bell" with unbelievers who can sense that our hearts vibrate in tune with the heartbeat of our heavenly Father. Thus we are God's artistic expression. Our lives reflect a purpose, a meaning, a message to fallen humanity that our Lord can take a life that is in total chaos and can turn it into His *poiema*, His workmanship.

I will work and who can hinder or reverse it?
Isaiah 43:13 AMP

For the Christian, deliverances and answers to prayer are always a result of divine intervention. Waiting for the answer to come, however, can cause spiritual tension. Especially when the answer is delayed. Negative or unchanging circumstances tend to produce impatience, anxiety, and doubt: "Will God hear me and help me, or not?" is often the question the weary soul asks.

What a reassurance then is this word from the Lord in Isaiah 43:13: "I *will* work. I *will* intervene. I *will* exert divine energy in your behalf. My power is being released. Your answer is on its way." Ten thousand malevolent voices may be screaming at you that your situation is different, that things will never turn out right for you, that your deliverance will never come. These are the voices of the accuser and his hosts of demons; they are lying vanities. But when the voice of the Lord pierces through the gloom and despair with these reassuring words, "I *will* work," all the harassing demons of doubt, fear, and uncertainty are immediately silenced.

...**I will work**....is a word of truth that builds faith and confidence; it steadies the soul to a posture of assured expectancy.

...**And who can hinder or reverse it?** lets us know that God's power can flood in on us in such a powerful way that no earthly or devilish force can possibly hold it back. A person may as well stand on the beach with a broom in his hand trying to sweep back the incoming tide as to attempt to reverse the flow of God's blessing into the lives of those whom He has determined to bless.

The joy of the Lord is your strength.
Nehemiah 8:10 NKJ

This word translated **strength** has a military connotation. The original Hebrew word is *ma'owz* *(maw–oze')* and indicates a fortified place, a citadel, a place of defense or a stronghold. Thus, the joy of the Lord is our fortified place, our place of safety and protection.

Since I was the only born-again, Spirit-filled person in a barracks of 24 men, my military experience was a time of extreme testing. Standing alone against ridicule, rejection, social ostracism, group humiliation, and constant verbal harassment made this one of the most difficult times of my entire life. The Lord graciously compensated me for it by giving me holy laughter and overwhelming joy. I had so much inner joy during that three-year period that it seemed like an inward buoyancy was suspending me. The more the demonic hostility surfaced, the more inwardly fortified I became with the joy of the Lord. I understood what the Apostle Peter meant when he wrote: **If ye be reproached for the name of Christ, happy are ye....**(1 Pet. 4:14).

The happiness that we experience at the human level always comes as a result of good things happening to us. In the spiritual walk of faith, happiness can be imparted to us even when bad things are taking place in our lives. When things go wrong and our Christian witness is being violently opposed or even mildly criticized, God imparts His tranquilizing joy that takes all the pain of ridicule and rejection from us. The joy the Lord gives us is our stronghold. It is a place of safety were Satan's darts cannot touch us.

**Now the manifold wisdom of God might
be made known by the church to the principalities
and powers in the heavenly places.
Ephesians 3:10 NKJ**

This word **manifold** is very interesting. It is the word used in the Septuagint to describe Joseph's coat of many colors. Designer fabrics in Bible days were usually made of one solid tint. Joseph's coat of many (manifold) colors was a radical departure from the custom of that day.

The verse we are looking at here assures that God's wisdom has a great deal of variety to it. Human methodologies tend to become structured. Whenever spontaneity does occur, our tendency is to imitate it, syndicate it, franchise it, and capitalize off of it until it becomes one of our set traditions. Not so with God. It is through His Church that His much-varied and multi-colored wisdom is to be displayed to the principalities and powers in the heavenly places. During the first two centuries of its existence, the Church displayed one shade or special tint of God's wisdom. The Reformation showed forth another hue. Wesley and his revivals demonstrated another facet of wisdom. Restoration movements and renewal groups all display hues, tints, and shades of divine wisdom.

In the ending of the Church Age, there will be yet new demonstrations of divine wisdom. This means that all the shades and hues of God's manifold wisdom have not yet been exhausted. In the days ahead we will be seeing new expressions of divine wisdom never before displayed. Be ready for new dimensions of God's many-colored and much-varied wisdom.

**If two of you agree on earth concerning
anything that they ask, it will be done for
them by My Father in heaven.
Matthew 18:19 NKJ**

In giving us this promise of answered prayer, Jesus used a musical term. In the original Greek the word translated **agree** is *sumphoneo (soom–fo–neh'–o)*. It is a compound word. *Sum* means "with" or "together." *Phoneo* is a form of the word *phone* meaning "sound."

So *sum-phoneo* means "to sound together." It is from this compound word that we get our word *symphony*. Imagine how symphonic prayer must sound in heaven! Prayers of agreement are melodic. Praying without agreement produces disharmony and discord.

Jesus is encouraging not only the blending of voices, but the harmonizing of wills, hearts, souls, and minds. It is an accomplishment to bring people together to worship the Lord. It is an even greater achievement to get them to sit in silence and receive instruction. The ultimate in church harmony is for everyone to agree or harmonize in prayer and praise.

This verse is the great equalizer. Leaders and followers can agree. New converts and old veteran saints can blend. Rich and poor, educated and uneducated, conspicuous and inconspicuous believers can all pray together in unity, harmony and symphony. What a joy to know that agreeing in prayer brings desired results. For the sake of answered prayer, we need to set aside personal preferences and harmoniously blend our prayers with others. The symphony of sound moves heaven to action for all of us.

Praise is awaiting You, O God, in Zion ....
Psalm 65:1 NKJ

The original Hebrew version of this verse reads: "Praise is silent before You, O God, in Zion...." This "silent praise" (as one writer has defined it) is not a resignation or a submission. It is a silence that comes from the sense of majestic awesomeness and expectancy that knows deliverance is at hand.

Resignation has an air of futility, finality, and fatalism about it. It really robs one of spiritual aggression, spiritual ambition, or spiritual desire. Praise is silent, but not for the wrong reasons.

Submission often implies an uncertainty as to God's will. The voice of submission says: "Since you do not know what God's will is in this situation, it is best to be docile and submit to whatever comes along." The problem with this attitude and approach is that it teaches people to humbly submit to and patiently endure many things they should be vigorously opposing. Uncertainty about God's will leads to submission to fear, poverty, sickness, discouragement, intimidation, and insecurity. Such negative things are not to be submitted to; they are to be refused.

Praise is silent before the Lord. This kind of silence is a majestic expression of faith, confidence and expectancy. It is outward evidence of an inner peace which says: "I have prayed, fasted and confessed the Word of God. I have received the promise. Now, free from any stress, tension or pressure, my soul quietly waits for the manifestation of my answer." Knowing that the answer is forthcoming produces a calm repose which can praise in total silence.

**For all the promises of God in Him are Yes,
and in Him Amen, to the glory of God ....
2 Corinthians 1:20 NKJ**

The test of validity of a promise is its performance. In Luke 1:45 we are told in essence: "...There will be a fulfillment of those things promised you by the Lord." So, standing on a promise from God is not mere wishful thinking or clinging to an impossible dream. A promise from the Lord carries with it its own assurance of fulfillment. In Numbers 23:19, the writer says of God: **"...Has He said, and will He not do it? Or has He spoken, and will He not make it good?"** (NKJ).

But between promise and performance is a time frame marked *patience*. It is harder to wait than to move. It is easier to run than to stand still. Waiting for an answer that seems unnecessarily delayed is not really to our liking.

Patiently waiting is valuable because the Lord has instruction for us. While we are waiting, He has our attention. We are ready for correction...reproof...personality adjustment...lessons in obedience. In our times of waiting we learn that we cannot program God, instead we must place our total trust and reliance in Him. We come to realize that the Lord is our sole source of supply.

The benefit of the patient time is two–fold: 1) we receive the answer which is so encouraging to our faith, and 2) we learn valuable lessons of trust and reliance. We learn the power of confessing the promises of God and of obedience to the leading of the Holy Spirit. Not only does a promise assure an answer, it also assures us of valuable instruction in the school of faith!

Thy visitation has preserved my spirit.
Job 10:12

There are several reasons for the Lord's visitation:

1) The Lord visits us as a doctor makes a house call. The doctor does not come to see us for social purposes. His coming is not for afternoon tea with relaxing conversation. Neither is the Lord's visitation. Like the doctor, He wants to "tune us up" spiritually so we can experience the best of spiritual health. By His coming, He is really looking out for our best interests.

2) Visitation is like a military inspection. The purpose behind inspection is to check to see if the troops are properly equipped and attired for combat. Our Commander-in-Chief Jesus Christ has issued us the whole armor of God, including the sword of the Spirit. Then He inspects us to see if we are wearing that armor and wielding that sword.

3) Visitation is a search, a test, and an exploration. The Lord visits us primarily to test our reactions. A pure heart is vital for spiritual health. He searches and explores the depths of our heart. This helps us to discover resentment, bitterness, and unforgiveness. We could read this verse: "...your exploring search is a preservative to my spirit."

4) Visitation is providential care. We could also read this verse: "...your care for me preserves my spirit." Job asks the Lord: "What is man that you care for him the way you do?" (Job 7:18.) This care watches over our progress, looks us over for improvement, prepares us for the future, and leads to our perfection. Do not fear the Lord's visitation. It is for our good. It will not destroy us, but will preserve us.

And from the days of John the Baptist until
now the kingdom of heaven suffers violence,
and the violent take it by force.
Matthew 11:12 NKJ

This verse is an encouragement to intercessors. The
word **violent** speaks volumes to us. A violent person is
defined as "one who feels an eager, vehement desire for
something." Praying people understand such language.
Some other possible translations of this verse are:

"...the kingdom of heaven is eagerly sought and
forcibly snatched at. The forceful press forward through
vehement desire and pursue it eagerly." "...the kingdom of
Heaven has been taken by storm and eager men are forcing
their way into it." "...the kingdom of heaven has been
rushed. The impetuous seize it by force."

In our times, the lateness of the day, the brevity of the
hour, the hostility of our enemies, the desperation of our
society, the urgency of the situation, the vital need of the
20th-century Church is all we really need to incite and
excite intense prayer.

Like a fortress in war, the kingdom of heaven must be
taken by storm. He who besieges the throne of grace by
faith and prayer is sure to prevail. Like a crowd bursting
into a house and like an army taking a city, this is no time
for hesitation or delay. Those who wrestle in prayer, those
who will not be denied, those who strive will succeed.

For praying people, Matthew 11:12 could read: "The
kingdom of heaven has available great answers to prayer.
The determined, persistent, fervent and energetic take it by
storm." What an incentive for a consistent disciplined life of
prayer!

The yoke shall be destroyed
because of the anointing.
Isaiah 10:27

The yoke shall be destroyed because of the anointing. The thought expressed is that the Holy Spirit's empowering of our lives turns the dull, drab routine existence into an invigorating, exciting, exhilarating experience. Prayer can change from lifeless formality to energized petition by the anointing of the Holy Spirit. Song services looked upon as a preliminary "warmer-upper" can become exciting worship to the Lord by the anointing of the Spirit. Preaching that is MONOTONOUS and BORING can become ALIVE and STIMULATING by the anointing of the Spirit. Witnessing that is dreary, drab drudgery performed out of compulsion and guilt can easily become electrifying by the anointing of the Holy Spirit. With this anointing upon us, you and I can face the future with confidence, expecting that our circumstances are not going to keep us in bondage.

In Isaiah 58:6 the Lord says: **Is not this the fast that I have chosen?...that ye break every yoke?** The anointing of the Holy Spirit on our lives not only will break the yoke that is intended to keep us in bondage, but will also enable us to reach out to others and break the yokes that are keeping them in personal subjection.

Psalm 92:10 says that you and I will be anointed with fresh oil. Our God refreshes us so we can refresh others. He invigorates us so we can invigorate others. He liberates us so we can liberate others. The yoke shall be destroyed because of the invigorating, refreshing anointing of the Holy Spirit.

A still small voice.
1 Kings 19:12 NKJ

The Hebrew word translated **still** here comes from the root word *damam (daw–mam')* which is an imitation of the sound made with the mouth shut, such as dmmmm or hmmmm. It applies to the sound made by one who is lost in wonder and astonishment. It is also used to refer to hearing someone without their speaking — a voice of silence.

I believe this passage of scripture has a great deal to say to us as individuals. I believe the Lord wants us to function free of stress. The Prince of Peace has a majestic quality of serenity and composure to exhibit to a tense and hyper world. The nonbeliever living in a tension-filled climate of stress and anxiety is unable to cope with life's hassle. The Christian, by contrast, has been promised **quietness and assurance for ever** (Is. 32:17). We believers are like an island of peace in a sea of turmoil. This "still small voice" represents to us a total absence of agitation and turmoil. We have something to give to a world that is in trouble and desperately calling for help.

The significance of the still small voice in Elijah's case can be measured by the end result it produced. After heeding it, his depression was gone, his courage revived, his calling restored, and his strength renewed. He was able to return to his normal duties without fear and with a new appreciation of God's gentle dealings. The same still small voice is speaking to you and me today. It is the voice of Jesus saying to us: **Take my yoke upon you, and learn of me; for I am meek and lowly in heart: and ye shall find rest unto your souls. For my yoke is easy, and my burden is light** (Matt. 11:29,30).

**For I know the plans I have for you, declares
the Lord, plans to prosper you and not to harm
you, plans to give you a hope and a future.**
Jeremiah 29:11 NIV

In other translations the Lord assures us in a variety of ways that He has good things in store for us: "plans for peace, not disaster"; "thoughts of peace and not of hurt"; "intentions of prosperity, and not suffering"; "to make you happy and not to harm you." It is your welfare I have in mind," He assures us, "not your undoing." In a world full of bad news where the mood of pessimism is strong, it is good for us believers to hear from the Lord Himself that He has good plans for us.

God has promised us a hope and a future. This age is not the post-Christian-era, as some are saying, because we are assured of a future. There are yet chapters to be written in the history of the Body of Christ.

One writer says of God's plans for His people that it is His purpose to give them literally an end and hope. End is like "happy ending" or "reward." He is the covenant God of unchanging grace. His plans concerning His people are always thoughts of good, of blessing. There is not a single item of evil in His plans for His people; neither in their motive, nor in their revelation, or in their consummation. All is good, all is blessing.

This verse can be claimed by you for your personal comfort and encouragement. God's plan for *you* are good plans, giving you so much to look forward to. You have so much to live for! Instead of despair, you have hope. All because of Him!

In a moment, in the twinkling of an eye....
1 Corinthians 15:52 NKJ

Paul describes the Second Coming of Christ as happening in a **moment.** In the Greek New Testament this word is *atomos (at'–om– os).* It is the word from which we derive our English words *atom* and *atomic.*

Paul had in his vocabulary the following words to indicate time: *millennium* (1,000 years), *century* (100 years), *decade* (10 years), *year, season, month, week, day,* and *hour.* (These are all Bible words. Paul did not have the words *minute* and *second;* these came later). Yet when describing the return of the Lord, none of these words would suffice. The Holy Spirit inspired Paul to write "in an *atomos,*" "in the twinkling of an eye." Jesus is coming in an atomic second. A second can be calibrated to a half-second, a tenth of a second, a hundredth of a second, even a thousandth of a second. But an atomic second is a unit which is incapable of being further divided.

We are not expecting the world to slowly improve in quality until at last the golden age will be ushered in. The Bible tells us conversely that perilous times are ahead. But it also tells us that Jesus is coming back to redeem His Church in an atomic second.

Since none of us knows when that atomic second will click off, our attitude and stance is one of hope. We live in what the Bible calls a blessed hope. We know a better day is coming. Some day, in an atomic second, Jesus will return!

Throughout the time of your sojourning....
1 Peter 1:17 NKJ

One Biblical word for **time** is the Greek word used here in this verse, *chronos (khron'–os)*. *Chronicles, chronic, chronological,* and *chronometer* are some of the English words which can be tracked back to this word. *Chronos* refers to time by the clock, time by duration, time that can be measured.

The Apostle Peter says that all believers in Christ are to pass the time *(chronos)* of their sojourn here in reverence. This reference points out the lapse of time involved between accepting the Lord into one's life and the event of being ushered into His physical presence. Bible writers are telling us to spend that intervening time wisely, not carelessly. In this case, *chronos* refers to a duration of time that has a definite starting point (the New Birth), a progress (our walk of faith), and a consummation (the Second Coming of Jesus). Time should never weigh heavy in the life of a Christian. Each tick of the clock brings us closer to the glorious realization of Christ physically appearing to us.

God eternal, dateless, and ageless introduced time only for our convenience. *Chronos* allows us to relate to the past historically, to interpret the present realistically, and to face the future confidently. Our heavenly Father originated time. He controls time. One day He will bring time *(chronos)* to an end and will usher us into eternal life. That life has no clock, no calendar, and no schedule. But it does have meaning and purpose. The one outstanding feature of eternity is unceasing fellowship with our Lord. When our earthly sojourn is over, time will be swallowed up in eternity.

Redeeming the time....
Ephesians 5:16 NKJ

This verse contains an illuminating Greek word for **time**: *kairos (kahee–ros')*. This is time adapted to circumstances. *Kairos* can be defined as: 1) A set time for action, 2) the right moment, 3) the opportune point of time when a thing should be done, or 4) the time appointed to accomplish a certain task.

In Ephesians 5:16 we are admonished by Paul to "redeem" the time (*kairos*) appointed to us by the Lord. Newer translations render this phrase, "buying up the opportunity", indicating we need a natural acumen to help us to interpret our spiritual opportunities. Revelation 12:12 says that Satan is furious because he knows his time (*kairos*) is short. His opportunities for going to and fro will shortly be curtailed. Part of the reason he is so furious is because he knows that his restless roaming will soon terminate in his being chained to the bottomless pit.

In 1 Chronicles 12:32 of the Greek Old Testament, we read that the children of Issachar had understanding of the time (*kairos*) to know what Israel ought to do. The distinctive feature of the children of Issachar is their sensitivity to their situation. They not only were cognizant of their opportunities, but also had a wise plan of action. As Christians we must remember that opportunities we have today will not last forever. Jesus said it succinctly: **"I must work the works of Him who sent Me while it is day; the night is coming when no one can work"** (John 9:4 NKJ). The tribe of Issachar had a contemporary understanding of their surrounding society and all its problems. They were also able to determine the best course to take. We can, too!

Nor give place to the devil.
Ephesians 4:27 NKJ

In the original Greek the word **place** reads *topos* *(top'–os)*. From this word *topos* we derive our English words *topography* and *topographic*. It has to do with place, locality or territory. This verse admonishes us to be so consistent, so dependable, and so trustworthy in our walk of faith that we surrender no *topos* — no ground — to the enemy . The stratagem of our adversary is to exploit our weaknesses or catch us off guard. When he can find an opening in our armor, he can weaken our effectiveness. In Ephesians 4:27, the Apostle Paul exhorts us to avoid giving the devil an opportunity.

Never give the adversary any topography *(topos)*. As believers we have the possibility of making forward progress without ever having to lose any ground.

By putting on the whole armor of God, it is possible to have the entire Christian personality and character completely covered. We can stand our ground in the battle between light and darkness, good and evil. (2 Sam. 23:12.) We can stand and, having done all, continue to stand. (Eph. 6:13.) Best of all, we can move ahead even though every inch of our progress is contested. (Ex. 14:15.) And we can be assured that God is with us to help us and to fight our battles. (2 Chron. 32:8.) For the believer, there is no turning back, no lost ground, nothing but continual forward progress in the good fight of faith.

They shall be fat and flourishing.
Psalm 92:14

This promise in Psalm 92:14 is for faithful and abiding believers. The end result of their consistency is that they will be **fat and flourishing.**

English words have changed a great deal since the year of our Lord 1611. In our days, *fat* refers to obesity; it has a connotation of overweight and being out of shape. At the time the *King James Bible* was written, however, to the English-speaking Christian the word *fat* meant "blessed with God's prosperous abundance".

The original Hebrew word translated **fat** in this verse is *dashen (daw–shane')*. Various lexicons define this word as "fresh," "rich," "fertile," "affluent," "abundant," "wealthy," and "satiated." This promise is an assurance of a fruitful life for those who have been faithful in the house of the Lord. They are also assured a life of consistency and stability. The verse ends in the *King James Version* with these words: **...they shall be fat and flourishing.** A look at other translations gives us a wider range of expression:

"...they will be fertile and full of growth." "...always green and strong." "...fair and desirable." "...vital and green." "...full of life and vitality". Others translate this phrase: "...they shall still multiply; and continue prosperous." "...their lives are rich and productive..." One version reads: "...and even when advanced in years they shall, like tall and sturdy trees, bring forth good fruit for years to come."

So the Biblical definition of *fat* is not "corpulent" (body heaviness), but "opulent" (having abundant resources).

And my God shall supply all your need...
Philippians 4:19 NKJ

In researching particular verses, we notice that certain words have the great possibility of further augmentation.

One such case is the word **supply** here in Philippians 4:19: **And my God shall** *supply* **all your need...** In the original Greek New Testament this word is *pleroo (play–ro'–o)*. It is akin to another great word *pleroma (play'–ro–mah)* used to describe the fullness of God.

Pleroo is a verb infinitive meaning "to fill to the full." It might be defined as "to cram the net," "to fill up a hollow place," "to cause to abound," "to load down," "to fill the stomach," "to fill the void," "to pay off a debt," "to complete a person so that there is no lack in him." By consulting certain key lexicons and translations, we could translate this verse to read: "But my God shall [liberally, fully, gloriously, amply, abundantly] supply all your need [by imparting richly and furnishing abundantly, in a lavish and magnificent way]..."

Try reading out loud as one composite verse all the above amplifications and I believe you will be quickened by the Holy Spirit to discover the immensity of God's provision.

We should notice that God's promise to supply all our need was spoken to those who had voluntarily and sacrificially given of their means to relieve the needs of one of God's servants. It is the abiding Christian whose heart is sensitive toward God and His people who has been given the Lord's promise for the supply of all his needs.

He who supplies the Spirit to you...
Galatians 3:5 NKJ

In this verse the word **supplies** is the Greek word
choregeo (khor–ayg–eh'–o). The history of this word is
illuminating and inspiring. It comes from the Greek word
choros (khor–os') which referred to the ring in which round
dances were held (hence our word *chorus*). It came to be
both a noun meaning "a chorus leader" and a verb meaning
"to lead a chorus of singers." Later it was applied to the act
of furnishing the chorus at one's own expense, to supplying
everything necessary for the entire production. At the
community level, it became a position of honor and
importance to *"choregeo"* any function, because of the great
personal expense involved.

The word thus suggests an abundant supply, both
materially and spiritually. So we could translate this
phrase: "...He Who *lavishes* the Spirit on you...," or "...the
One Who is constantly supplying the Spirit to you *in
bountiful measure...*"

Paul is not writing to these people of one single isolated
incident of God's provision in their lives. Rather, he is
referring to a continuous floodtide of answered prayers,
miracles, healings and deliverances. Although unbelievers
may question God's existence or His provision, the believer
soon discovers a lavish supply of blessing from His
generous nature.

God is the patron, the sponsor, the "angel," the backer
— the *choregeo* — the One Who has underwritten lavishly
the total cost of our lifetime walk with Him. Jesus paid the
total price of our redemption. Accepting Him starts us on a
journey that is fully and lavishly provided for — from New
Birth to New Jerusalem.

The gates of hell shall not prevail...
Matthew 16:18

In Bible days the gates of the city were the ordinary place for transacting business, administering justice and conducting trials. People met there to discuss news, engage in commerce (buying and selling), and make communal plans. Lot sat in the gates of Sodom. (Gen:9:1.) Abraham negotiated a land purchase with Ephron in the gates of the city. (Gen. 23:10.) Sometimes the word *gates* (or *gate*) conveys the idea of people meeting in a forum setting to discuss and decide outcomes of certain issues. In Genesis 34:20, two men, Hamor and Shechem, came to the gate and in a forum asked if Israel would approve of a marriage between Shechem and Dinah. Boaz conducted the kinsman redemption of Ruth with the elders in the gates. (Ruth 4:1.) Eli conducted priestly administration in the gates. (1 Sam. 4:13.) Absalom made kingly decisions in the gates while stealing the hearts of the people away from his father David. (2 Sam. 15:2.) Nehemiah 8:1 tells us that Ezra the scribe read the law to the people gathered together in the broad place before the water gate.

The Greek word translated *gates* in Matthew 16:18 is *pule (poo'–lay)*. The gates stood for those who governed or administered justice there. Jesus was telling us that neither the plots and strategies nor the strength of Satan and his angels will ever prevail against His Church. The gates of death are a citadel. The Church of Jesus Christ is a stronghold built on a firm foundation: "All the plots, stratagems and crafty plans of the enemies of the Church shall not overcome it." This promise has been remarkably fulfilled.

Thinketh no evil.
1 Corinthians 13:5

The brain of modern man has been compared to a complex computer. Information is constantly being fed into it, each occurring incident in life being stored away in its inner recesses.

Many behavioral activities are a result of (or result in) the recall or retrieval of data stored away in the brain's "memory bank." In 1 Corinthians 13:5 when Paul wrote that love **thinketh no evil,** in the language of his day he used a metaphor concerning love that was a description of an accountant filing information into a bookkeeping system.

The Greek word translated **thinketh** is *logizomai (log–id'– zom–ahee)*. This word is traced back to *logos (log'–os)* which is defined basically as "a word; speech; a declaration; a matter; an account." *Logizomai* takes the word *account* and makes it into *accountant* — one who keeps records. Life is one big ledger, with our minds and hearts recording and reacting to all the debits and credits, positives and negatives, pluses and minuses which we encounter day by day.

Paul is saying that love (*agape* – the divine love of God in our heart and life as a fruit of the Spirit) does not count up the evil done to it with a view to settling the account. Love does not enter offenses into a notebook for future revenge. Love keeps no record of evil done to it. It has no memory of injuries. *Love is a poor accountant.* It would prefer to leave a blank page in our "memory bank" than to record all the distasteful things that happen to us. Thank the Lord for such a poor bookkeeper as divine love!

They have proved to be a comfort to me.
Colossians 4:11 NKJ

In Colossians 4:10,11 Paul names three dear Christian friends who were a comfort to him: Aristarchus, Mark and Justus. The Greek word translated **comfort** in this passage is *paregoria (par–ay–gor–ee'–ah).* It is from this word that we get our English word *paregoric* which is a medicine that soothes and settles. Rubbed on the gums of teething infants, it immediately brings soothing relief to irritated tissues.

Paul, in a Roman prison, is chafing. He is irritated. The prison has no air-conditioning, no creature comforts, and no room service. Paul is suffering most of all from the inconvenience, the delays the wasted time spent chained up to a Roman guard. In His mercy and grace, the Lord sends three men to act as a "paregoric" to Paul. They soothe him. They calm him down and refresh him in spirit.

You can either be an irritant or a balm. You can hurt or you can heal. You can be part of the problem or part of the solution.

It is interesting to note that Job had three "consolers." He ended up calling them **miserable comforters** (Job 16:2) because they added to his grief instead of relieving it. Here Paul lists three consolers who were true comforters.

Only by being indwelt by the Divine Comforter, the Holy Spirit, can we bring needed comfort to others.

Blessed be the God of all comfort, who comforts us in all our adverse circumstances, so we can comfort others in their adversity with the same comfort with which we have been comforted. (2 Cor. 1:3-4.)

He gives His beloved sleep.
Psalm 127:2 NKJ

This verse is to remind us that a good night's sleep is really a gift from the Lord.

Since God's whole nature is giving, this word from Psalm 127:2 stresses that He is continuously giving, even while we are asleep. The *Good News Bible* translates this verse by saying that the Lord provides for those He loves while they are asleep. One writer stated that God works when men do not work at all. He blesses and prospers them without any effort on their part. He blesses all who love Him whether they know it or not. He blesses and furthers the work of spiritual life even while we work not. He blesses us silently, as if in the watches of the night, when we are all unconscious of it. Yes, truly He does give to His beloved while they sleep.

Not only does the Lord give physical refreshment to His beloved in their times of repose, He also has other things to give them while they sleep. Guidance can come while the conscious mind is at rest. (Job 33:14-16.) In the Bible we read of warnings which were given to key people while they were asleep. Healings, deliverances, visions, courage, strength, and new insights often come to saints during the sleep process. Gifts of spiritual illumination and direction have come through sleep. When God shuts the door of the senses, He opens the door into the spirit. Many times He gives His beloved thoughts of truth and desires for good that surprises them when they awake. *The Amplified Bible* sums it all up: **...He gives [blessings] to His beloved in (their) sleep.** James Moffatt adds: **...God's gifts come to his loved ones, as they sleep.**

Forgetting those things which are behind and reaching forward to those things which are ahead.
Philippians 3:13 NKJ

Wouldn't it be wonderful if we could open the top of our head like a lid, reach inside our brain, and clear out all the traumatic memories? The next step would be to put the lid back on and go on our way with a mind cleared of painful and hurtful associations with our past.

It can be done. This verse tells us that we can turn 180 degrees from looking into our past and can begin to confidently peer into the future.

One time a very godly person had a vision of me bound to past memories. A prayer went up: "Lord, free Dick Mills from being chained to the past, even if You have to give him a vision to do so." It happened that very evening while I was in prayer. I saw a vivid picture of myself sitting in a chair with chains linking me to the past. I could see many signposts all in a row. The closest signpost was marked with the date of the preceding year. The one behind it showed the date of the year before that. There were twenty posts in all, receding in time. (I was 24 when this event took place.) In the picture I was chained to all twenty of those past years of my life. My back was to the future and I was facing the past. In desperation I cried out to God: "Lord, I will never be able to adequately minister to the needs of people until these chains are removed. Dear Jesus, free me from this bondage." This verse in Philippians 3:13 and others came to me, and immediately the chains came off. I did a complete turn around. I was gloriously freed so I could get on with what the Lord had called me to do.

The wicked one (Satan) does not touch him.
1 John 5:18 NKJ

Here is a precious promise assuring you and me of immunity from Satan's assaults. He cannot touch us. We are covered with a divine protection that wards off direct attack. Unprotected people become victims of a hateful enemy who goes around as a devourer, but in Christ we are protected.

In the Greek this word translated **touch** is *haptomai (hap'– tom–ahee)*. It gives the picture of a wedge being driven between the believer and his God with the idea of separating him from his divine source or connection. It is also used in what is called the "middle voice." This means that a person acts on his own for his own purposes. Though our foe be malicious and hostile, he cannot pick us out as his target and sever us from God. You and I are united to the Lord. We are welded to our God, glued to our Savior. The enemy would like to get the wedge in, but he cannot. That wicked one cannot touch us. (Luke 10:19.) No one, not even Satan, can sever our relationship with Christ.

Early in life I had a fear of Satan overwhelming me like a flood and sweeping me away from God's protective care. The Lord helped me by giving me a mental picture of myself in a heavily fortified citadel. Satan was outside screaming threats and vile accusations. Somehow I felt safe, secure, and peaceful, like a person in a comfortable home by a fireplace while a bad storm rages outside. That is when this verse came to me: "The enemy by his own design cannot attack you or assult you in order to sever you from God's tender loving care or your peace of trust and rest."

**My presence will go with you,
and I will give you rest.
Exodus 33:14 NKJ**

Rest is total absence from stress, conflict, turmoil, tension and hassle. This is not a rest "from" activity, but a rest "in" the midst of activity. Have you not been impressed by certain people who seem to be the epitome of composure and total serenity while everyone else around them is going to pieces or "coming unglued"? What is it that allows these people to show such inner strength and continual tranquility?

Years ago, the old saints of God called this state of continual peace and quiet "the rest of faith." The writer of Hebrews assures us: **There remains therefore a rest for the people of God** (Heb. 4:9 NKJ). He also exhorts us to make every effort to enter into that rest. This rest is a place of faith that allows us to function free of stress, tension and pressure. In that place we can be at rest while going about our normal activities of life, while busy with our responsibilities. This almost seems like a contradiction in terms: resting while laboring...resting while exerting energy. This is not laziness, shirking duties, neglecting responsibilities, or sleeping on guard.

Rest is the capacity to function at full capacity and strength all the while sustained by an "in-working," "in-strengthening," God-given ability. Jesus as our role model is a good example. He was never caught off guard or taken by surprise. Even when trick questions were thrown at Him, He handled His opponents with a disarming ease. His inner peace kept Him unruffled even in the face of resistance and opposition. In this verse, He promises us that same inner peace and rest.

To another...special faith...
1 Corinthians 12:8,9 Weymouth, N.T.

This verse refers to the gift of faith that God has for each of us to equip us for any special need that may arise in our life. One translator calls it "heroic faith." Another scholar calls it "wonder-working faith." This promise lets us know that we do not have to be anxious or insecure about the days to come. Some people dread the uncertain future and are tense and nervous as they look ahead to tomorrow. Some carry on as though the fuse has been lit and now we are waiting for the bomb to go off.

The gift of faith is special to the occasion. It rests in the confidence that Jesus is the same yesterday, today, and forever. (Heb. 13:8.) The gift of faith confidently states: "God has met us in the past, He is meeting us in the present, and we know He will still meet us in the future. He brought us out to bring us in. He has brought us this far and He will see us through." (2 Cor. 1:10.) When the Lord imparts this gift of special faith to us, great peace and inward calm comes to our soul. Our spirit confidently proclaims to us: "It shall be well with you." (Is. 3:10.)

Aren't you glad the future is all known to the Lord? Aren't you glad the steps of the righteous are ordered by the Lord? (Ps. 37:23.) For all emergencies and special times of need that may arise, He has the gift of "special" faith just for you. It is the God-given ability to trust your situation into His hands and see Him work it out for your comfort and for His glory. Special faith is yours for the asking!

**To him who overcomes I will grant
to sit with Me on My throne...
Revelation 3:21 NKJ**

In the book of Revelation, each of the seven churches in Asia is promised a different reward for overcoming the flesh, the world and the devil. These rewards include the privilege of eating of the tree of life and the hidden manna, power over the nations, being clothed in white raiment, and being made a pillar in the temple of God. The last church mentioned was Laodicea. The reward offered them was this promise to be enthroned with Jesus in a place of glory and honor.

There are many similarities between tendencies of the Laodiceans and the modern-day Church. Their lukewarmness, complacency, smugness, and spiritual conceit are characteristics we see prevalent in many of our churches today.

I used to think the greatest rewards were reserved for the martyrs. Surely, I thought, giving up one's life for the cause of Christ would bring great rewards. Second on my reward list were the missionaries. If anybody deserved special rewards for self-sacrifice, doubtless was this group of brave people who have given up everything to go witness to foreign people.

But the truth is, the greatest reward is promised to those who can keep a zeal alive, a flame of devotion, and a spiritual intensity in a world filled with apathy and spiritual indifference. Keeping the fire of the Holy Ghost burning in the midst of ineptitude, mediocrity, and spiritual lethargy results in the privilege of sitting on the throne with Jesus.

Wisdom and knowledge will be the
stability of your times...
Isaiah 33:6 NKJ

Wisdom and knowledge go together like a husband and wife. They complete each other.

Knowledge is facts; it is informational. Wisdom is understanding; it is directive, procedural. Knowledge provides data needed to be informed and aware. Wisdom provides the insight necessary to know how to proceed based on facts at hand. For example, Noah had the facts about the coming worldwide flood 120 years before it arrived on the scene. But he really didn't know what to do about that flood until a word of wisdom came to him saying, "Build an ark."

You and I can be intuitively and sensitively cognizant of coming events in our own life. But knowledge alone is not enough. We need to wait for wisdom to show us how to proceed. James tells us if anyone lacks wisdom, it is available for the asking.

Lot and Abraham both knew that Sodom was going to end up at the bottom of the Dead Sea. Abraham knew it a week before it happened, and Lot knew it a day ahead of time. To those who are truly in tune with the Lord, knowledge always comes first because God is omniscient; He knows *all* things. Proverbs 14:6 says that knowledge is **easy** to the person who understands. (NKJ) There is not anything the Lord doesn't know. He even invites His children to be curious enough about their future to ask Him about it. (Jer. 33:3.) Once we have done that, once we have the facts, then we are to inquire and ask for wisdom and direction. With both wisdom *and* knowledge, we are standing on solid ground.

**For the iniquity of the Amorites
is not yet complete.
Genesis 15:16 NKJ**

Here the Lord is telling Abraham that occupancy of the
land promised to his descendants can only take place when
the depravity of the Amorites who lived there has reached
its zenith. This event took place over 400 years later. The
land literally vomited out the Amorites because of their
total degeneracy and depravity. It was then that Israel was
able to go in and possess the land as their inheritance.

This event explains why the Lord Jesus has not yet
returned to the earth. Over 318 verses in the New Testament
point to Christ's Second Coming. Right now we are seeing
all the malignant forces of evil heading towards a
culmination of total depravity. This action will produce the
man of sin — the antichrist. He will be spawned in a
garbage-can society that reeks of filth and degradation.

At the same time all this is taking place, a work of
righteousness is being developed and orchestrated in God's
people. The loving, compassionate nature of Christ is being
implanted and formed in our hearts. Hate in the world is
making the sinners more like Satan. Love in the Christians
is making us more like Jesus. Earthly, sensual and devilish
wisdom is fully demonstrated in Satan's followers. The
pure and holy wisdom from above is conspicuous in the
followers of Jesus. When the iniquity of the latter-day
Amorites reaches its saturation point, the righteousness of
the bride of Christ will produce the Second Coming of
Jesus. (Rev. 19:7.)

**The people who know their God shall
be strong, and carry out great exploits.
Daniel 11:32 NKJ**

This verse covers life during times of great stress,
pressure, and turmoil. It is not speaking of a time of
unparalleled peace, prosperity, and plenty. It is a promise
that shows us how to survive in a climate of international
tension, economic upheaval, and spiritual change. This
word from the Lord tells us that persecution of the
Christians will result in greater knowledge ("they shall
know their God"), greater strength ("they shall be strong"),
and greater miracles ("they shall carry out great exploits").
The more difficult the days, the greater God's power will be
demonstrated. You and I should be encouraged knowing
that the Lord is fortifying us for the future. We are not only
going to survive, we have been promised that miracles will
accompany our Christian witness.

In times of great opposition to the Church of the living
God, the world becomes a combat zone between God and
Satan. Where sin abounds, grace abounds even more.
(Rom. 5:20.) The greater the darkness, the greater the light.
Right in the midst of the devil's revival of occultism and
mystic religions, the Holy Ghost is being poured out in
copious measure.

The Church of Jesus Christ is not getting weaker and
weaker as the end of time approaches; it is getting stronger
and stronger. We believers are going out in a blaze of glory.
We will know the Lord intimately, have a prevailing
strength, and do notable feats and miracles in His name!
Our future prospect is victory all the way!

Because they do not change,
Therefore they do not fear God.
Psalm 55:19 NKJ

How resistant to change are you? How much pain does a new idea cause you? How willing are you to discard a method that no longer works, a tradition that has lost its meaning, a methodology that has become ineffective? Would you agree with the statement that sameness begets tameness, and tameness begets lameness?

Changes do not come easily to any of us. Especially to those in the church world. But change we must, because of the condition of the lost and needy world. The unsaved world is rushing downhill to eternity. It is going to take something drastic to catch their attention and stem the tide of this self-destructing society in which we live. To refuse to adapt to changing circumstances is to ignore the cries for help of a lost society. Being locked into our traditional ways of doing things could keep us from a readiness to respond to the calls for help that our lost world keeps sending forth.

The verse for today says that if you and I will not change, it is because tradition means more to us than the reverential fear of the Lord. You and I have a lot of reasons for not changing, but our God wants us to trust Him completely for the future and allow Him to make any necessary adjustments. Such trust qualifies us for the capacity of reverentially fearing the Lord.

**But the path of the just is like the shining sun,
That shines ever brighter unto the perfect day.
Proverbs 4:18 NKJ**

One day my dad and I went hiking all night in the Sierras. We parked the car at a trail head and began an eight-mile hike by flashlight into the back country. Between 4 and 5 a.m. a transition began to take place. All the nocturnal activity terminated. Although we were in an area populated by marauding bears, stealthy mountain lions, howling timber wolves, and barking coyotes, everything became unearthly quiet. Total silence settled over the forest. It was as though the stalking creatures had retired to their lairs and dens and gone to sleep. There was not yet any light so the daytime creatures were still inactive. There was an indescribable hush which lasted for about an hour. Then about 5 a.m. the first ray of light appeared over the horizon.

From that moment on, the forest gradually became a bedlam of noise from chipmunks, stellar jays, golden mantled ground squirrels, quail, and other chattering creatures. By the time the full rays of the sun finally broke through the heavy foliage about 6 a.m., the forest was alive with the vibrant sounds of life.

This verse tells us that our Christian journey is like that time just before the sunrise. The night is far spent and the day is at hand. (Rom. 13:11.) For the believer, the long dark night is being replaced by a new day at which time...**shall the Sun of righteousness arise with healing in his wings** (Mal. 4:2). His glory shall light up the earth. For us who believe, it is getting brighter and brighter!

**My glory is fresh within me,
And my bow is renewed in my hand.
Job 29:20 NKJ**

The bow represented the livelihood of ancient peoples. Not only was it used for military purposes, but also to obtain wild animals for food. In other words, early people lived by the bow. For it to be renewed in the hand meant that the archer was getting stronger and stronger. This verse is thus an assurance that we can function in life and not be fatigued in our everyday activities. We can be refreshed as we go about doing God's will.

Stringing the bow took a great deal of exertion and energy. When not in use, it would be left unstrung because it was discovered that the bow left strung up would lose its tensile strength and elasticity. We derive our word *delente* from this concept of a bow being unstrung. You can readily see that in primitive times stringing and unstringing the bow would be a time-consuming and strenuous exercise. Job is telling us here that ordinarily he would be completely worn out when doing his normal work. Instead, God's glory and honor refreshed him, and his bow was renewed or changed in his hand. As a result, he did not get weaker and weaker, but stronger and stronger.

Use your faith and you will get more faith. Use your strength for the Lord and He will give you more strength. Give joy to others and God will replace it with more joy. Impart courage and courage will be imparted to you. Give and it shall be given. Getting stronger while exerting energy may seem a reversal of the natural order, but it is a spiritual truth from which we can all benefit.

**Call to Me, and I will answer you, and show you
great and mighty things, which you do not know.
Jeremiah 33:3 NKJ**

One post-war development of which we are all aware
are the giant underground missile silos.

The Hebrew word translated **mighty** in this verse
implies the same kind of invisible sources of power. It has
to do with the hidden, the inaccessible, that which is
subliminal or below the surface of normal vision. This
promise reassures us that if we will but call upon the Lord,
He will bring such things into the scope of our vision: "I
will show you great and fortified things that up to now
have escaped your attention."

While I was in the service, the Lord began dealing with
me about forgiving a sergeant who had been making my
life miserable. My chief concern at the moment was an
overdue auto payment. The Lord was zeroing in on my
need to forgive while I was concentrating on a threat by the
bank to repossess the car. In keeping with my priority list, I
kept insisting in prayer that the Lord help me with the car,
and then we could discuss the sergeant. God conveyed to
me that top priority was an act of forgiveness on my part.
Once that issued was settled, then we could talk about the
car payment.

The Lord won out. I had a beautiful release of love, joy,
and peace as true forgiveness came. At that time, a family
member called my attention to a letter on my dresser. It
contained more than enough money to make the car
payment. The sobering fact surfaced that the letter had
been lying there for three days unnoticed. God is thus
saying to us here: "Your answer is there; call upon Me, and I
will make it visible to you."

**I have loved you with an everlasting love;
Therefore with lovingkindness I have drawn you.
Jeremiah 31:3 NKJ**

Have you ever seen the letter TLC written on a bedside hospital chart? This symbol is used to tell all personnel that this patient needs a lot of "tender loving care." This verse in Jeremiah lets us know that TLC originated with the Lord: "I have loved you with an *everlasting love*," He says. This is an eternal love. It never oscillates, vacillates, or fluctuates. It does not freeze over in winter or dry up in summer. It is constant and perennial.

How often we encounter conditional love. Our society is structured on it. We soon get the message: "If you want to be accepted, measure up." Conditional love sets achievement levels and goals that are usually beyond reach. It forces us to compete for acceptance, approval or affection. Such competition produces alienation. One person wins the prize, the rest are losers who must learn to cope with rejection.

God has an unconditional love for us. He does not love *us* because we are somebody; He loves us so we will *become* somebody. He loves each of us as though there were no one else to love but us. He will never love us a bit more in the future than He loves us right now. We can grieve the Lord, insult Him, resist Him, and even disobey Him. None of these things removes or lessens His love. Our perverse actions only hinder His blessings, because God can only bless obedience. But we cannot add to God's love or subtract from it. The good news is that we can cooperate with His love and enjoy it forever.

The message is: God loves *you*.

Do not remember the former things,
Nor consider the things of old.
Behold, I will do a new thing,
Now it shall spring forth...
Isaiah 43:18,19 NKJ

Former things are those that have occurred during the last few years...recent things or things that are still fresh in our memory...those things people talk about for days afterwards. They seem to be conversation pieces. This verse challenges us to turn 180 degrees and start planning for a good future.

Things of old go back in time...back to antiquity. History, tradition, and past ages can be included in these things of old. The verse commands us to leave the past and get ready for the future. The Lord has new things for us. It is impossible to look in two directions at the same time. Clinging to past memories could cause us to pass up the new things and miss out altogether on good things He has planned for us.

A new thing is challenging. It refers to something fresh, exciting and exhilarating rather than predictable, lackluster, dull, boring, or routine. The Lord promises to put us on a daily diet of challenges all to stimulate and build our faith. Each day can be another unfolding of the divine drama in our life.

Now it shall spring forth. This phrase **spring forth** means the same as *to sprout*. It refers to a plant growing out of the ground. God's Word is a seed planted in the heart. Faith causes it to germinate and sprout. The end result is fruitfulness. Instead of living in the past, you and I can now lead fruitful, productive lives.

Then you will have good success.
Joshua 1:8 NKJ

Success is a Bible word. As the power center of the universe, Jesus is a success with a capital S. He was a success in the dawn of time when an enemy tried to unseat Him from His throne of authority. (Is. 14:12-15.) He was a success in the Garden of Eden when the messianic promise was given concerning the defeat of Satan's realm. (Gen. 3:15.) He succeeded at the crucifixion and at the resurrection. (1 John 3:8; Col. 2:14,15.) He will succeed at the Second Coming, on the day of judgment (Phil. 2:10,11), and in eternity.

Serving the Lord lines a person up with the victorious cause — past, present, and future. Joshua 1:8 tells us that by following the Lord you and I will make our way prosperous and experience good success. God's standards for evaluating success are even higher than those established by man. The original Hebrew word translated **success** in this verse is *sakal (saw–kal')*. Besides indicating the ability to accomplish or achieve some goal, *sakal* includes the possession of discretion, intelligence, prudence, wisdom, and good understanding.

We attribute success to winning athletes, popularly elected politicians, self-made millionaires, and all kinds of achievers. The Biblical principles of success are built on faithfulness, trust, integrity, discipline, and obedience. When you and I are promised success in Joshua 1:8, we are assured of arriving at our destination safe and sound. We are also assured of the expertise and ability to achieve our goals. We succeed not only in reaching our objectives, but also in the methods chosen to attain those high ideals.

Whoever believes will not act hastily.
Isaiah 28:16 NKJ

It is too late in the day for rash action. You and I have been serving the Lord too long to begin making snap judgments, jumping to conclusions, or becoming impulsive. This promise is an assurance that we can avoid the mistakes that come from impatience or acting on impulse.

If you have a history of precipitating crises by acting too hastily, would not this be a good day to begin overcoming that tendency? Remember: "He that believes shall not make haste."

One of the things that helped me in this area was the discovery that most of my hasty acts occurred because I did not have all the facts. Later, after all the needed information had surfaced, then I regretted my premature action. In 1 Corinthians 4:5 the Apostle Paul encourages us to...**judge nothing before the time....**(NKJ). Then we will be fully cognizant of what is going on and can act with confidence and assurance.

Another cause of hasty action is frustration. We would like to see things happen. Everything seems to be standing still. We get impatient. We feel that a slight nudge will get things rolling. We try to hurry up God's plan. In so doing we create a new set of problems. This verse was placed in the Bible just for those of us who could easily take things into our own hands and try to "get on with it" — only to botch things up worse than if we had done nothing at all.

Note Psalm 37:5: **Commit your way to the Lord, trust also in Him, and He shall bring it to pass** (NKJ). You might want to add these three verses to your active vocabulary. If so, do it today.

My people will dwell in a peaceful habitation,
In secure dwellings,
and in quiet resting places.
Isaiah 32:18 NKJ

Have you ever walked into a home and felt peace and serenity? Have you ever been in a home that gave you a feeling of turmoil, confusion, or even hostility? A home will take on the very nature of its residents. Disciplined and well-adjusted families give a home the feeling of teamwork and harmony. A home filled with bickering and strife exudes a spirit of tension and dissension. A home in which love resides reflects an atmosphere of peace and joy.

This verse promises peace, security, and tranquility. Since we are called God's people, it is reasonable to expect His attributes to be demonstrated in our lives and in our homes. Since God is not the author of confusion, but of peace, we can believe for peace to rule and reign in our homes.

Our God also promises us secure dwellings. I believe we can claim a good foundation for our natural homes. Security is assured us against flood, fire, earthquake, tornado, hurricane, or any other natural disturbance.

We know the world is full of potential natural disasters. We also know the Word of God promises us a secure dwelling. I would rather stand on God's promises and be secure than to allow the fears generated by the news media to dominate my life and make me feel insecure.

> When the enemy comes in like a flood,
> The Spirit of the Lord will lift up a
> standard against him.
> Isaiah 59:19 NKJ

The original Hebrew word translated **standard** is this verse is *nuwc (noos)*. It is an unusual word signifying something displayed in order to put to flight or to chase away opposition so that a person can escape or be delivered. The Spirit of the Lord will lift up a standard *(nuwc)* not only to turn back the floodtide of the enemy that comes against us, but also to deliver us and give us a way of escape. Our God not only promises to stop the opposition in its tracks, but to show us the way through to our next point of victory.

The image *nuwc* gives is that of a brake and an accelerator on an automobile. The Lord tells us that He will put the brakes on the enemy and at the same time will accelerate our forward progress. The enemy will go back to his starting place, turned back by the Spirit of God. We, on the other hand, will get on with living. We will be set free to go ahead and fulfill the will and call of God on our lives. Satan goes backward while we go forward. This exchange puts us way ahead of the opposition and the competition.

Isaiah referred to **...those who turn back the battle at the gate** (Is. 28:6 NKJ). As in the expression "the gates of hell" (Matt. 16:18), this alludes to the place from which Satan's malignant forces issue. To "turn back the battle at the gate" is to drive Satan back to his starting place. This action frees us to get on with our journey, to press on to even greater levels of victory and triumph in Christ.

> **Now when they began to sing and to praise,**
> **the Lord set ambushes against the people...who**
> **had come against Judah; and they were defeated.**
> **2 Chronicles 20:22** NKJ

Think of it! Singing and praising your way to victory. Singing and praising your way through discouragement, oppression, depression, fear, and worry.

...And they were three days gathering the spoil (the loot) **because there was so much** (v. 25). In Bible days, driving an enemy out entitled the victor to all the spoils of the battles. The army of Judah so routed the enemy that it took three days to collect all the booty the enemy had left behind. And the victory was wrought not by fighting but by singing and praising the Lord!

God responded to the prayers of His people with these reassuring words: **"...the battle is not yours, but God's"** (v. 15). With this assurance, the king of Judah appointed singers and praisers to go out before the army and to praise the Lord. When they began to praise, the enemy was defeated. The key word in this passage is **began.** Your victory is dependent upon your doing something. You need to *begin.* Begin to count your blessings. Begin to enumerate past deliverances. Begin to praise the Lord. Begin to sing your song of deliverance.

The Bible says the Lord inhabits the praises of His people. (Ps. 22:3). When the Lord's presence comes into our setting of praise and worship, the enemy is powerless against us. We can literally sing our way through every battle and win the victory the same way Jehosphaphat's army won. Singing and praising the Lord is an effective weapon in our spiritual warfare!

**And shall make him of quick understanding
in the fear of the Lord...
Isaiah 11:3**

In the original Hebrew this expression **quick understanding** is "quick scented." It is the Hebrew word for spirit, *ruwach (roo'akh)* which has to do with breathing, respiration, perceiving by scent or smell, discerning by aroma, or detecting by breath. It is the ability to detect, judge and determine a thing by the way it smells. Thus, "quick understanding" is equal to instantaneous discernment by the sense of smell.

All living organisms have a distinctive fragrance or aroma. It is the breath of life. Everything God touches comes alive and emits the aroma of life. Everything Satan touches dies and produces the aroma of death. Everything the unregenerate human spirit (or man in his natural state) touches gives forth the aroma of his perspiration (his ego-drive). So, three distinct aromas can be detected for discerning purposes: 1) The perfume that accompanies and identifies the true worship of God in spirit and in truth, 2) the stench of death that is evidence of Satan at work, and 3) the smell of human perspiration produced by man in his own self-efforts. To have "quick understanding" or to be "quick scented" in the things of life means that we are able to instantly discern what is happening, to know what is behind every activity with which we come in contact. What a blessing to be spiritually *scent*-sitive!

Beloved, I wish above all things that thou mayest prosper and be in health, even as thy soul prospereth.
3 John 2

In Greek the word translated **health** in this verse is *hugiaino (hoog–ee–ah'ee–no)* from which we derive our English word *hygiene*. It is defined as "sound," "healthy," free from disease or void of the viruses that cause sickness and disability."

This wish by John was expressed to a man named Gaius who worried himself sick over his problems. John was sending traveling ministers to Gaius' church. An influential member of that church by the name of Diotrephes did not want these ministers to come so he vigorously opposed the plan, apparently threatening to cut off his financial support if it was carried out. Gaius was thus caught in the middle.

This verse is part of John's letter written in response to the situation. In it, John is telling Gaius: "Look, you do not need to worry over this situation. Diotrephes does not have all the money in the world. He is causing problems because he loves to have pre-eminence. But, Gauis, God wants you to look to Him as your sole source of supply. I am praying that you will prosper financially, and be in health, even as your soul prospers."

Hugiaino is used for sound doctrine and sound teaching. Your body is the temple of the Holy Ghost. You are storing in it massive amounts of the Word of God. That Word is sound and healthy. You can do more for the Lord with a healthy body than with a sick one. A sound and healthy body is the ideal receptacle for the sound and healthy scriptures which you have hidden in your heart.

Taking the shield of faith...to
quench all the fiery darts of the wicked one.
Ephesians 6:16 NKJ

Crimes of passion take place when the enemy ignites an inflammable area within the human personality. We hear of flaming anger, fiery jealousy, burning passion, of people being afire with lust, consumed by hatred, devoured by the flames of prejudice. All these can occur when a person has no guard to protect him from the fiery darts of Satan.

The word *diaballo* (the original Greek word for the devil) is composed of two words: *dia* meaning "through" and *ballo* meaning "to throw." *Diaballo* is thus the evil who tries to throw fiery darts through the believer. These darts will ignite trouble in some area of life if a shield is not used. In Roman days the shield was as big as a door. With it a soldier could advance under attack knowing that he had no vulnerable areas exposed.

As mature Christian soldiers we are called out of the comfort zone into the combat zone, out of the nursery into the trenches. We are to get off the charismatic love boat where life has been all fun and games and onto the spiritual battleship from which we can shell the enemy's fortresses and demolish his strongholds.

The shield of faith enables us to remain unscathed in the very midst of battle while the onslaught is at its worst. No area of our life or personality can be touched. The shield of faith completely covers every area of our existence. We are not only protected, we are gaining ground against our adversary. The Church of God is moving onward to great victories.

Make no provision for the flesh, to fulfill its lusts.
Romans 13:14 NKJ

You have doubtless heard the old saying: "People do not plan to fail, they just fail to plan." This verse addresses those who actually do plan to fail. They work failure into their confession, their plans, their expectancy. You can hear it in their conversations: "If this marriage doesn't work, I can always get a divorce." "If this business goes under, I can always file bankruptcy." "If the Lord doesn't heal me, I can always use Blue Cross and Medicare." Such words are more than attempts to plan for contingencies, they are actually attempts to justify failure before it ever happens.

In Romans 13:14 the Apostle Paul warns against such pre-planned failure. He tells us in essence: "Don't work failure into your plans. Don't allow for it. Don't even put it on the agenda."

Provision is an interesting word. In the original Greek it is *pronoia (pron'–oy–ah)*. *Pro* is a prefix meaning "before, in front of, prior to, ahead of time" (compare *pro*logue — words spoken before the main dissertation). *Noia* comes from *noieo* referring to the mind, perception, the intellect, the thoughts. Thus, *provision (pronoia)* is thinking about something ahead of time. People plan their vacations, their holidays, their income tax filings, and a myriad other happenings during the course of a year. That is good — if it's positive. Negative planning is disastrous.

Don't plan on bankruptcy. Don't plan on trouble. Don't plan on losing your temper. No general ever goes out to battle planning on losing. Plan on winning. Plan on victory. It is in Christ. It is in this verse.

But without faith it is impossible to please Him...
Hebrews 11:6 NKJ

According to scripture, pleasing the Lord is within the reach of all of us. Out of the Dark Ages came a concept of God as One Who was vindictive. He angrily watched every move people made. If they strayed or erred one bit, He was quick to "zap" them. He was out to get people. Unfortunately, this concept still exists today. Sadly, it disregards everything the Word of God has to say about His goodness and merciful lovingkindness.

Our heavenly Father says in His Word that there are things we can do to please Him. They are not impossible. Having faith and trust in Him pleases Him. Colossians 3:20 tells us that God is pleased when children obey their parents. Second Samuel 7:29 indicated that it pleases God to bless our homes. Keeping His commandments is pleasing in His sight. (1 John 3:22.) Any recognition or acknowledgement we give to His righteous Word is well–pleasing to the Lord, according to Isaiah 42:21. The psalmist tells us that praising, singing, and worshipping the Lord pleases Him. (Ps. 69:30,31.) Solomon says that our journey or pathway can be pleasing to God, resulting in His favor and blessing. (Prov. 16:7.) In Isaiah 55:11 (NKJ), the Lord Himself tells us that His Word will not return to Him void (unfulfilled or unrealized) but will accomplish what He pleases, and will prosper in the thing for which He sent it. (NKJ). The writer of Hebrews says that Enoch had...**this testimony, that he pleased God** (Heb. 11:5.) If you look up the words *please* and *pleased* in the concordance, you will be happily surprised to discover how often things were said and done that pleased the Lord.

**And there will be great earthquakes
in various places....
Luke 21:11 NKJ**

Revivals seem to parallel natural phenomena.
Occurrences in the natural world are usually accompanied
by similar events in the spiritual world. The San Francisco
earthquake happened at the same time that the Welsh
revival and the Pentecostal outpouring were taking place in
1906. Natural shaking and spiritual shaking go together.

In our verse in Luke, we are told of great earthquakes
which will happen all over the world in the last days.
Haggai 2:6 tells us that heaven, earth, the sea, and the dry
land will be shaken and God's house will be filled with
glory. In Ezekiel's valley of dry bones, a shaking took place
as bone was knit to bone. In the days of Uzziah, king of
Judah, a great earthquake occurred. We read in Amos 1:1
that recorded time is built around events happening prior
to the earthquake. When Moses received the Ten
Commandments, the mountain quaked. When Jesus died
on the cross, the whole world shook. On resurrection
morning another earthquake took place. Hebrews 12:26,27
promises that prior to the coming of the Lord Jesus there
will be more earthquakes.

Perhaps reading prophecies about earth shaking is not
your way to start the new day. But with the natural goes the
supernatural. The good news is, "The Lord is stirring His
people." His Church is being jolted out of her lethargy. Old
antiquated and absolute traditions are being shaken to the
very foundations. This shaking has to take place before we
will accept the new things God has in store for us.

See if there is any wicked way in me....
Psalm 139:24 NKJ

In the Greek Old Testament (LXX), the word translated
wicked here is *kakos (kak–os')* meaning "ill." David is
praying for the Lord to check him over to see how
spiritually healthy he is. He is saying to the Lord: "How
about my attitude? Do I harbor resentment? Is there
repressed anger lurking inside of me? Do imaginations and
fantasy dominate my thinking? Do hurts, real or imagined,
constantly occur?" By asking the Lord to make a spiritual
x-ray of his inner man, David is risking the pain and
embarrassment of being found guilty of hidden and
presumptuous sins. Can we take the same risk and ask the
Lord for His inspection?

Man has explored everything but the explorer himself.
He has climbed all the mountains of the world, but has not
penetrated or searched out all the ridges of his own heart.
Jeremiah labored with this truth when he posed the classic
question: **"The heart is deceitful above all things, and
desperately wicked** (Heb., *anach*, "sick"); **who can know
it?"** (Jer. 17:9 NKJ). In the very next verse, the Lord responds
rapidly with these reassuring words: **"I, the Lord, search
the heart, I test the mind, even to give every man according
to his ways, and according to the fruit of his doings"** (NKJ).

Heart searching is painful, but it is part of the purifying,
purging, pruning, perfecting, and polishing process
designed by the Lord to bring us to full maturity in Christ.
It is possible to approach the Lord with "clean hands and a
pure heart," but it does take honesty and a commitment to
truth that will not allow us to hide anything in our heart
that displeases the Lord.

O Lord, correct me, but with justice;
Not in Your anger,
lest You bring me to nothing.
Jeremiah 10:24 NKJ

Take a lump of clay or a clod of earth. Tell this muddy mass that there is a chance that he can be worked over, improved upon, changed, remade, and then fashioned after the very nature of the Designer who created him in the first place. Call this process re-creation, regeneration, or rebirth. Then show him the majestic qualities of the Architect. Tell him that he can be just like that. Tell him it is a lifetime process, but the end result is being conformed to the image of his Savior and Lord. That earthy person is going to respond very favorably. Some people may think it too good to be true, but most will think it worth striving for. From the earthy first Adam to the heavenly second Adam is quite a journey. The long-suffering God waits patiently while the corrective work is going on.

In this verse Jeremiah, acknowledging his need for adjustment, fine tuning, finishing, and correcting, asks the Lord to remove carnality and replace it with spirituality. He knows it will take time so he asks the Lord to be patient with him. Jeremiah is negotiating with the Lord. He tells Him he needs correction (who doesn't?). He asks the Lord for justice. He wants to be right. He wants the truth. He wants to be totally honest. He appeals to the mercy side of the Lord. So can you. Ask the Lord to give you a heart after Him and inclined toward Him. His attribute of mercy will permeate you, for to the merciful He will show mercy.

Faint, yet pursuing....
Judges 8:4

Athletes claim that fatigue can improve their performance. Getting tired during the contest moves them from reason to instinct. They accomplish things in their automatic output of energy they would not be able to do if they were figuring things out mentally.

"Faint, yet pursuing" is used to describe the condition of the three hundred men assigned by God to Gideon to fight Israel's battles for her. The enemy was being routed and put to flight. In order to capture them, Gideon's little army, hungry and tired as they were, had no choice but to continue pursuit. Smelling victory and tasting success, they were highly motivated to carry on. They were willing to forego the usual eating and sleeping schedule in order to press the battle to the gates. (Is. 28:6.) This is a message to intercessors as well as soulwinners.

There are times in our lives when we need Gideon's mentality. Sometimes we, too, are exhausted but still in pursuit with victory in sight, the enemy is on the run, and a few extra hours are needed to wrap things up. This does not mean that we advocate a disregard for proper rest and nourishment. Many articles have been written about revivals that ended prematurely because the participants ignored the body's natural need for food and rest. "Faint, yet pursuing" does reveal how the thrill of conquest, the assurance of victory, and the joy of knowing we are winning in the contest against our enemy will spur us on. This spiritual "second wind" is a priority item to the Christian.

**Let not the one who puts on his armor boast like
the one who takes it off.**
1 Kings 20:11 NKJ

The one who takes his armor off is the tried, tested, seasoned veteran who has been in battle and lived to tell about it. He has learned to survive. He understands his opponent. He knows the stratagems, designs, ruses, and cunning of the enemy. He has also found from his battle experiences that as tough as his adversary may be, he is vulnerable and can be defeated. The one taking off the armor has a victory to report. He has earned the respect of his fellow soldiers by helping the cause of truth to gain new footholds and win new ground. He could write the manual of fighting and winning. He also keeps the victory in right perspective. He knows all triumph is a result of teamwork. A true hero wisely recognizes that victory is always the fruit of combined effort. He takes the armor off as a real winner, humbly grateful to be alive.

The one who puts on the armor (for the time) is a rookie. Inexperienced, untested, unproven, full of enthusiasm, and even a little conceited: "Let me at 'em; just wait till I get into combat, I'll show 'em a thing or two." These are invariably the words of the one putting on the armor. Such bravado is rarely heard issuing from the mouth of the veteran. It is typical of the untried youth full of his own eagerness and supposed prowess. Soon enough his boasting will be replaced by a more sober, mature viewpoint. The one who takes off the armor has a different attitude from the one who puts it on.

He stretches out the north over empty space....
Job 26:7 NKJ

It has been conjectured that in our universe there is an area to the north of our earth in which there are no stars, planets, or other heavenly bodies. It is supposed to be sort of a void, an empty nothingness. Along with this "empty north" verse in Job, there is a statement in Isaiah 14:13 about Lucifer aspiring to sit in control **"...on the mount of the congregation on the farthest sides of the north"** (NKJ). Apparently the Lord announced in the dawn of time that the north was designed with something special in mind. Made empty on purpose, it was destined to be filled with a congregation of worshippers. In Psalm 48:2, Mount Zion is identified as being **...on the sides of the north....** (NKJ). Zion is always symbolic of the place where true worshippers gather together to celebrate the Lord's name.

John the revelator saw something that could be fulfillment of these verses. In Revelation 21:2 he writes: **Then I, John, saw the holy city, New Jerusalem, coming down out of heaven from God, prepared as a bride adorned for her husband** (NKJ). Here we have the potential for full drama: 1) At creation God deliberately leaves a square slot in the universe with nothing in it. 2) He announces that this space is reserved for a future bride for His Son. This bride will be a large number of people. They will make up the congregation in the mount on the farthest sides of the north. The empty north will soon be occupied. The void place will be filled in with the redeemed. This is the true dignity and destiny God offers to the human race!

And God hath set...in the church...helps, governments.... 1 Corinthians 12:28

According to the usual interpretation of this verse, **helps** refers to those people in the church who serve as deacons and deaconesses, along with the other unpaid, volunteer workers who assist the employed staff members who occupy positions of leadership. **Governments** are the church administrators, those on the payroll, the titled staff. Thus, as a rule, helps and governments are assumed to describe officers in the church and those who assist them. However, there are some options that are worth considering.

J.R. Pridie wrote a book (circa 1926) on the healing ministries of the church. In this book he suggested that **governments** could be interpreted to include words of knowledge and wisdom, as well as the discernment, diagnosis and treatment of sickness. Likewise, **helps** was translated "nursing" or any beneficial acts aimed at helping a sick person to recover or mend. It is very interesting that helps and governments in the text occur right after the phrase **gifts** (plural) **of healing**. It is as though these two words, helps and governments, are an extension of the healing ministries.

I visualize one team having a capacity to minister to the sick with revelation knowledge, compassionate words of wisdom, a penetrating discernment that sees the cause of the sickness, knows how to get to the root of the problem and even be able to minister healing to the person in need. Then the helps ministers would set in and begin nursing the person to spiritual health, stamina and vitality. Any volunteers for these ministries?

**And they heard the sound of the Lord God
walking in the garden in the cool of the day....
Genesis 3:8 NKJ**

The cool of the day is around 4:00 p.m. It is the time when the evening breeze begins to stir. The Hebrew word translated **cool** in this verse is *ruwach (roo'ach)*. Elsewhere in Scripture, this same word is translated *breath, wind, breeze, spirit,* and *Holy Spirit.*

God is a spirit. When the afternoon breeze began to stir in the Garden of Eden, God as a spirit came to Adam and Eve in the wind. Although it is not stated that this was a daily occurrence, most Bible scholars consulted seemed to feel that this was the case.

David Kimchi, a Jewish scholar living in Spain in the 12th century, wrote that Adam and Eve sinned around the 4:00 p.m. time. Satan's stratagem was to tempt Adam and Eve into disobedience, thereby casting a sin barrier between them and their God.

Matthew Henry, an 18th-century scholar wrote: "There is an evangelic note to this passage. God knew they had sinned, but it did not keep Him from coming to meet them. Even though they had miserably failed and caused a separation between God and the pair, He still came looking for them. His grief and compassion effected a reconciliation and a promise of a coming Messiah."

To this day, man is still feeling the effects of that separation. I believe modern man is still lonely for his Creator's fellowship. There is a void, a darkness, in his heart. Jesus came to fill that void. To those who believe, He has promised the light of His eternal presence — 24 hours a day. To the Christian, there is no such thing as a "twilight zone"!

To make ready a people prepared for the Lord.
Luke 1:17 NKJ

Even though these two phrases, **make ready** and **prepared**, are seemingly synonymous, they have opposite meanings in the original Greek. The word translated **make ready** is used to describe thorough preparation by an internal fitness. The word rendered **prepared** refers to external equipment and adjustment. One describes a work of grace going on outside of the Christian Church, the other a work of grace going on within the Church.

Make ready in this verse covers the whole range of internal qualifications necessary to meet the Lord Jesus at His return. The Holy Spirit is working inside each believer in the areas of honesty, integrity, humility, holiness, obedience, attitude, and motive. An invisible work of grace is going on in God's people helping them to overcome resentment, bitterness, hurts, wounds, unforgiveness, and general unbelief.

Prepared is a description of the external work of grace, including the Church's coming into unity. Revival fires burning, true worshippers showing forth the praises of God, Christians standing shoulder to shoulder against the common enemy, and rallying around to help in international disasters: these are externals that are visible to the unbelieving world.

In this prophetic note, the Lord declares that an internal work is going on that will cause the Church to be externally prepared for His Second Coming. God is at work externally in the world at large, getting His Church ready. The Bride of Christ is becoming more beautiful every single day!

The Egyptians whom you see today,
you shall see again no more forever.
Exodus 14:13,14 NKJ

How would you like to bid a "final farewell" to your problems as you go on to your promised land? How would you like to say goodbye forever to worry, fear, and anxiety? To cancer, arthritis, diabetes, heart trouble? To poverty, debt, unemployment, and money worries? Does this sound too good to be true? Can you accept this promise from the Lord: **"...the Egyptians whom you see today, you shall see again no more forever?"** Can you claim this promise without a qualifying "Yes, but...."?

In Biblical topology, Egypt is a picture of the world system and everything related to it. When we read that Israel was told not to look to Egypt for help (Is. 30:2), it is a message for us today to rely completely upon the Lord as our sole source of supply. Israel was warned of the Lord: **"...the Egyptians shall help in vain and to no purpose"** (Is. 30:7 NKJ). So Egypt can be compared to dependence upon man and man's resources. Such faith is always misplaced. We Christians are urged to put our total trust in the Lord.

Biblical Egypt also represents the opposition and hostility shown to God's people, as in Moses' day. This situation can be likened to the modern-day problems we Christians face with persecution, poverty, pressure, and life's adversity.

Praise God, there is a time of deliverance. No trouble was ever intended to be permanent. The "Egyptians" you see today, you will see no more. The problems you have been facing up till now, you will never face again.

But we have this treasure in earthen vessels.
2 Corinthians 4:7 NKJ

This verse presents a divine paradox: immutable deity dwelling in a breakable container...the Creator of the heavens and earth residing in a clay vessel...eternal permanence abiding in a time-captive housing.

The paradox has to do with completion and incompletion. As human beings, we are not complete till our divine Creator has taken up His abode in our hearts. For some reason known only to Him, the Almighty, the Eternal, has chosen the human heart as His place of rest. We are created with a void in our hearts which only He can fill. By His own design, neither creature nor Creator function properly till He becomes incarnate in us. Without His Spirit, we can do nothing in our weak flesh. In His infinite wisdom He has chosen not to manifest Himself in the universe without our mortal bodies. Therefore, neither of us functions adequately without the cooperation of the other.

In the original Greek, this word translated **earthen** is *ostrakinos (os-tra'-kin-os)* which is defined as "made of clay, brittle, fragile, easily broken." God has chosen to invest His frail human creatures with a treasure of inestimable value. **Treasure** is also an interesting word. In the original Greek, it is *thesauros (thay-sow-ros')*. It refers to deposited wealth, amassed riches, reserves of great value, a hoard of priceless valuables.

God's Spirit in us is like all the country's gold in Fort Knox. He is the treasure, we are the vault. God has taken the riches of His Holy Spirit and stored them in our bodies. The contrast between the two is so great, He gets all the focus, the attention and the recognition!

You shall be witnesses to Me....
Acts 1:8 NKJ

Jesus promised His followers an enduement of power. The end result would be their witness to the world. The Greek word translated **witnesses** here is *martus (mar'-toos)* from which we derived our English word *martyr.* We usually think of martyrs as those early Christians who were fed to the lions or burned at the stake. Church history records thousands of heroic deeds of Christian martyrs who gave their lives for the faith. Their stories have inspired many believers with new courage and strength.

Martus has other meanings in addition to martyrdom. The verb form of this word means "to testify." The Holy Spirit empowers the believer to live a life that is a testimony to others. Perhaps you are the only Christian in your office, factory or department. If so, your lifestyle should be a testimony of your Christian faith. Those around you who do not know the Lord should be able to see in your life a quality that is missing in their own. We "testify" with more than just words. How we live, we conduct ourselves, how we react and respond in awkward and unpleasant situations is also a witness or testimony to our faith (or lack of it!). An overcoming and victorious life is a great testimony to the world.

To testify means "to give evidence or produce facts," "to exhibit truth," or "to confirm claims." One form of evidence is signs, wonders, and miracles. The early Church depended upon the Lord to confirm their witness with supernatural signs. In Acts 1:8 the Lord Jesus declared His disciples would be filled with the Holy Spirit. In Mark 16:17,18 He promised that their witness would be backed up with divine evidence.

**You will also declare a thing, and
it will be established for you.
Job 22:28 NKJ**

The word **thing** in the original Hebrew is *omer (o'–mer)* and is similar to the Greek word *rhema*. The promises, the sayings, the word, the utterance, and the confessed word are included in *omer*.

"You will also declare the Word of God, the promises of God, the sayings of God, and these things will happen." This implies more than just cheerful optimism, wishful thinking, or positive affirmation. When we speak forth the Word of God, we are not just blowing smoke, filling the air with clever rhetoric, or mouthing platitudes. We are declaring with our lips what God has spoken to our hearts. The power is not in our speaking; it's in the Lord Who gives the message.

When we're in distress, people can tell us, "Don't give up; hang in there. Remember, it's always darkest before the dawn." And all that may be true and some comfort. But it really does more for us to hear the Lord say to us personally, **...not a hair of your head shall be lost** (Luke 21:18 NKJ). All the cute aphorisms and clever slogans in the world are anemic compared with a solid word from the Lord.

This word **declare** (or "decree") means "to decide, predetermine, and declare the outcome of a matter before it comes to pass." If your declaration is in line with the word you have received from God, you can "declare a thing, and it will be established for you!" Weak or timid faith is too cautious to make any kind of pronouncement before it sees the outcome, but strong faith says, "It shall be done just as the Lord has said!"

I will instruct you and teach you in the way
you should go; I will guide you with My eye.
Psalm 32:8 NKJ

This is a good verse for those of us who seek guidance and direction from the Lord. It is an assurance that our heavenly Father is going to move us from a weak transmission to a "clear-channel station with no static." We will be able to hear the gentle voice of the Good Shepherd without interference.

The Lord makes three direct promises in this verse:

1) **I will instruct you**...This is like having a private tutor. The purpose of the instruction we thus receive is to make us more intelligent, skillful and circumspect in our dealings, more adept in making decisions.

2) **...and teach you in the way you should go;**...The original word used here indicates the pointing of a finger in a certain direction. It also implies shooting an arrow at a target in such a way as to avoid missing the mark. This word from the Lord is an assurance that we will not drift aimlessly through life, but that He will give us a definite direction and a clear goal to aim for.

3) **...I will guide you with my eye.** One translation of this phrase says: "I will keep my eye upon you to see how you are doing."

Here is my paraphrase of this verse: "I will make you skillful and proficient in decision-making and will aim you in the right direction; I will watch your progress and see how you are getting along; My eye will be upon you for your benefit.

If by any means I may provoke to emulation them which are my flesh.... Romans 11:14

The English word *emulation* is only used twice in the *King James Bible* — both times by the same author, Paul. He uses the singular form in a very positive way in Romans 11:14, but the plural form in a very negative way in Galatians 5:20.

In the passage in Galatians, **emulations** (plural) is listed as one of the works of the flesh. The original Greek word used here is *zelos (dzay'–los)*. When used in this context, it refers to hatred, wrath, variance, strife, jealousy or malice, the indignant zeal of an enemy. It portrays destructive energy that should be avoided at all costs.

In the passage above from Romans, **emulation** (singular) is used in a good sense. The original Greek word here is *parazeloo (par–ad–zay–lo'–o)*. It refers to stimulating another person by example, or to a good-natured rivalry that brings out the best in another person. It also implies challenging or motivating a person to become more ambitious or more aggressive.

Thus, *emulation*, as used here by Paul, is a "good example." Paul is saying: "I hope my Jewish friends will see something in my life that will stir them to action to become just like me." You and I can lead lives so full of the love of God that others are inspired to become just like us. In a time when there are few heroes or positive role models, the Lord can cause us to be "exhibit A" of what Christianity is all about. Our lives should make others want what we have.

And strengthen your bones....
Isaiah 58:11 NKJ

This word *strengthen* has quite a few interesting definitions which can speak to us today. *Chalats (kwaw–lats')* is the original Hebrew word used by Isaiah. The King James translators rendered it "make fat" your bones. As people get older, their bones get brittle and break easily. This promise to "make fat your bones" is an assurance of plenty of moisture or marrow in the bones throughout life. Instead of our bones getting old and brittle, this word guarantees that we will remain limber and pliable all our days. For the child of God, the aging process can be reversed by this word from the Lord.

One translator reads *chalats:* "He will *arm* your bones." This translation has a military overtone. Not only are we Christians marching through life, we are traveling as soldiers to fight a war. To "arm the bones" is the same as to provide with protective armor so as to render us invulnerable to attack.

Chalats is also used in the sense of stripping off excess baggage, cargo or unnecessary weight. A person who is going on a long journey is not going to overload himself with useless and cumbersome burdens. Most wilderness backpackers learn to carry only vital provisions so they can travel light. Our God has promised to lighten our load and free us for unimpeded travel. What a wonderful word for the Lord's traveling soldiers: Plenty of moisture for the bones, arming and fortifying for battles, lightening the load so the bones can be agile and limber. It's all there to help us reach our destination and accomplish our mission.

**For He will finish the work and cut it
short in righteousness, because the Lord
will make a short work upon the earth.**
Romans 9:28 NKJ

Your God is saying to you: "Your prayer has been heard. I am intervening and responding to your petition. The answer is on its way. I am speeding up the answer, so get ready for a quick and sudden release of divine power in your situation."

The context of this verse is God's dealing with Israel, but the word expressed here can be applied to all individuals who put their trust in the Lord for answers to their prayers. When scholars attempt to confine a scripture to a certain community, society, or nation, we must remind them that such masses of people are made up of individuals. A verse spoken to a city is also a word spoken to the individual citizens of that metropolis. This is a verse for us personally, as well as a group of people.

In the Greek text of this verse, the expression **short work** is *suntemno logos (soon-tem'-no log'-os)*. *Logos* has many definitions, among them "topic," "matter," "a thing," "a report," "a subject," and "a word." *Suntemno* means "to reduce or contract the size of a thing by concise and speedy cutting." Thus we are promised here that God's Word covering final things and the consummation of time will be speeded up and shortened.

The Lord is doing a "quick work" in His Church. Do not be surprised when He accelerates: 1) your answers, 2) your growth and maturing, 3) your ability to worship Him in spirit and truth, and 4) your desires to please Him and do His will.

Reaching forward to those things which are ahead.
Philippians 3:13 NKJ

Craning the neck, scanning the horizon, and shading the eyes with the hand in order to see at a distance: these are all expressed by the phrase **reaching forward.** Paul is telling the Philippians to forget the past and start looking ahead. He knew what he was talking about. Since he had earlier persecuted the Church and consented to the stoning of Stephen, Paul had to learn to put such negative memories behind him and get on with life. Instead of allowing the past to become an unbearable burden and weight to him, Paul simply dropped it to the ground and used it as a stepping stone to the future.

Reaching forward is a good exercise for all of us. It stimulates hope. It puts us in a state of expectancy. It declares that what has been is only a prologue to what will be: Yesterday was good, today is better, tomorrow will be better still. Reaching forward anticipates miracles, revivals, outpourings of the Spirit of God, deliverances, and answered prayer. It looks to the future with intensity and great expectation, as Isaac looked and waited eagerly for the arrival of his new bride. (Gen. 24:63.)

As Christians we have so much to look forward to: 1) the salvation of our families, 2) the evangelization of the world, 3) the reviving of our churches, and, 4) most of all, that blessed hope, the return of Christ the Bridegroom for His Bride, the Church.

"For I know the plans I have for you," declares the Lord, plans to prosper you and not to harm you, plans to give you hope and a future" (Jer. 29:11 NIV). What a future we have to look forward to!

> 'Not by might nor by power, but
> by My Spirit,' says the Lord of hosts.
> **Zechariah 4:6** NKJ

Not by **might**. The word **might** in the original Hebrew has to do with military strength. In Bible days Israel was not a war-like nation. Its rural lifestyle consisted of peaceful farming and herding of sheep and goats.

The Lord was the Israelites' defense, and they knew it. As God's people walked in obedience and trust, He defended them time after time. This verse reminded them that victory is not assured by massive numerical strength. Although they had warriors to defend them, just as we have the military today to protect us, they knew that the Lord was their real security **...except the Lord keep the city, the watchman waketh but in vain** (Ps. 127:1).

Nor by **power**. Whereas *might* is a team word, *power* refers to what one person can do. It has to do with native ingenuity, with putting one's nose to the grindstone, one's shoulder to the wheel. It implies single-handedly taking the initiative and pushing past all opposition. It is a word which speaks to loners who would rather do things alone than to work with others. Soloists, lone rangers, prima donnas, and superstars like the word *power* because it glories the individual.

But this message from the Lord says that it is neither by the might of men nor by the power of any one person that you and I are kept. Our security is solely dependent upon God's Spirit. We are reminded that with the Lord there is no restraint to save by many or by few. (1 Sam. 14:6.) Our reliance is not on numerical strength or human cleverness. Our reliance is on the Lord!

**Until the time that his word came to
pass, the word of the Lord tested him.**
Psalm 105:19 NKJ

Tried by the Word. Tested by a promise from the Lord.
Joseph was 18 years of age when the Lord gave him the
promise of a miraculous ministry. Joseph waited 12 long
years for the fulfillment of that promise. The waiting period
was not easy, but he had a promise to cling to. That very
promise tried him as a person. The Hebrew word translated
tried in this verse means "to purify and refine." It is a term
used to describe the removing of impurities from gold ore
in order to produce pure metal. The Word of God refined
and purified Joseph.

Many Christians are taught that God uses
circumstances to purify and refine them. There is a suffering
cult which holds that human misery has redemptive value.
"Suffer and win points with God," they seem to say.
Jeremiah would not agree, because he says of God: ...**He
does not afflict willingly, nor grieve the children of men**
(Lam. 3:33 NKJ).

It was not circumstances which tested Joseph and
refined him, it was the promise of God. His adverse
circumstances cried out, "No way." But the promise came
back emphatically: "There shall be a performance of those
things promised you by the Lord." (Luke 1:45.)

When your situation contradicts the promises and
assurances God has given you, you have two choices: you
can confess the circumstance or confess the word of
promise. Remember: circumstances can change, but the
Word of God will never change. Like Joseph, you can live to
see a beautiful fulfillment of all those things promised you
by the Lord. (Num. 23:19.)

The Lord Himself will descend
from heaven with a shout....
1 Thessalonians 4:16 NKJ

Israel of old had three kinds of shouts. All three could adequately be represented in this particular verse.

First, there was a vintage shout. During the period of the judges, Hebrew life was very precarious. Due to the uncertainties of life, no one was really sure of seeing a crop all the way through from planting seed to threshing grain. Gathering in a bountiful harvest became a cause for rejoicing. In our verse, Jesus could be giving a vintage shout because the harvest of souls is finally being reaped and gathered into the garner. (James 5:7.)

Israel also had a nuptial shout. This happy, joyful shouting occurred during wedding festivities. (Is.62:5.) At His coming to redeem His Bride, the Church, and to proclaim the wedding feast of the Lamb, Christ may give forth a nuptial shout of joy.

Finally, there was a shout of war. This was the jubilant war cry given during battle in confident anticipation of victory. In the original Greek text, the word translated **shout** is *keleuma (kel'–yoo–mah)* or "shout of war." It includes *incitement* (**"Gather My saints together to Me...."** (Ps.50:5 NKJ) and *command* ("Satan, step aside, I am coming through your territory to receive My Church!").

The Second Coming of Christ will involve conflict, but *once* the Lord leaves heaven and descends with the shout of victory, the battle is over right then. The next verse joyfully declares, **...And thus we shall always be with the Lord** (v. 17 NKJ). Hallelujah!

In My Father's house are many mansions....
John 14:2 NKJ

Have you ever wondered what heaven is like? Since we believers will be there for all eternity, it does seem that we should give some thought to our future home. Our stay on earth is transient, while our dwelling in eternity is called our **long home** (Eccl. 12:5). Jesus described that "home" as a mansion. The Greek word used here is *mone (mon–ay')*, which has a lot of interesting possibilities worth considering.

Out of the economic depression of the 1930s there came the "mansion mentality." Many of God's people, having lost all hope of ever prospering in this life, began to dream of one day moving into stately and ornate dwellings. "Mansion songs" sprang up during this time as a reassurance to the numberless earth-bound vagabonds that their eternal destiny was a place of dazzling white palaces — much like the antebellum "Southern" mansions they saw portrayed in Depression–era movie epics such as *Gone With the Wind*.

We should not discount entirely the hope of a residence that will far exceed in stateliness and beauty anything we have ever lived in on earth. However, *mone* carries with it a connotation not of stability, but of mobility. Some lexicographers have defined it as "way-stations on the journey," or as "stopping places along the road." Heaven could easily be a place of unfolding vistas, horizons, plateaus, and new sights.

Thus Jesus' use of the word *mansion* suggests rest in the midst of continual progressive activity. What He might have been saying was: "In My Father's house are many way-stations where you will stop in between the continuous unfolding of God's eternal purpose."

All the children of Israel
had light in their dwellings.
Exodus 10:23 NKJ

What a study in contrasts! Egyptian homes shrouded with darkness like a blanket — darkness so thick you could almost cut it with a knife. By contrast, all the children of Israel flooded their dwellings with light. Using the symbolism we find in Scripture, Egypt is a type of the world system. Israel is a type of the Church. This verse is thus telling us that believers walking in the light of truth will carry that light right into their homes. Likewise, those following the prince of darkness will live in homes which are an extension of that darkness.

This promise assures you and me of light in our dwellings, regardless of world conditions. The ending of the Church Age is likened to a setting sun. Jesus said that He was working while it was yet day because the night was coming when no man could work. (John 9:4.) It is evening time for the Church. In Zechariah 14:7, the Lord promises that His followers will have light even in the evening of life. We who believe will be bathed in light even when the sun is setting upon the world.

According to Esther 8:16, light in the dwelling is accompanied by gladness, joy and honor. Not only is the home of the believer assured illumination, but also a general profusion of God's blessings. It is possible, probable, and preferable that our homes be so filled with the presence of the Lord that all non-Christians visiting there will be touched and impressed with that light. It can happen!

That He would show you the secrets of wisdom!
For they would double your prudence....
Job 11:6 NKJ

Here is a word from the Lord that links the best of two realms. It blends natural skills, understanding and expertise with supernatural insight. It is the Lord's way of adding the wisdom from above to the natural common sense and native ability He has given each of us. God's superior knowledge coupled with our natural human instinct produces an unbeatable combination.

This verse is especially vital to salesmen, executives, factory foremen, employers, business owners, and all those who must compete daily in the market place of life. Our God is telling us to be knowledgeable, informed, aware. Each of us needs to know everything he can find out about his occupation if he expects to succeed in this competitive world. The Christian has to think faster and better than the competition if he is to survive. The non-Christian's thinking is pre-occupied with self-aggrandizement. The Christian, on the other hand, has a clear channel to wisdom because the Holy Spirit of God has shown him how to get the victory over selfishness.

Here, the Lord is promising to add His knowledge, understanding, insight and expertise to ours. That gives us a double portion of wisdom — or what one translator calls "two-sided wisdom."

Make this fourfold confession of faith: "With God's wisdom I can have: 1) twice the results with half the effort, 2) the competitive edge over the non-Christian, 3) a doubled output, and 4) a double portion of God's blessing on my life and work." Praise the Lord!

> They shall be Mine," says the Lord of hosts,
> On the day that I make them My jewels....
> Malachi 3:17 NKJ

This verse has always stirred my imagination to visualize the great circle of celestial beings gathered around the throne of God. The throne is majestic and awesome because the Lord God of Hosts is seated on it. Around Him all the angels are in attendance and the whole heavenly assembly stands and gazes with rapture upon the power center of the universe.

I also visualize a circle of redeemed saints encompassing the throne like a great rainbow. The beautiful and most breathtaking aspect of this magnificent assembly is the fact that the circle is unbroken. The reason it is complete is because God's will has finally been done on earth as it is in heaven.

The Lord's promise that all those who are to come to know Him will be there on the day He makes us His jewels has guaranteed the completion of the circle of the redeemed. I know from Scripture, however, that not every person on earth will be there in that circle. I have met people who say they do not want to be there. God will not force them to come. He invites people to enter the Kingdom of heaven; He doesn't coerce them into it. But He does declare in His Word that His place is for the salvation of the *whole* family. If there are members of your family who do not yet know the Lord, quote Malachi 3:17 aloud and make it part of your fourfold confession of faith: 1) "There is a circle around the throne of God." 2) "It is a family circle." 3) "It is my family circle." 4) "The circle will not be broken! All my family will be there!" Praise the Lord!

I am the Lord, I do not change....
Malachi 3:6 NKJ

This is an encouraging word for those seeking stability in a changing world. In the creation, God set up the succeeding seasons, the alteration of day and night, the incoming and outgoing tides. He placed man in a world in which the sun rises at a different time every single day and sets at a different time each evening.

Life is so filled with activity that we must constantly adjust, adapt, and accommodate ourselves to changing situations — even in nature. Behind all this ceaseless motion, there is one constant: God. Whatever may be going on about us, we can always know that He is the same, day in and day out. He can be depended on. He does not change. He is not fickle. He is not moody. He does not feel good about us one day and bad the next. His love is always steadily on course.

This verse can be especially helpful when we find ourselves in situations that seem rather shaky. We speak about having to walk on egg shells, tread on thin ice, or build on shifting sands. That kind of feeling does not give us much of a sense of stability.

The Scriptures liken the Lord to a rock. A rock is stable. It will be there after the storm has passed. Rain doesn't wash it away, lightning doesn't move it. This promise from our Creator, "I am the Lord, I change not," tells us that day after day He is "on the job." He never takes vacations, days off, or leaves of absence. Anytime, anywhere, under any circumstance, we can breathe His name and be assured of an instant audience with Him. What an encouragement to know that the Lord Who watches over His people neither slumbers nor sleeps. (Ps. 121:4.)

There shall enlargement and deliverance arise....
Esther 4:14

In this verse, the Lord promises us not only a deliverance from every dilemma, but also an enlargement in our particular calling and station in life. The text reverses their order, but for the sake of clarity I would like to present these two occurrences this way: 1) deliverance or liberation of a person from a temporary state of confinement, followed by 2) enlargement or expansion of his sphere of influence.

We see this sequence in the life of David. In his youth as a shepherd he slays a marauding bear. Reports of this incident reach his family. Next he overcomes a lion which is attacking the flock of sheep. A lion is more ferocious and destructive than a bear, so news of this exploit reaches all the shepherds.

Next David faces the giant, Goliath. He draws upon his past experiences to declare openly: "The Lord who delivered me from the paw of the bear and the lion will deliver me from the hand of this uncircumcised Philistine." Again David's enlargement grows. This time to the whole Israelite army. The Lord then rescues David from the hand of King Saul, enlarging his reputation in all of Israel and Judah. Finally, David becomes king himself and is delivered from an insurrection lead by Absalom, and his sphere of influence reaches the nations.

Every time you faithfully trust the Lord for His deliverance, two things happen: 1) He sets you free, and 2) He enlarges your potential. You will not stay in the same trying circumstances perpetually. You will come out, and with expansion. It is worth pursuing after deliverance in order to reap the reward of enlargement!

Do not listen or consent.
1 Kings 20:8 NKJ

King Ahab of Israel was being intimidated by a bully. Ben-hadad was putting fear in his heart by threatening to move into Israel, take over Ahab's kingdom, and carry off all his possessions. Fearfully Ahab offered no resistance, but instead caved in to Ben-hadad's outrageous demands. Ahab's spineless reply was: "Just as you say, all that I have is yours."

The elders of the land responded differently. "Do not listen or consent," they advised Ahab. "You're listening to the wrong voice. You're accepting what you should be refusing."

We receive mail from people who have recurring nightmares. Usually their dreams are about accidents, injuries, or personal harm coming to loved ones. My response is always to send them this verse, urging them to take a stance of refusal and denial. I remind them that as believers related to the Lord, we are told to yield no topography or ground to the enemy.

One time, our family was scheduled to take a trip over a treacherous mountain road. Three times I dreamed that we had an accident at a certain bad curve on that road. After the third time, I quoted this verse, declaring: "This could happen, but it doesn't have to. I don't believe an accident would glorify God or serve any purpose. Since it has no utility, I refuse that dream in Jesus' name!" We made the trip both ways with no problem.

You can do the same thing with negative dreams, visions, or apprehensions. Refuse to receive them!

___

You brought us out to rich fulfillment.
Psalm 66:12 NKJ

This term **rich fulfillment** is translated from a Hebrew word *revayah (rev–aw–yah')* meaning total satisfaction. This word is derived from a primitive root word *ravah (raw–vaw')* which means "to slake the thirst," or "to abundantly satisfy the appetite."

David lists the trying circumstances he and the people of Israel had to face and how the Lord had led them through all their difficulties. He relates how the enemy had tried to enslave them, to submerge them, to overcome them with fire and flood. But then he tells of the Lord's gracious dealings with him and his people:

"Because of You, Lord, we are actually better off now than we were before our trial. We held on to Your promises and You fulfilled them all. You gave us the courage to endure, led us through the tests, and then rewarded us by bringing us out to total satisfaction." (Author's paraphrase.)

Sometimes a greater insight into a word can be gained by comparing it with other usages in the Scriptures. *Revayah* appears one other time in the Old Testament: in Psalm 23:5 where David declares of the Lord's blessings,...**my cup runneth over.** The word translated "runneth over" and "rich fulfillment" are one and the same *(revayah)*. Moisture, satisfaction, and abundance are all embodied in this one word.

Never give up. The effort it takes to get through trying situations is always worth it when you come out to the **wealthy place** (KJV). Satan wants to discourage you into quitting and missing the blessing. Jesus wants you to persevere, to get past the place of difficulty, and to come out to *revayah,* the place of fulfillment. The effort is worth it!

Knowledge is easy to him who understands.
Proverbs 14:6 NKJ

The Lord is omniscient; He knows *all* things. In His Word He has promised to make available to His children all the treasures of His wisdom and knowledge. Our tendency is to complicate matters and make it difficult to obtain divine knowledge. This verse assures us that knowledge is easy for the person who understands the ways of God.

One time I was walking through a public place of business headed for a conference room where I was to take part in a seminar. Suddenly I noticed a man sitting all alone. Instantly the Lord put it in on my heart to witness to the man about the love of God. I have a natural reluctance to go up to people I don't know and start talking. I did have a burden for the man and knew that the Lord was putting him on my heart. My spirit was saying to me, "Share God's love with him," but my flesh was saying, "But you don't even know this man!"

Inwardly I was praying for help. In answer to my prayer, the Lord imparted the knowledge about the man that I needed in order to approach him. Knowledge is factual. The Lord gave me the complete facts about the man's situation, his occupation, his relationship with his wife and children, and his attitude toward God. The man was so overwhelmed with my knowledge and concern that he broke into tears and surrendered his life to the Lord then and there.

The knowledge you need to be an effective witness is available. It is easy to come by. Jesus said that His yoke is easy. (Matt. 11:30.) Teamed with Him in service, His knowledge easily becomes your knowledge!

**Commit your works to the Lord, and
your thoughts will be established.
Proverbs 16:3 NKJ**

To "commit your works to the Lord" is to "roll" onto Him all your plans and schemes. It means to come to the place where you are willing to trust yourself and your future totally to His keeping, watchful care.

Before you and I became Christians, we learned self-preservation from the world system. Before conversion we thought we had to depend upon survival instinct based on human cleverness and native ingenuity. It is quite a transition from "Look out for Number One" to "The will of the Lord be done." To get self-will to God's will takes quite a bit of doing. This verse placed in the Bible was to help us make the necessary adjustments to our attitude and actions.

Rolling your plans and activities onto the Lord can be done only when you are convinced that He is more interested in your happiness and well-being than you are. ...[He will cause your thoughts to become agreeable to His will, and] so shall your plans be established and succeed.

Your thoughts are the equivalent of your plans, aims, objectives, hopes, and desires. Turn your future over to the Lord 100 percent, and then you can *know* that your plans will succeed. It is a paradox: hold on too tightly and you lose, release the Lord and you win! Try it!

You have cast all my sins behind Your back.
Isaiah 38:17 NKJ

This verse has universal appeal to everyone who has experienced genuine sorrow for sins committed. When we confess our sins to God, not only is He faithful and just to forgive us our sins (1 John 1:9), He also removes them from us and puts them behind His back.

All through Scripture we find references to the face of the Lord and the eyes of the Lord. For example, the prophet Habakkuk said of his God: **You are of purer eyes than to behold evil, and cannot look on wickedness** (Hab. 1:13 NKJ).

So confessed sins are removed from us and also from God's gaze by a process that puts them out of sight forever. Since God puts our sins out of His mind and view, we need to learn to do the same. I continually meet people whom God has forgiven, but who have never forgiven themselves. That is not only tragic, it is also unnecessary — and spiritually unproductive.

Don't keep punishing yourself and carrying a load of self-imposed guilt when simple repentance and confession of sin removes completely and forever all condemnation and feelings of failure.

Since God is omnipresent — filling all of heaven and earth with His presence (Jer. 23:24) — we may ask where His "back" is? The answer is: In the opposite direction from His face and eyes. This verse lovingly assures us that the sins we have confessed to our heavenly Father are no longer visible to Him. What blessed release!

For every idle word men may speak, they
will give account of it on the day of judgment.
Matthew 12:36 NKJ

Put your words to work for you! Speak words that produce action, results or wages. This word *idle* is quite interesting. In the original New Testament writings, it is *argos (ar–gos')*. In the Greek, *a* is a privative negative, or as we say an "un" word. *Argos* refers to toil, labor, or any activity or work that pays wages.

Thus, "idle" words are words that are non-working unemployed, inactive — words having no utility. Jesus used the word *argos* in the parable of the laborers in the vineyard in which the owner asked the eleventh-hour workers, "Why have you been standing here *idle* all day?" In other words, "Why are you not gainfully employed when there is work to be done?"

This verse is not an indictment against a sense of humor. Some Christians are so somber, joyless, and legalistic that they resent happy, joyful, or humorous people. Idle words are not anecdotes, aphorisms, metaphors, maxims, proverbs, or humorous stories.

Idle words are word that are unproductive. Since death and life are in the power of the tongue (Prov. 18:21), we are challenged to speak only words that generate life. Fill your mouth with praises. Let your speech be full of promises of God. Every time you quote a scripture at the prompting of the Holy Spirit, you are releasing faith. With careful attention, your words can be fully active, fully employed, fully working.

**But others fell on good ground and yielded a crop:
some a hundredfold, some sixty, and some thirty.
Matthew 13:8 NKJ**

The context of this verse seems to indicate three types
of Christians with varying percentage of return on the seed
of the Word of God planted in them. It implies that some
have the capacity to produce a 100 percent return on God's
investment, while others can only muster 60 percent, and
others even less. Each person is thus thought to have his
own *set* "personal production potential."

Some scholars, however, see in this verse a *progress* in
the life of each believer. To them, this verse says that each of
us has three phases in our Christian life: PHASE ONE is
when are babes in Christ; PHASE TWO is when we are
young, growing servants and handmaids of the Lord;
PHASE THREE is when we are mature saints, grown-up
adult Christians. "Thirtyfold," or phase one, could include
the blessing that accompany the New Birth. "Sixtyfold," or
phase two, would refer to the blessing of growth, expansion,
enlargement, and development into spiritual adulthood.
"A hundredfold," phase three, would entail all the blessings
that come with the patience, faithfulness, consistency, and
endurance of our later years.

If so, then the famous and eagerly-sought instant
"hundredfold return" on our giving would not be a "wind-
fall profit" at all, but rather on a "long-term capital gain"!

The encouraging thing about this progression is that it
is on-going. Thank God right now for raising your
"personal production potential" and preparing you for the
next phase of your unfolding life and ministry.

Bear fruit...bear more fruit...bear much fruit....
John 15:1–8 NKJ

We are living in an age that wants instant results. Ours is a push-button society that is turned off by delays, slowdowns, or obstructions. We want our photos, our printing, our cleaning and our answers — right now!

In the story of the tortoise and the hare, we are more impressed with the rabbit than with the turtle because the rabbit is speedy. Like us, he's anxious to be "off and running." He appeals to us because he's a "shaker and mover," the type that "makes things happen."

The turtle, on the other hand, is just not "with it." He's a slow mover, a plodder, a "real stick-in-the-mud type." He has no "pizazz," generates no excitement, no glamour. He's just plain dull!

Lost in our comparisons is the fact that the lowly turtle won the race while the speedy rabbit never made it to the finish line.

There are dozens of books on the market these days on how to go from kindergarten to graduate level in one quantum leap. Even many Christians seem to want to go from spiritual babyhood to manhood in "one giant step."

By contrast, this verse indicates a "longevity mindset." First we bear fruit. Then as we persevere and faithfully continue, we bear more fruit. If we keep at it, ultimately we bear much fruit. I certainly don't mean to extinguish the fires of enthusiasm or spiritual desire. But the message remains the same: It's the long haul which counts. Time is on our side. Sooner or later faithfulness and consistency produce fruit, then more fruit, then much fruit. It's just a matter of time!

We will give ourselves continually
to prayer....
Acts 6:4 NKJ

The key phrase here is **give ourselves continually**. It is a statement indicating great intensity and exertion. This is not a casual, ho-hum, business-as-usual type activity, but one involving concentration and determined effort. My only intent in defining this expression is to open the way for all of us to have a more effective prayer life.

In the original Greek text, **give ourselves continually** is only one word: *proskartereo (pros–kar–ter–eh'–o)*. It is a compound word made of two components: 1) *pros*, meaning "toward, in the direction of, forward, or pertaining to," and, 2) *kartereo*, meaning "endurance, strength, steadfastness, and power."

To "give oneself continually to prayer" is to engage in an activity requiring time, energy, commitment and disciplined effort. It demands prayer habits that are consistent, persistent, and insistent. *Proskartereo* has thus been defined as "persevering diligence," "close adherence to a task," "constant diligence in exercise," and "steadfast earnestness." It implies taking prayer very seriously and working at it very hard.

One great writer on the subject of prayer has defined this expression as "making a business of prayer; surrendering oneself totally to prayer; putting fervor, urgency, perseverance, and time into prayer."

If your own prayer life does not match these descriptions, begin today to "give yourself continually to prayer." It is never too late to begin!

So the word of the Lord grew mightily and prevailed.
Acts 19:20 NKJ

The book of Acts makes three progressive statements about the Word of the Lord:

PHASE ONE is found in Acts 6:7 in which we read that in the infancy of the Church, the Word of God **increased**. This is what happened to us at our conversion. Before we came to know the Lord, our knowledge of Scripture was quite limited. Upon our conversion, however, an awakening to the beauty of the Word of God stimulated an appetite for more. In our Christian walk, His word increases in us as we become more and more enamored with His marvelous promises.

PHASE TWO is found in Acts 12:24 which tells us that the Word of God **grew and multiplied** (NKJ). Applying this verse to ourselves, we experience an expanding consciousness of scriptures through an on-going, on-growing practice of daily studying of the Word of God. The multiplying of that Word comes as we share it with others.

PHASE THREE is found here in Acts 19:20 where we read that the Word of the Lord **grew mightily and prevailed** (NKJ). In the original Greek, these words denote dominion and force. They are indicative of a heavily armed military unit triumphing in combat, driving out the enemy, and occupying territory as a conqueror with a great show of force.

As we grow in the Lord, we can experience: 1) an increase in knowledge of scriptures, 2) a normal growth in ability to multiply that knowledge by sharing it with others, and 3) a relationship with the Lord in which His Word becomes the one motivating factor of life.

Let this mind be in you which was also in Christ Jesus.
Philippians 2:5 NKJ

The key word in this sentence is **mind.** In the original Greek, it is *phroneo (fron–eh'–o)* and covers a wide range of meanings. Each definition of *phroneo* can speak volumes to us.

In *The Amplified Bible* this word is translated "attitude." We are urged to let the same attitude that Christ displayed govern our activities. Jesus came to earth to do His Father's will. He showed forth that purpose when He prayed: **...not my will, but thine, be done** (Luke 22:42). He attributed all His activities to a desire to please His Father. We can have the same attitude.

Phroneo can also be translated "opinion." We can have the same opinion about life that Jesus had. He loved truth. So can we. He detested hypocrisy. We too should be turned off by plastic artificiality. We can have His opinion of right and wrong. If we will, we can let the same opinion be ours which was in Christ Jesus.

Finally, *phroneo* can be translated "interest" or "motivation." We can be interested in and motivated by the same things which interested and motivated Jesus Christ. Our Lord was motivated to pray, to attend to the house of God, to fellowship with God's people, to care for the needy, and to go about doing good. (Acts 10:38.) We too can allow the same motivation to be in us which was in our Lord and Savior. He is our role model.

The old hymn expresses this attitude, opinion, interest and motivation best when it declares: "All I ask is to be like Him."

The peace of God...will guard your
hearts and minds through Christ Jesus.
Philippians 4:7 NKJ

This verse calls to mind an armed sentinel standing by to prevent intrusion. Soldiers guard fortresses; sentries watch over premises. But here is peace which stands guard. Peace does not seem militant enough to do any "guarding," yet it is God's choice to protect our hearts and minds.

The Greek word translated **peace** here is *eirene (i–ray'–nay)*. It includes the idea of joining and reconciling forces or factors to produce quietness, harmony, and unity. *Eirene* says: "Be reconciled with God, and you will have rest and contentment. All division, disunity, distrust, and disruption will be removed when peace intervenes and takes over."

The lexicographers tell us that *eirene* implies more than concord, harmony, or just getting along with one's neighbor. Included in this word is the idea of security, safety, prosperity, and happiness. Your thoughts and affections can be in perfect harmony and you can enjoy total rest — all because of Jesus.

The verse adds the name of the Lord like a signature on a check. A check without a signature is worthless. Jesus gives validity to this promise by adding His name to it.

Peace not only guards heart and mind, but also reconciles both areas. Sometimes your heart will tell you one thing and your mind another. Pray for God's peace to reconcile the divided factions and bring them together. Oh happy times when heart and mind are in one accord!

**God also bearing witness both with signs
and wonders, with various miracles, and
gifts of the Holy Spirit....
Hebrews 2:4 NKJ**

Just when you feel your witnessing is ineffective, your testimony discredited, your words falling on deaf ears, the Lord comes to add His testimony and witness to yours. This action gives instant credibility to your Christian witness.

The Greek word translated **bearing witness** here is a triple compound: *sunepimartureo (soo–ep–ee–mar–too–reh'o)*. It is composed of three elements: *sun* ("alongside"), *epi* ("in addition to"), and *martureo* ("to witness and testify"). Thus this verse says that if you will give your testimony to an unbelieving world, the Lord will come alongside and add His witness and testimony to yours. When the Lord bears witness, it will be with signs, wonders, diverse miracles, and gifts of the Holy Spirit. Supernatural confirmation is thus promised you.

In the original Greek, the expression **gifts** is *merismos (mer–is–mos')* which is defined as "distribution, division, portion." We can be in a position where the Lord will distribute to us a share of His miraculous and supernatural power. At conversion, He gives each of us a measure of faith. John 3:34 indicates that the Holy Spirit comes without measure, but apparently His gifts are apportioned and measured out individually as the Lord sees fit.

This verse reassures us that if we will give our testimony, the Lord will come and corroborate our witness by distributions of the Holy Spirit's ministry. Have you claimed your share? If not, do so right away!

Casting all your care upon Him, for He cares for you.
1 Peter 5:7 NKJ

This verse contains a play on words: your care becomes God's care. Reading in the original language helps add a dimension not always evident in the English version. The words "care" and "cares" in this verse happen to be two entirely different words. Looking closely at their meanings makes this promise even more precious to us.

In the Greek text, this word translated **care** is *merimna (mer'–im–nah)*. It is a noun which has to do with anxiety, stress, distraction, preoccupation with insecurity, or worry. It suggests the kind of thoughts that trouble us and keep us from peace of mind. Jesus used this word when He said to His disciples: **...take no** (anxious) **thought for your life...**(Matt. 6:25). This is a reminder that time spent in anxiety could be better invested in Bible reading, prayer, praising the Lord, and waiting upon Him for direction.

The second word translated **cares** is *melo (mel'o)*, a verb meaning "to be concerned about or interested in." God is aware of you. He is interested in you. You can cast all your worries, anxieties, and insecurities upon Him because your well-being matters to Him.

Don't carry around any unnecessary burdens; the Lord invites you to shift them onto Him. He has a 2000-year head start on you when it comes to burden-bearing. He can be trusted. Give Him your cares; He cares!

**These things says He who is holy, He who
is true, ...*He who opens and no one
shuts, and shuts and no one opens*:**

**See, I have set before you an open
door, and no one can shut it....**
Revelation 3:7,8 NKJ

This verse presents an area called *the transition zone.*

Think about the scene: Behind you is a door which the
Lord has closed. You know you cannot go back. There is
nothing to go back to. In front of you stands a door to new
opportunities, new challenges, new ministry, new spheres
of influence, a whole new future. In this transition zone in
which you find yourself, the door to the past is sealed shut,
but the door to the future has not yet opened. You know it is
time to progress. There are all kinds of indications that the
new door will open, but so far you are at a stand still. What
is expected of you in this situation?

You must maintain a good level of trust in your God.
This is no time to oscillate, fluctuate, or vacillate. This is the
time to be reassured that the same Lord who closed the old
door behind you will also open the new door in front of
you. His leading you into the transition zone is not a sign of
abandonment, but of His confidence in you and of your
need of confidence in Him. Remember: He did not bring
you out to desert you; He brought you out in order to bring
you in! (Deut. 6:23.)

**This wisdom descendeth not from above, but
is earthly, sensual, devilish...But the
wisdom that is from above is first pure....
James 3:15,17**

There is a sentence in the Anglican prayer book that
reads: "Deliver us from the world, the flesh, the devil." that
sentence was drawn from this verse in James. **Earthly** refers
to the world. **Sensual** is the equivalent of the flesh. **Devilish**
has to do with Satan and his demons. Verse 17 of this
passage contains a reference to the true wisdom which is
from above. Thus these verses deal with four kinds or
sources of wisdom.

Earthly wisdom is centered in the human intellect. As
beneficial as it may be to us in this life, since it deals with
matters of time and not eternity, it does not adequately
prepare us for the other world.

Sensual wisdom is centered in the human body. This
wisdom comes to us through the senses and relates to the
world of entertainment, advertising, art, fashion, and
recreation. It appeals to the flesh or physical side of man. It
too fails to equip for eternity.

Devilish wisdom is centered in the spirit realm. It can
be found in horoscopes, Ouija boards, tarot cards, seances,
and other occultic activities. Its danger is that it leads
people away from the truth of God and opens them up to
the lies and deception of the enemy.

Wisdom from above is centered in the Holy Spirit. It is
God–given wisdom. It originates from outside of man, but
is available to him for the asking. (James 1:5.) The beautiful
thing about this wisdom is that it is three-dimensional: with
it we can be in good relationship with God, in good
harmony with our fellowman, and at peace with ourselves.

He has made us accepted in the Beloved.
Ephesians 1:6 NKJ

Accepted in the Beloved. What an encouraging word. In this world, with its constant search for affection, approval, and acceptance, it is good to know that we Christians are accepted in the Beloved. We do not have to struggle for acceptance, we already have it. How comforting to know that our Father will not love us any more (or less!) in the future than He does right now.

Sometimes the best way to understand a word is to find out how it is used elsewhere. This word *accepted* is no exception. In the original Greek text, it is *charitoo* *(khar–ee–to'–o)*, and is closely related to the grace word *charis. Charitoo* is defined as "highly favored," "graced with honor," and "accepted." It only appears one other time in the New Testament and that is in Luke 1:28 when the angel appeared to Mary and called her by her name..."**Rejoice, *highly favored one*, the Lord is with you; blessed are you among women!**" (NKJ). The word used to tell Mary that she was highly favored by being selected by the Lord for a very special task is the same word used to describe all Christians. We have also been highly favored by being selected of God.

Mary was chosen to bring about the Lord's first coming into the world. All believers have been chosen to bring about the Lord's Second Coming into the world.

Quit putting yourself down. If you are a Christian, you are not an outcast, you are *charitoo* — accepted in the Beloved!

**Who comforts us in all our tribulation, that we may
be able to comfort those who are in trouble....
2 Corinthians 1:4 NKJ**

This is a case of "freely you have received, freely give."
Each of us has received something from the Lord (in stress
situations) that we can pass on to others. This makes us a
channel of blessing.

In this verse, the Apostle Paul says that not only do we
receive comfort from the Lord, but that we can also pass
that comfort on to others. Comfort is that special
"something" the Lord imparts to us to sustain us, undergird
us, and reinforce us in times of trial and tribulation. The
very word itself paints an image of the Lord leaning over
the portals of heaven and calling out to us words of
encouragement and reassurance. He does even more than
that. He comes down and stands alongside of us to speak
words of comfort to us in our time of greatest need. Then
He tells us to do the same for others. Be a comforter, a
consoler, an encourager to those who have needs like your
own.

There are people in our world who feel that no one
understands what they are going through. Furthermore,
they are convinced that no one even cares. When you have
been comforted by the Lord, you can say to such people,
'Look, I understand what you are going through and I care,
because I have been there myself." It is by undergoing —
and overcoming — our own trials that we are able to
comfort others in their times of testing. The Lord has
comforted you in your time of need; now pass that comfort
on!

Some say...Elijah, and others Jeremiah....
Matthew 16:14 NKJ

Jesus had just asked His disciples how the world viewed Him. They relayed to their Master that people saw Him in different capacities. Some felt He was a reflection of Elijah, while others felt He was of the Jeremiah mold. The thing that is interesting here is that Jesus is a fine blend of many characteristics of both men which we would do well to emulate.

Elijah was Mr. Firm. He was as straight as an arrow. One of his many positive qualities was manliness. He was strong spiritually, physically, mentally, emotionally, and volitionally. Elijah comes across as a no-nonsense type with unusual strength of character, intense spiritual drive, and a determined will. The people saw these same qualities in Jesus when He refused to be intimidated by the religious leaders. It was easy to associate Jesus with Elijah because of His strength.

Jeremiah was the exact opposite. He was gentle, compassionate, kind, merciful, patient, genteel. He was known to weep openly, was highly sensitive, and had a great capacity for love and kindness. Like Jeremiah, Jesus was tenderhearted and possessed great feelings.

Put Elijah and Jeremiah together and you have a person who is tough but gentle, firm but compassionate, rugged and strong but blessed with great sensitivity. It would be good if each of us could incorporate the same qualities in our own life. We too need to be firm against sin, but compassionate with the sinner. What an ideal!

But at evening time it shall...be light.
Zechariah 14:7 NKJ

This verse speaks of a phenomenon of light at evening. It refers to a future time when Jesus will bodily return to earth and His feet will touch down upon the Mount of Olives. According to verse 4,...**the Mount of Olives shall be split in two, from east to west, making a very large valley**...In the midst of all of the descriptions of things which will then come to pass, we find these words of comfort, "And at evening time, it will be light." What would ordinarily be a time of the setting of the sun will, instead, become a scene of great illumination.

In the Bible, the Gospel era is likened to a day. Sunrise is a type or symbol of the Upper Room when new light shone down upon the disciples and the birth of the infant Church ushered in the dawn of a bright new day. Noon time is like the Middles Ages. It is the heat of the day, a time of scorching sun, a moment of slowed activity and lessened productivity. Three p.m. is like the Reformation period. The 4 p.m. time is like the evening breeze or the revival times of the last days. Genesis 3:7 calls this period the cool of the day.

Evening time, sunset, or suppertime is like the ending of the Church Age. This Scriptural promise of phenomenal brightness at day's end assures us that we can be bathed in light all the way up to the Lord's coming. The sun will set on civilization, but we who look for His coming will be lit up with the glory of the Lord. Cheer up, your light has come! (Is. 60:1)

**My flesh and my heart fail; but God is the
strength of my heart and my portion forever.
Psalm 73:26 NKJ**

This verse was visibly demonstrated to me in an intensive care unit. Leitha, a friend of the family, was rushed to the hospital suffering from a severe heart attack. Hovering between life and death, she was being monitored closely by the hospital staff. The machine attached to her showed a dot and a wavy line, a dot and a way line. It was explained to me that this was an indication that the heart beat was normal and that Leitha was resting comfortably.

Due to the serious nature of Leitha's condition, the nurse in attendance limited my wife and me to a visit of five minutes or less. She also expressed a great concern that any "excitement" could cause Leitha irreparable damage. For four minutes my wife and I carried on the normal social amenities with Leitha. How are you? Are you eating? Are you resting well? All the time we were talking, I kept watching the monitor. There it was, steady as a clock: dot, wavy line; dot, wavy line.

With one minute to go, I quoted Psalm 73:26. Immediately the lines on the monitor jumped. They began to go up and down, even disappearing off the top and bottom of the screen. Quickly the nurse hurried us out of the room thinking that Leitha was going to die from the sudden burst of excitement. A few days later, however, Leitha was released from the hospital completely healed. Those lines running up and down and off both top and bottom of the monitor were visible proof that God's Word is living and powerful, able to penetrate joints and marrow. We saw it with our own eyes!

**Thine enemies shall be found liars unto
thee; and thou shalt tread upon their high places.
Deuteronomy 33:29**

He was in tears and visibly shaken by his circumstances. He was the proprietor of a local doughnut shop
and had been doing well until trouble came his way. An
unscrupulous person came into his store and staged a
phony accidental fall. Right behind the "injured party" was
a person with a camera to take a picture of the "accident."
Behind that person was another man ready to take down
the names of convenient "witnesses." A lawsuit for an
exorbitant sum of money was then filed by the "victim"
who had staged the whole scenario.

This dear brother told me, "Dick, I could lose it all. My
insurance policy for this type of accident is minimal at best.
If this fellow wins this case, I could lose everything I own."
I stood in agreement with the shopkeeper, praying with
him that the Lord would work a miracle of deliverance.
How I appreciate the faithfulness of the Lord in these
situations. I was not familiar with Deuteronomy 33:29, but
the Holy Spirit quickened it to me: "All your enemies shall
be found as liars unto you."

The next day, in his private chambers, the judge in
charge of the case began to read over the records. The trial
was to start in one hour. Suddenly the magistrate was heard
to make this statement in disgust: "This is a travesty of
justice. The plaintiff is obviously a pathological liar. I refuse
to hear this case. I am throwing it out of court."

An overnight fulfillment of a word from the Lord! Case
dismissed! Another enemy found as a liar!

How should one chase a thousand, and
two put ten thousand to flight, except
their Rock had sold them?...
Deuteronomy 32:30

You and I really do not need another sermon on the necessity and value of unity and teamwork. Common sense tells us that cooperation is vital to accomplishment. We know there is a great need for people to work together for the good of the cause. It is the actualization of what we already know about unity that is needed now.

One can stand against a thousand discouraging things, but two can stand against ten thousand. Having another person alongside to help increases one's potential by nine thousand. That should be a great incentive for working harmoniously with others. As I travel widely, I am constantly meeting Christians who are getting the exact same word from the Lord: *cooperation.* Christianity is not for soloists, prima donnas, lone rangers, heavyweights, or superstars. The Body of Christ is one unit, but it is made up of many components. None of us is a law unto himself or herself. We must work together as a team to represent Christ to the uncommitted. Just as the world needs us, so we believers need each other.

Our Lord has promised to bless cooperation. Alone you or I can push back a thousand obstacles. Together we can push back ten thousand. The more we cooperate, the higher the percentage of results. By taking this promise to heart, we can go from "fruitfulness" (John 15:2) to "much fruitfulness." (John 15:5) Let's do it!

Why was not this ointment sold for three hundred pence, and given to the poor?
John 12:5

Mary is remembered for breaking an alabaster box and anointing Jesus for burial with costly spikenard ointment. Judas Iscariot was critical of the action, placing a cash value of 300 pence on the contents. Since one pence was a day's wage, Mary was actually pouring on Jesus the equivalent of a year's salary.

In the parable of the vineyard, the employer...**agreed with the labourers for a penny a day**...(Matt. 20:2). When Jesus asked Philip how much it would cost to buy food for 5,000 people, Philip replied,....**Two hundred pennyworth of bread is not sufficient**....(John 6:7). This does not equal two dollars, but 200 days' wages!

So Mary actually had, by Judas' evaluation, "wasted" 12 ounces (a Roman liter) of ointment which, if sold, could have brought in enough cash to feed 7,500 people. No wonder Judas reacted as he did!

One sidelight of the incident: This "waste" to which Judas was referring is also translated "perdition." In Greek it is *apoleia (ap–o'–li–a)*. Later when Judas had left to betray His Master, the Lord used this same word to describe His betrayer. He spoke of Judas as the son of "perdition" (*apoleia*) (John 17:12.) It may be some consolation to realize that when you are being criticized, invariably the things you are accused of are the exact things your accusers are guilty of. Mary's act of devotion and love is branded a "perdition" by the very "son of perdition." That ought to take the sting out of the criticism you have been getting lately!

**He who is in you is greater
than he who is in the world.**
1 John 4:4 NKJ

Someone once asked me why a football never gets deflated in a game. Twenty-two huge, burly men kick it, throw it, pounce on it, fumble it — yet it never gets "squashed" or loses its size to deflation. The answer is a simple law of physics. It seems that the internal pressure of the ball is much greater than all the pressure 22 men can place upon it externally.

This verse says the same thing about the Christians. The power of the Holy Spirit residing in our hearts and lives is greater than all the pressure the external world can place upon us.

You could list all the different opponents who come against you to impede or block your forward progress. Satan's strategy is to deflate you and render you inoperative, but the Holy Ghost gives you a buoyancy. You can roll with the punches. It may seem sometimes that you are being tossed around by circumstances, but with the Lord's power within, you will always bounce back.

This verse is a great comfort to many people who are not having it very easy in life. It is a constant reminder of God's sustaining grace, Christ's resident peace, and the Holy Spirit's indwelling power. Greater is the power within us than the pressure upon us. So hang in there, teammate; despite the hard hits, we're winning!

He who waters will also be watered himself.
Proverbs 11:25 NKJ

Our English language sometimes confines our understanding of Biblical principles. Twice in this verse we find a form of the word *water*. At face value, we could assume we are being told here that if we give someone a cup of water, then sooner or later someone else will give us a cup of water in return. That interpretation is only partially accurate.

This principle of reciprocity is found throughout the Bible. For example, **Give and it shall be given unto you....**(Luke 6:38); **Draw nigh to God, and he will draw nigh to you....**(James 4:8). However, this verse promises far more than a simple "tit for tat." It has a greater dimension than reaping (*only*) what we have sown.

A look at a Hebrew-English lexicon will reveal there are two different Hebrew words used here — both highly significant. The first word translated **waters** is *ravah* (*raw–vaw'*) and has to do with satisfying a thirst. In Christian circles, this action would be the same as giving a person a cup of cold water in the name of the Lord.

The second Hebrew word translated **watered** is *yara* (*yaw– raw'*), meaning "to pour out like rain, descend like a shower, fill up by a deluge, flow like waters from a cloud-burst."

So, with a little imagination, we could interpret this verse: "If you give someone a cup of cold water in the name of the Lord, He will give back to you the whole reservoir!" What a promise!

**He who loves Me will be loved by My Father,
and I will love him and manifest Myself to him.
John 14:21 NKJ**

This is a very intimate promise. It speaks to those who want more than a shallow, superficial relationship with the Lord. As I travel, I meet precious saints of God everywhere who say they want more out of life than what they are now experiencing. They have a yearning for a deeper, closer spiritual relationship with the Lord than what their church is able to provide. They are on a personal quest for "more" of the Lord. I pray that you, too, will sense that yearning and embark on that quest.

In this verse, Jesus is promising that to those who truly hunger and thirst for Him, He will manifest Himself personally. This manifestation is more than a conversion experience. It is even more than a baptism with the Holy Spirit. In addition to all these beautiful and dynamic encounters with the Lord, He is promising each of us a personal visitation.

In the original Greek text, this word translated **manifest** is *emphanizo (em–fan–id'–zo)*. It is a verb meaning "to disclose by appearance." Literally, it could be interpreted as "to shine within," "to exhibit plainly," or "to appear openly." All you need to receive such a disclosure is a heart-hunger for more of Jesus and His power and love. He will meet you in an individual way.

Blessed are you who hunger and thirst for righteousness. You shall be visited — and *soon*!

The Lord is able to give
you much more than this.
2 Chronicles 25:9 NKJ

How often are we willing to settle for less than God's best for our lives? Sometimes when a step of faith requires some real effort, it seems easier to give in to pressure and accept substandard arrangements or provision. This verse assures us that the Lord is trying to raise our sights in order to raise our levels.

Whatever you may have in life right now, the Lord is able to give you much more than this. His plans for you, if accepted and implemented by you, will improve your quality of life. Good will become better. Better will become best. God is able to do much more for you. Best of all, He is willing to do it. All it takes is faith.

But faith is not a struggle to convince your "spirit" of something your mind knows is really not so. It's not saying "I believe" over and over until you "psyche" yourself into believing by force of sheer repetition. Faith is not brainwashing or mouth wishing.

Simply stated, faith is more than believing God. We have all heard of the great faith of Abraham. Yet what he did, we can all do:...**Abraham *believed God,* and it was counted to him for righteousness** (Rom 4:3). Abraham became known as the "father of faith." Why? Because of his attitude and actions...**before him *whom* he believed, even God**....(v. 17).

The Lord is able to give you much more than this. If you have faith — if you believe God — then take Him at His Word. Do what Abraham did: Believe God, agree with God, obey God. Do that, and you will receive "much more than this" from Him! Amen!

Healing all who were oppressed by the devil.
Acts 10:38 NKJ

You have wanted more power in your life. You have desired to see more miracles in your ministry. You have fasted and prayed for a revival of signs, wonders, and miracles. One thing that will help speed the answer to those prayers is a clear understanding and appreciation of Satan's tyranny over the human race.

Jesus contested the malignancy of Satan and, by the powerful anointing of the Holy Spirit, healed the oppressed ones. The key word in this great description of Jesus' healing ministry is this reference to the oppression of the devil. The word *oppression* is defined as "domination, total control, tyranny, lordship; the exercise of authority over another person or persons as a potentate or dictator."

By their sin in the Garden of Eden, Adam and Eve abdicated their position as reigning over the earth. By default, they surrendered their dominion and authority to the usurper, the prince of darkness, who now holds the unbelieving world in a cruel vise-like grip. (1 John 5:19 NKJ.) Jesus came to destroy the works of Satan. (1 John 3:8.) According to this verse in Acts, He went about doing good and breaking the stranglehold of Satan upon people.

In Psalm 97:10, David challenges us to love the Lord and hate the Evil One. You and I must look upon Satan's victims with great compassion, and at the same time hate the enemy for what he is doing to them. This will qualify us for miracles quicker than anything else we could ever do.

Sin lies at the door.
Genesis 4:7 NKJ

Here is another verse that has great potential for personal encouragement. The Lord is speaking to Cain and describing two conditions to him: 1) what happens if he does well (acceptance), and 2) what happens if he does not do well (a chance to make amends).

The usual interpretation of this verse is that sin is like a ravenous animal at the door ready to pounce on and devour the one who sins. But that is not what God is really saying here. Without getting too technical with the language, we can interpret the Hebrew word translated **sin** (*chatta'th*) (*khat–tawth'*) as a "sin *offering*." Thus this verse is really extending God's mercies to cover the failure areas of human life.

What the Lord was saying is: "Cain, if you do well, you will be accepted. If you do not do well, there is still a sin offering available for your reconciliation to Me. You don't have to go through life hounded by failure feelings, carrying a load of guilt and condemnation, defeated by your sins. There is a sin offering. Forgiveness can be yours. Reconciliation is to be preferred to alienation."

We do not have to go through life carrying the sin load. Jesus is our sin offering. He is the Lamb of God who takes away the sin of the world. (John 1:29.) Mercy triumphs over judgement. (James 2:13 NKJ.) This is good news for all of us. Doing good is great. Not doing good is tragic. But even then a way out has been provided. A sin offering is available. (Jesus bore our sins to free us from bondage to sin.) Call on the Lord and He will deliver you once and for all from guilt and condemnation. (Rom. 10:13.)

**It is possible to give away (release) and
become richer! It is also possible to hold
on too tightly and lose everything....
Proverbs 11:24 TLB**

Here is a paradox. Letting go is enriching; holding on is impoverishing. It almost sounds the very opposite of everything we have ever been taught. Our crass world says: "Get all you can, and can all you get!" "Get while the getting is good!" "Opportunity only knocks once, so you'd better seize it when you get the chance!"

This verse is a confirmation of the Biblical admonition of Ecclesiastes 11:1 to "cast your bread upon the waters" (give to others), in confident assurance that "it will come back to you" (greatly multiplied).

While the Bible encourages thrift and preparation for emergencies (Prov. 22:3), it discourages unhealthy hoarding, insecure stockpiling, and anxiously awaiting some dreadful calamity.

Generosity is the key to prosperity, and outflowing is the key to contentment. Givers are fulfilled; takers are unfulfilled. This verse actually implies that giving people get richer while miserly people get poorer. Generous folks can always find something to give to worthy causes. Stingy folks find it extremely hard to find even a ten-cent piece for anybody else's welfare.

What a challenge to be generous! Give away and become richer. (It is the heavenly Father's nature to be giving.) Try it! You'll enjoy it! You're in for a very pleasant surprise when the full impact of this verse falls on you and its results start appearing in your life!

The houses you broke down to fortify the wall.
Isaiah 22:10 NKJ

This verse warns us about being hollow on the inside and placing our whole emphasis on externals.

Israel was facing a siege. The enemy was pounding at the gates of Jerusalem and trying to demolish the city walls. In order to provide materials to use to fortify the outer defenses of the city, the people began dismantling their own houses. The walls were thus kept at the expense of private homes.

People in the world today will often do the same thing: sacrifice their homes for a facade. Some people spend more time, energy, and money on external appearances than they spend on internal strengths and inner resources. You and I continually meet people who are hollow. They are empty inside. They have concentrated so much on putting up a good front (that is what this verse is all about) that they have never developed any character or solid-quality integrity.

Happy is the Christian who has Christ enthroned in his heart. He can say confidently, "Greater is He who is in me than he who is in the world."

Christ dwelling in our hearts enables us to be strong in the Lord and in the power of *His* might. We do not have to sacrifice inner resources to beef up external walls. We are strong both inside and outside. The Lord in our life makes the difference.

**If the ax is dull, and one does not sharpen
the edge, then he must use more strength....**
Ecclesiastes 10:10 NKJ

Sometimes we have to make serious decisions that mean severing someone or something from our life. We painfully face the prospect of making unpleasant "cuts." A long-time employee must be released. A major household move has to be undertaken. (Sometimes moving from one location to another is as disruptive to a family as chopping is to a tree.) A life-time behavior pattern has to be changed drastically. All these "cuts" are hard, but they don't have to be brutal or bloody.

This verse tells us that a sharp cutting edge makes the difference. Dullness means that our action done in the power of the flesh will not only require much strength, but will also be messier.

Jesus prayed all night before making His greatest decisions or changes. You and I rush in with a dull axe and chop away, but it is preferable to face major "cuts" with spiritual preparation. Fasting and prayer will sharpen the cutting edge of our faithful action.

Sometimes removal of persons from our association is like a surgeon cutting away an abscessed part of the body. With skill and speed he makes a deft incision, removes the poisonous mass, closes up the wound, and lets the healing process begin. The sharper the cutting edge, the quicker the recovery.

This verse urges "sharpness" in removing unpleasant elements that are keeping our "tree of life" from becoming as healthy and vigorous as it should be. Prayer "sharpens" us up for even the distasteful things we are called to do.

I will stand upon my watch....
Habakkuk 2:1

Watchmen on the wall were on the lookout for four things: 1) fires from brush areas reaching the city, 2) wild animals which lived in the jungle-like vegetation along the Jordan River and which stealthily approached inhabited areas when driven out of their dens by flood, 3) invading armies which sometimes crawled into position under cover of darkness, and 4) the dawn.

Once the sun rose, the watchmen were relieved of their responsibility. Along with fire, wild animals, and enemy forces, the rising sun occupied the thoughts of the watchmen of ancient times.

Habakkuk had a great hunger and thirst for the Son of righteousness. He had spiritual longings and desires. More than anything else, he wanted to meet God. He had an intensity that drove him relentlessly in his pursuit of God's visitation. We learn a great lesson from Habakkuk. The Lord honored his quest and fulfilled his heart's desire. All because he was faithful at his post of duty.

"I will stand upon my watch." In other words, "I want the Lord so much I will not be satisfied until He comes and meets me." Going away is not the answer to your situation. Taking a sabbatical will not do it. Retreats, advances, seminars, and conferences all add something of value to life. But Habakkuk would tell us his answer came when the Lord visited him at his post where he stood guard with commitment and fidelity: "I will stand upon my watch. I will wait and see." The Lord answered Habakkuk. He will answer you. Stand upon your watch. Bloom where you are planted!

**In a dream, in a vision of the night, when deep sleep
falls upon men, while slumbering on their beds, then
He opens the ears of men, and seals their instruction.**
Job 33:15,16 NKJ

Guidance while sleeping. Does that sound mystical?
Esoteric? Metaphysical? Does it sound practical? Are you
willing to trust God to provide you with guidance and
direction while you are sound asleep?

This verse is meant to assist people who are facing
major decisions, but who must cope with myriad
distractions. You have a serious decision to make. The
phone is ringing off the wall. People are continually asking
you, "What are you going to do? Have you made up your
mind yet? Which way are you going to go?"

You have the heavy responsibility of making the right
decision. You also have a lot of pressure placed upon you
by those around you who want to know what you are going
to do. If that is your situation right now, take heart. This
verse promises divine assistance in the whole matter.

Here the writer assures us that God is going to speak to
us. In a dream. In a vision. In the night when deep sleep
falls upon us, He will open our ears to hear. He will seal up
our instruction. He will even warn us if we need warning.
All this through the sleep process.

When the phone rings incessantly and all you hear is,
"What are you going to do?" your response should be,
"Sleep on it!" Good answer!

**The God of peace will crush
Satan under your feet shortly....
Romans 16:20 NKJ**

Two keys phrases here are **crush** and **under your feet.**

In the original Greek, the word translated **crush** is *suntribo (soon–tree'–bo),* meaning "to shatter, annihilate, torpedo, disintegrate, totally demolish." This verse assures that God has a victory in store for us in every testing area of our lives. That victory will be so complete, the enemy will never again try to put that particular obstacle in our pathway.

Take heart! You have been assured that the victory your God has planned for you is so tremendous your enemy is going to be sorry he ever bothered you in the first place! Your triumphant deliverance is going to be such an embarrassment to the enemy that he wouldn't dare try the same tactic the second time to oppose you!

In Romans 1:17 Paul writes that we believers will go "from faith to faith" — from *victory to victory!*

Under your feet indicates that you and I must actively engage in the good fight of faith. To do that, we must go forth in battle array. Part of the armor of God which we wear is the covering for our feet. (Eph. 6:15.) We need that covering to tread on serpents and scorpions in the name of the Lord. (Luke 10:19.) It's worth it, because every place the sole of our foot trods on is ours! (Josh. 1:3.)

Get your marching shoes out! Get ready to tread down fear, insecurity, poverty, sickness, trouble, discouragement, and all the other works of the enemy. The God of peace is about to shatter Satan's opposition under our feet. Let's go! Onward Christian soldiers!

The spirit indeed is willing, but the flesh is weak.
Matthew 26:41

There is a real study in contrasts in the words *willing* and *weak*. One describes a forwardness, the other a backwardness. One denotes eagerness, the other reticence. One is forthright and aggressive, suggesting taking the initiative; the other is reluctant and apathetic, implying indecisiveness or a lack of ability. Let's take a closer look at each word individually:

The Greek word translated **willing** in this verse is *prothumos (proth'–oo–mos)*. The Greek prefix *pro* means "in front of" or "ahead of." *Thumos* refers to passion, ardor, enthusiasm, hard breathing. Thus, *prothumos* is a description of the spirit of man activated and energized by the Holy Spirit. In that case we could say, "The spirit indeed is ready, alert, forward, eager, prompt, willing; the flesh is not."

The **flesh** is a good description of human nature or the qualities man inherited from Adam. You would think that with all his other improvements, man would have learned to sharpen his spiritual capacities. Not so. In John 6:63, Jesus says: "The flesh (human nature) profits nothing; it is the spirit that quickens and makes alive." Paul tell us in Galatians 5:7 that the fleshly man and the spirit man are at war with each other.

The word translated **weak** is *asthenes (as–then–ace')*, meaning "impotent" or "powerless." It is very close to the Greek word *asthma*, "shortness of breath." We could read this verse: "The spiritual man is breathing hard, eager and ready for action while the natural man is out of breath and unable to participate." To resolve this dilemma, we are told by Paul to walk in the spirit, and then we will not fulfill the tendencies of the flesh.

There His power was hidden.
Habakkuk 3:4 NKJ

The original *King James Version* of this verse reads:
...there was the hiding of his power. This passage describes
a potency not visible to the human eye. It is a power that is
not for public display, a power kept from the view of the
mass of society.

Many believers long and pray for a ministry of the
miraculous. Our world needs ministries which are
accompanied by the supernatural evidences of miracles,
signs and wonders. However, there is a danger in *seeking*
these things. Unconsciously, prayers for manifest power
usually imply huge crowds of people, amazing results,
large offerings, great publicity, world-wide recognition and
popularity. It seems that generally all of that "goes with the
territory." Meet the needs of people, and they will come
running. We see it in Jesus' ministry. He healed people, and
the result was that multitudes followed Him.

But this verse declares that God also has a hidden
power. That sobering fact causes us to ask ourselves some
important questions about our motives in seeking divine
power: Would I be willing to have God's power, and yet
work behind a cloak of anonymity? Would I still seek a
deliverance ministry if I knew it would mean spending the
rest of my life in a mud hut in the jungle? Do I seek signs
and wonders because they have become synonymous with
"successful ministry?" Should miracle power ever be
equated with popularity and fame?

Let us seek the "power gifts" for one reason only — not
to magnify ourselves, but to bring glory to God by meeting
human needs. Seeing God's power at work, whether
conspicuously or inconspicuously, is reward enough!

That ye might be filled with all the fulness of God.
Ephesians 3:19

Fulness is the key word here. In this verse, it is the Greek word *pleroma (play'–ro–mah)*, which has an interesting sidelight.

When the ancients conducted a census of a city, if every dwelling place in it was occupied, then the town was listed as *pleroma*, fully occupied. When the crew of a ship attained full strength, it was listed as *pleroma*, indicating a full complement of officers and men. In addition, *pleroma* was used to describe a cargo net when it was "crammed full" of goods, or a hollow place which had been completely filled in. Inherent in its meaning also was the idea of a full-term of office or the completion of a task.

Paul's prayer is that you and I might be filled with all the fulness (the *pleroma*) of God Himself. We need this fulness in order to be able to complete our assigned tasks in life, to finish out our earthly service to the Lord. It is this fullness which will fill up the hollow places as yet unfulfilled in our human natures and characters. *Pleroma* will fill our lives with God's surplus abundance. In turn, it will allow us to fill up God's crew on the old ship of Zion and, one day, to occupy our mansion and have our part in completing heaven's population.

To be filled with God is wonderful. To be filled with the fullness of God is super wonderful. To be filled with *all* the fullness of God has to be a mind-boggling experience. This *pleroma* was Paul's prayer for you and me. Let's receive it and enjoy it!

**The eternal God is your refuge and
underneath are the everlasting arms....
Deuteronomy 33:27** NKJ

A *refuge* is a place of safety. In a game refuge, the animals instinctively know they will not be trapped or shot at. Likewise, we Christians have a refuge, a place of safety and security from the traps and direct attacks of the enemy.

In speaking in this sense of security in the Lord, the psalmist David wrote: **Great peace have they which love thy law: and nothing shall offend them** (Ps. 119:165). In modern versions, this word **offend** is usually translated, "snare, trap, capture." Thus, this is Biblical terminology for Satan's attempts to capture believers and make them into prisoners of fear, poverty, sickness, anger, lust, insecurity, etc.

In the original Hebrew, the word translated **refuge** here is *me'ownah (meh–o–naw')*, meaning "a lair, den, asylum, retreat, or home." As believers, our place of safety, of retreat, of refuge from the assaults of the enemy, is the Lord God of hosts.

Refuge (*me'ownah*) is also the word used for the tabernacle or temple where God dwells. We Christians have our individual dwelling places, our *me'ownah*. God also has His tabernacle, or *me'ownah* — His dwelling place. We not only have the security of our own homes, but we also have an added spiritual security in the place of worship. When we worship the Lord in spirit and in truth we find a beneficial refuge from doubt, disbelief, distrust, despair, dismay, and disturbance.

The Lord is our refuge: our lair, den, our retreat, our home, and our tabernacle!

He who is of a merry heart has a continual feast.
Proverbs 15:15 NKJ

A feast is more than an ordinary meal. It includes the idea of company, music, entertainment, unusual or special gourmet foods. In general, a feast involves eating plus having a good time.

In our world, we see a great pursuit of "good times." People are trying so hard to find pleasure and satisfaction. You often hear the question, "Are we having fun yet?" The world is trying to find the right things in all the wrong places.

In John 4:32, the Lord Jesus told His disciples, ..."**I have food to eat of which you do not know**" (NKJ). Our text verse confirms this truth. *The Amplified Bible* version reads: **...he who has a glad heart has a continual feast [regardless of circumstances].**

Believers do not have to spend a lot of money to go to a music concert. They have a song going on inside of them continuously. It is the song of the Lord. Jesus is singing it within their hearts. (Zeph. 3:17.) Christians don't have to wait up and hear some stand-up comedian on T.V. tell the latest jokes. They have the joy of the Lord within them giving them "a merry heart."

When the world comes up with a booklet called "How to Party Every Night of the Week," the Christians response is, "I don't have to clutter my life with a lot of socializing; I'm so contented serving the Lord that I don't need partying."

The joy of the Lord is like a continuous feast. We are not anti-social, just contented and happy. We don't have to go around looking for what we have already found.

**He shall not be afraid of evil tidings:
his heart is fixed, trusting in the Lord.
Psalm 112:7**

Out of our twentieth-century culture there has come a familiar expression, "getting a fix." This term usually refers to taking drugs. Because of his dependency upon artificial stimulants, the drug addict is continually in the position of craving a "fix."

In this verse, David states the person who trusts in God is never really afraid because his heart is "fixed" on the Lord. That's good news for us today, because in our society it seems that everyone has a dependency of some kind.

Materialistic people are dependent upon money for their happiness. Egocentric performing artists must have a continual supply of adulation and applause from their adoring fans. Authority figures are driven by a consuming hunger for power. Perverts have an insatiable appetite for "kinky" sex. Alcoholics lust after liquor to slake their never-ending thirst. Smokers crave nicotine constantly.

We Christians are dependent also. The difference is, we look to the Lord as our sole supply. Our dependence is on Him. This is not a mark of weakness; it is a mark of intelligence. Our reliance is upon the only absolutely dependable thing in the universe: the Lord Jesus Christ. Our heart is "fixed," because we trust in Him.

**When he (a thief) is found, he must
restore sevenfold; he may have to give
up all the substance of his house.
Proverbs 6:31 NKJ**

This Bible verse tells us that a thief, when caught, has to make up to his victims seven times over what he has stolen from them — even if it means he has to empty his house to do so.

In John 10:10, the Lord Jesus Christ speaks of Satan, the original thief, who has come to steal, kill, and destroy. The Apostle John declares that Jesus was manifested to destroy the works of the devil. (1 John 3:8.) One of the works of Satan is stealing. He has been "found out" as mankind's greatest thief.

Jesus exposed the works of the enemy and showed him up for what he really is, the prince of thieves. Our text verse says that when a thief is discovered, he has to restore sevenfold what he has taken.

Some police departments, when apprehending a thief in possession of stolen goods, will ask property owners to make out a list of things missing so they can be returned to them.

Make out your list and present it to the Lord: "Lord, the enemy robbed me of peace of mind. I want it back sevenfold." "Lord, the enemy robbed me of health. I am requesting that health be returned to me, multiplied by seven." "Lord, the enemy has robbed me of financial blessings. He has been found out as a thief, and I want my money back seven times over!"

The list could include anything you previously owned that has been stolen by the enemy. What you have lost to the devil, you can have restored to you sevenfold!

Go therefore and make disciples
of all the nations....
Matthew 28:19 NKJ

The original *King James Version* of this verse begins with this familiar injunction, **Go ye....**This has probably been the one phrase which, more than any other, has inspired believers in every age to go forth to mission fields and proclaim sacrificially the Good News. "Go ye" has a certain ring to it. It is a commanding imperative. It motivates believers for a commitment to a life of unselfishness. "Go ye" moves people to disregard creature comforts and to boldly declare with the hymnist: "I'll go where you want me to go, dear Lord, O'er mountain or plain or sea; — I'll say what you want me to say, dear Lord, I'll be what you want me to be."

In addition to the challenging command "go ye," there is another option, an alternative reading of this verse. Beside "go ye," the opening phrase can be interpreted, "As you go...."

All Christians are in motion. We are on a path leading to our eternal home. We are going through this life, led by the Spirit, and strengthened by the Word of God.

"As you go, make disciples of all nations." When you go to the post office, when you go the store, when you go to work, to school, or to church. When you go on vacation. Whenever and wherever you go, be on the lookout for opportunities to share with others the Good News!

Not only go, but as you go — make disciples!

**The Lord has given Me the tongue
of the learned, that I should know how to
speak a word in season to him who is weary.
He awakens Me morning by morning, He
awakens My ear as the learned.**
Isaiah 50:4 NKJ

Here Isaiah tells us how he received his messages from
the Lord. Evidently, the prophet was just like other normal
human being. He seems to have kept the same laws of
health that we do today. He ate and slept regularly. At
morning time, when he was most rested and refreshed,
most sensitive to spiritual response, he would get a "nudge"
from the Lord who would say to him: "Wake up, Isaiah, I
have many things to tell you."

If you would like this to happen to you, then claim
Proverbs 6:22 as a personal promise from the Lord to you:
...when you awake, they (the words of God) **will speak
with you.**

After the Lord had awakened Isaiah, He then opened
his ears. Jesus often challenged His audiences: "He who has
an ear, let him hear." Waking up is the first step. Hearing
from the Lord is the next step. This is why a consistent plan
of daily devotions is so vital to spiritual health.

As a result of awakening and listening to the Lord,
Isaiah had the ability to say the right word to the right
person in the right place at the right time. First his eyes
were opened from sleep, then his ears were opened to God.
Then was his mouth opened to speak sustaining and
refreshing words to the languishing, weary followers of the
Lord.

Eyes open, ears open, mouth open. That is a good
sequence — for us as well as for Isaiah!

Go in and out and find pasture.
John 10:9 NKJ

"Go in and out." This is one of those balance verses. It tells us how to keep life on a normal, even keel by avoiding extremes.

Going in describes an aspect of life that is inward in scope. It refers to the practice of prayer, contemplation, meditation, fasting, solitude, and spending time alone with God. It stresses the need for a time of private fellowship with the Lord. Even though the Church is a community, an organism made up of many members, we are still individual believers with a personal relationship with our heavenly Father. We have a bond with the Lord that is best nurtured by daily communion with Him. When we go in, we often receive our marching orders and directions for that particular day.

Going out speaks of service to others. After we have gone in, sat at the feet of the Master, and received our directions, then we go out and communicate that truth to others by word and lifestyle. Going out is both a missionary journey and a mercy mission — an encouraging word accompanied and confirmed by a helping hand.

The two extremes are represented by: 1) those who have dedicated their lives to going in to God, and yet never, ever going out to a lost world, and 2) those who are so restless, nervous and hyperactive that they never cease "ministering" long enough to wait upon the Lord.

The ideal is a balance between the two: going in and going out — in that order. Go in *for* the message, go out *with* the message. To do so is to find pasture (rest and refreshment for the soul).

When you roam, they will lead you;
when you sleep, they will keep you; and
when you awake, they will speak with you.
Proverbs 6:22 NKJ

Here Solomon is referring to commands, laws, precepts, and principles which his father and mother had taught him. He urges his son not to forsake or neglect them, but to keep them and value them highly. He assures his offspring that the Word of the Lord will lead him wherever he goes. It will stand guard over him as he sleeps. When he awakes in the morning, it will speak to him.

Years ago, I met people who told me they started the day with a scripture verse from the Lord. These dear friends were not mystical, ethereal, or metaphysically esoteric. They were down-to-earth, sensible, God-fearing, hard-working people devoted to serving the Lord and doing His will.

They shared with me how they had trained themselves to start the day with a "word from the Lord." This was the verse they used as a basis for their practice, for which they claimed three benefits: 1) their lives were serene, knowing they were guided by the Word, 2) their sleep was peaceful, knowing they were guarded by the Word, and 3) their waking was inspiring, knowing they would be given a word from the Lord for that day.

Tomorrow morning, instead of jumping out of bed and hitting the floor with a running start, why not wait 30 to 60 seconds and let the Lord give you a word of peace, joy or love. Proverbs 6:22 could read in this sequence: 1) *guided* by the Word, 2) *guarded* by the Word, 3) *goaded* by the Word. Try it; it works!

Say to the righteous that it shall be well with them.
Isaiah 3:10 NKJ

When you were a child, didn't you like to hear stories which ended with the time-honored words, "...and they lived happily ever after?" Didn't you give a sign of relief at the image of the hero and heroine finally having overcome all their obstacles and blissfully facing a wonderful new life together? Wasn't it satisfying to imagine the two of them — all their troubles behind them — happily riding off into the golden sunset?

This verse paints just such a bright, happy picture of the Lord and His Bride, the Church. It assures believers that they too will surmount the obstacles in their paths, overcome the difficulties which beset them on all sides, ride out the storms of life, and in the end find peace and joy and a marvelous new beginning. This verse expresses the Christian equivalent of "they lived happily ever after:" **...it shall be well with them....**

In the original Hebrew, the word translated **well** is *towb* *(tobe)* and can be defined as "good, gracious, joyful, prosperous, pleasant, precious." It denotes a state of general well-being. It is the word used to describe a person who has been ill but who has now regained his health. It is also used to speak of the state of an individual who has suffered financial reversal, but whose fortune has now been fully restored.

"Say to the righteous that it shall be well with them." Know that with God's intervention, things can always turn out the way they are supposed to. Don't expect the worst to happen, expect the best to take place. The Lord says that it shall be well with you. *Well.* Add this promising word to your vocabulary!

> I drew them with gentle cords,
> with bands of love....
> Hosea 11:4 NKJ

This verse shows us the compassionate side of the Lord in His dealings with us mortals. He draws us with gentle cords and with bands of love. Like the great lover He is, He woos us closer and closer to Himself. He leads us, not by severity, but with tenderness.

When I was growing up in church, I can remember hearing all the horror stories of how God takes out His fierce anger upon all those who are in rebellion against Him. Such stories are uncomplimentary to the nature of our loving heavenly Father. They make it appear that God is out to "get" people. Too often, the Lord is portrayed as vindictive and relentless in His determination to reduce to dust and grind to powder anyone who dares to resist Him.

The point of these stories seems to be that when all resistance against the Lord is finally crushed, the agonizing soul totally surrendered and thoroughly chastened, then and only then will the Lord have mercy and turn away His anger. Growing up with such a concept of God did not help me to understand Him, His nature or His attributes. It was a welcome relief to me to discover in Scripture that it is the goodness of God — not His wrath — that leads men to repentance.

It is as though the Lord is saying to us through this verse: "You are getting closer to Me every day. Not because I am laying on you terrible diseases, horrible accidents, traumatic losses, debilitating financial reversals, and crushing personal failures. Rather, you are coming near to Me because I am drawing you with gentle cords and bands of love."

**Judge nothing before the time, until the Lord
comes, who will both bring to light the hidden things
of darkness and reveal the counsels of the hearts....
1 Corinthians 4:5 NKJ**

You don't know what to do. You have to make a decision, but you know you need more information than you have at hand. This verse assures us that, regardless of the seeming urgency of the situation, it is best to wait until we are more knowledgeable than we are at present.

The usual interpretation of this verse by most scholars is that it concerns the *parousia (par–oo–see'ah)* or Second Coming, of the Lord Jesus Christ. When He returns, He will bring to light every hidden thing and rectify every injustice. "Wait till the Lord comes back to earth, and then we will see things in their true light."

This *is* the meaning of the verse. However, there are other events in our lives to which this verse can be applied equally as well. Besides the great *parousia* at the end of the age, Jesus comes to us in many ways: in salvation; in healing; in guidance; in deliverance from danger, crisis, and great need.

We could read this verse: "Do not take any hasty action; wait until the Lord has come onto the scene." There are subliminal factors hidden from your view. The Lord wants to bring to the level of your sight the things you need to know in order to make the right decision. You won't have to wait long. When you get the facts you need, you will know what action to take. Without those facts, you could do something you might later regret. When the Lord comes, you will be more knowledgeable and you will make the decision you can live with comfortably.

He has put eternity in their hearts, ...no one can find out the work that God does from beginning to end.
Ecclesiastes 3:11 NKJ

Here is a verse that explains why we go into all the world and preach the Gospel to every creature. God has put eternity in the heart of every person who has ever existed. Despite exterior appearance or attitude, deep down inside every living soul there is an inherent awareness of eternity. From the intellectual to the illiterate, all people have one thing in common — an intuitive inkling of the reality of life beyond death.

When He breathed into the first man the breath of life, the Creator placed within him an unextinguishable hope of another life beyond this present one. The presence of this deep-seated, universal hope is the basis of success for all evangelism, missionary outreach, and personal soul-winning. Knowing that God has already put into man's heart an awareness of eternity makes our job as witnesses not only possible but also much easier. We do not have to convict or convince anyone; all we have to do is to wisely and lovingly strike a responsive chord in the heart of each person with whom we share the Good News. When that chord is strummed, they *will* respond.

The second part of this verse says that although he is aware of eternity, man does not know the way to it. Our job as witnesses is simply to show people that way. We do that by telling them the Good News of Jesus, sharing with them God's plan for eternal life in Him.

Half of our job has already been done for us by the Lord when He placed within people the awareness of eternity. He has laid the foundation; we build His Church upon it — Jesus Christ being the chief cornerstone. (Eph. 2:20.)

**On some have compassion,
...but others save with fear....
Jude 22,23 NKJ**

This verse encourages sensitivity when dealing with unsaved people. Instead of strictly following a manual which purports to show how to witness to people, it is more preferable to let the Lord Himself adjust us and adapt us to each person's individual personality and disposition. Some people are farther along (in God's dealings with them) than others. We can be attuned to each person's capacity and spiritual receptivity. This verse tells us that there is a variety of ways people can be won to the Lord.

Instead of using the same technique with everyone, Jude tells us to use compassion with some and fear with others. Each case must be judged on its own merits. With sensitivity, we can adapt to each different situation. With some people I have had to be deadly serious, while with others I have been able to carry on light conversation which even bordered on levity. Yet both approaches have produced responses. What will "work" in one instance might be highly inappropriate or in poor taste in another.

Other translations of this verse suggest that we show compassion on those struggling with doubt, but fear with those who are arrogant, haughty, conceited, or rebellious. Proud, self-made people need breaking, broken people need mending. The Holy Spirit will show us each person's personal need and how to minister to that need.

Compassion or fear. They are both effective tools when used in the right way, at the right time, with the right person.

**We do not know what we should pray
for as we ought, but the Spirit Himself
makes intercession for us....**
Romans 8:26 NKJ

I have been in churches recently that were having "an hour of prayer" between 6 and 7 a.m. each day during the week. It has been quite encouraging attending gatherings around the world and finding sincere and conscientious working men, housewives, students, retired people, and church leaders all joining together to pray.

The comment is often heard from those not participating. "I don't know how to pray for a whole hour. I'm good for about five minutes of prayer and then my mind goes blank. What am I suppose to do the other 55 minutes besides let my mind wander?" That is an honest question. It deserves an honest answer: this verse assures us of divine assistance.

This scripture acknowledges our limitations. We *don't* know how to pray as we ought. This is not a reproof or rebuke. It is a statement of fact. But this verse also tells us that the Holy Spirit helps us by making intercession for us.

If we will give Him the opportunity, the Holy Spirit will move inside us, prompting us to pray along certain avenues and for particular subjects. Given free rein, He will actually energize our prayer life, stirring us to fervent intercessory prayer. Jude calls this action "praying in the Holy Spirit." (Jude 20.)

When we allow the Spirit of God to pray *through* us, time is no problem.

He has made everything beautiful in its time....
Ecclesiastes 3:11 NKJ

The original creation was so awesome, majestic and beautiful that morning stars sang together and sons of God shouted for joy. (Job 38:7.) Flawless, perfect, and magnificent was the creation. God Himself examined it all and declared that is was "very good." (Gen. 1:31.)

But then an oppressive shadow came over this divine work of beauty. One of the head angels became self-willed and instigated an insurrection against the divine Creator. (Is. 14:12–15; Rev. 12:7–10.) As a result, creation became marred and discordant.

As human beings, created by God, you and I are a miniature world, a microcosm of the original creation. We are a world of our own. Just as Genesis 1:1 tells of God's creating heaven and earth, so He also made us beautiful in our infancy. But under the influence of that fallen angel, like all of God's creation, we too became "damaged goods." When sin came into our lives, we became "emptiness and confusion." (Gen. 1:2.)

Salvation is a salvage work. Redemption is a restoration. Our Creator has intervened to give us beauty for ashes. Now that we are in Christ, we are no longer "damaged goods." His promise that He would send a Redeemer to beautify the meek with salvation has been fulfilled. (Ps. 149:4.) The defective has now been restored to its original pristine newness. (2 Cor. 5:17.)

Your God has made everything beautiful again. So...think beauty...talk beauty...walk beauty...believe beauty...behave beauty...enjoy beauty! Because of Whose you are, you are beautiful!

**This is the day which the Lord hath made;
we will rejoice and be glad in it.
Psalm 118:24**

Which day is this verse talking about? Is it confined to one isolated day in human history?

The "day which the Lord hath made" began with the day of creation when morning stars sang together and all the sons of God shouted for joy (Job 38:7).

Another day of rejoicing occurred when Israel was led out of bondage in Egypt. David spoke of this day, saying of the Lord: **...he brought forth his people with joy, and his chosen with gladness** (Ps. 105:43).

That was a day of joyful deliverance. But it was not the only one. The day of Jesus' resurrection from the dead is also included in this verse. The anguish of the disciples, the sorrow of the women, the heavy gloom of the crucifixion — all this was replaced by the joy of an empty tomb: **...Then were the disciples glad, when they saw the** (risen) **Lord** (John 20:20).

Other days of rejoicing are the day of our own personal conversion, the day set aside each week to worship in the house of the Lord, and the day the Lord returns to claim His Bride, the Church.

Besides all these special days, let us remember that this age is often referred to as "the Gospel days." It is a day of God's making and its blessings are ours because our Lord has been placed as the head of the corner.

So therefore every day we live is the Lord's day and is a cause of joyous celebration!

Let your speech always be with grace,
seasoned with salt, that you may know
how you ought to answer each one.
Colossians 4:6 NKJ

There is a vast difference between salty speech and speech seasoned with salt. Salty speech is offensive, sarcastic, sharp, bitter, biting. Speech seasoned with salt is attractive, appetizing, flavorful, tasteful. It fulfills the very words of Jesus who urged His disciples to "have salt in yourselves." (Mark 9:50).

In sharing our faith with others, we need to be able to capture their interest and keep their attention. One way to do that is to make sure that our speech is well seasoned with salt. Just as salt adds appeal to food, so it adds appeal to our witness to others.

Salt enhances and enriches; it adds flavor to that which is dull, bland, and tasteless. Well seasoned speech adds flavor to the Bread of Life which we share with others to enhance and enrich their lives.

Salt is used as a preservative; it prevents corruption in meat. Likewise, "meat of the Word" which we share with others can be kept pure and incorrupt when our speech is well seasoned with salt.

Salt produces thirst. Well salted speech can actually stimulate a thirst for the Water of Life.

In his New Testament commentary, Dean Alford states: "Salt as used by our Savior symbolizes the unction, freshness and vital briskness which characterizes the Holy Spirit's presence and work in a man."

Without salt in our speech, our words will be insipid, banal, and uninspiring. Prayer makes the difference. A consistent life of daily prayer keeps the salt in our lives from losing its savor.

The Lord called your name, Green Olive
Tree, Lovely and of Good Fruit....
Jeremiah 11:16 NKJ

As a man, do people call you handsome? As a woman, are you considered beautiful? Well, according to this verse, this is the Lord's opinion of you! Maybe you don't see yourself as handsome or beautiful, but the Lord does. In this scripture, three unusual adjectives are used to describe you: **Green, Lovely,** and **Good.**

In the original Hebrew, this word translated **Green** is *ra'anan (rah–an–awn')*. It is defined as "new, prosperous, verdant, flourishing, thriving." It denotes great potential for growth. Thus, your spiritual name is "One Who Has a Great Capacity for Fruitfulness and Productivity in the Lord."

Lovely is from an original Hebrew word *yapheh (yah–feh')* meaning "beautiful, excellent, good, handsome." Bible grammarians note that this word is used primarily to describe men and women who are serving the Lord. Our heavenly Father has no "ugly ducklings" or "plain Janes." He has given His children beauty for ashes. Instead of down-playing yourself, verbally state that in God's eyes, you are handsome (male) or beautiful (female).

Of Good Fruit in Hebrew is a combination of *yapheh* and *to'ar (to'–ar)*, meaning "shape, form, figure, outline." Thus you are "of beautiful form" or "of excellent figure." As a redeemed person, you have been translated from Satan's realm of little worth to Jesus' kingdom of great worth. He states you are: 1) good looking, 2) thriving, and 3) in great shape!

Get wisdom. And in all your
getting get understanding.
Proverbs 4:7 NKJ

It is possible for a person to increase in knowledge and yet still be devoid of wisdom and understanding. The Bible assures us that knowledge will increase. We are living to see this prophecy fulfilled. Yet the crucial need of every person alive today is wisdom and understanding of God's dealings and purposes in his or her own individual life.

Pursuit of knowledge is a worthwhile endeavor. But it's not enough. An astronomer may know 100 times as much now about the solar system as his predecessors did a century ago, and still have no personal knowledge of the God who created both him and the solar system he so admires. According to Proverbs 9:10, knowledge of the Holy One produces understanding.

Understanding is important. Proverbs 3:19 (NKJ) tells us: **The Lord by wisdom founded the earth; by understanding He established the heavens.** Verse 13 says: **Happy is the man who finds wisdom, and the man who gains understanding.**

It is possible to increase in knowledge and at the same time find wisdom and gain understanding of God's designs for us and our lives. Proverbs 2:2 (NKJ) exhorts us to incline our ears toward wisdom and to apply our hearts to understanding. Wisdom comes from an encounter with the Christ Who is the wisdom of God; understanding has to be sought and pursued. Success in life requires a solid edifice of wisdom and knowledge built upon a stable foundation of truth that cannot be swayed. That wisdom and knowledge can be acquired. It requires effort, but the reward is well worth the expense of time and energy.

**For exaltation (promotion) comes neither from the east
nor from the west nor from the south.**
Psalm 75:6 NKJ

This verse came to me when I was working in a group
of men doing road construction. The foreman told me I
would never be promoted as long as he was in charge. He
harbored hostility toward all Christians and bluntly stated,
"We don't give promotion to milk drinkers, only beer
drinkers." That left me out. When the promotion lists were
posted on the bulletin board, my name was always notably
absent.

I knew that I qualified for promotion, but I also knew
that I was being purposely passed over because of the
foreman's antagonism toward me. It was at that time that
the Lord gave me this scripture as a promise.

If you will notice closely, the word *north* does not
appear in this verse. As Christians, our promotion will
ultimately come from the north. Look up the word *north* in
the concordance and Bible commentary and you will find
that it has a great deal of future import. (Is. 14:13.) When
time runs out for this earth, you and I will say with the
redeemed of all ages: "Our promotion came from the north
from whence came our Savior to take us away!"

It was also during this time in my life that I received a
visitation from the Lord. He imparted to me the ability to
give "precious promises" to people by divine revelation. I
didn't get a raise in salary, but I did receive a spiritual
"boon." That should be no surprise: This verse tells us that
our promotion always comes from the Lord!

And that ye study to be quiet, and
to do your own business....
1 Thessalonians 4:11

Study is the key word here. Although not the same Greek word translated **study** in 2 Timothy 2:15 (**Study to shew thyself approved....**), its meaning is similar. The *King James* translation of both words as *study* often leads people to think they refer to academic instruction or scholarship, when they actually have no connection at all with mental activity.

In this verse from Thessalonians, the word **study** is a compound Greek word whose definition reads: "to make an effort," "to be ambitious," "to make it a point of honor," "to exert oneself from a sense of love," and "to be motivated by an intense desire." In other words, Paul is saying here: *"Have no other ambition* than that of a quiet, industrious life."

The existing society in Paul's day was given to riots, community unrest, mob incitement and meddling in the affairs of others. Paul is telling the believers in Thessalonica to have a different goal. Their neighbors loved to be idle, to carry gossip and rumors, to stir up strife and contention. Some of this activity had crept into the church. Paul urges the believers to march to a different drumbeat: *"Make it your aim* to dwell safely and securely in a quiet, peaceful setting."

One version reads: "Keep yourself from all gathering of the idle, the restless, and the dissatisfied." To "study to be quiet" in the Greek suggests an all-out effort to maintain a lifestyle that is tranquil, serene, calm, and peaceful. It is worth it. The results can be lasting peace and harmony.

Study to shew thyself approved unto God,
...rightly dividing the word of truth.
2 Timothy 2:15

In the original Greek of this verse, the word translated **study** is *spoudazo (spoo–dad'–zo)* and has to do with quickness or promptness in one's efforts. One writer defines *spoudazo* as "to speed, make haste, and manifest oneself in diligence, earnestness, and zeal."

Originally, *spoude (spoo–day')* ("speed," dispatch, eagerness) and *spoudazo* were external words denoting quick movement in the interests of a person or cause. They implied carrying out a matter with speed and enthusiasm. Christianity applied these two words to an inner sphere of action, using them to relate to zealousness or eagerness, desire or concern. The adjective form of these words could be defined as "busy, active, industrious." As a noun, they might be translated as "zeal, industry, effort, diligence or care (in contrast to laziness or sloth)."

For the person who is called to a career ministering the Word of God, this verse could be an incentive for an all-out, conscientious effort to please the Lord by prompt and eager obedience. Paul was saying: "The sooner you begin, the better. Don't delay. There's no time to lose. Get started, get on with it, get busy!"

Rightly dividing the word of truth is translated in *The Amplified Bible* as: 1)...**correctly analyzing**...2) **accurately dividing** — 3) **rightly handling** and 4) **skilfully teaching** — the Word of truth.** As Christian witnesses, we need to go "all out" in our eager, earnest efforts to learn to correctly handle the sword of the Spirit!

**A satisfied soul loathes the honeycomb, but
to a hungry soul every bitter thing is sweet.**
Proverbs 27:7 NKJ

Bitter herbs were part of the fare of the Jewish Passover.
Ordinarily, they were an item that was considered
unappetizing. Solomon is telling us here that if a person is
hungry enough, even the bitterest of herbs tastes good to
him.

Some missionaries have related this verse to overseas
missions. They tell us that approximately ten percent of the
world's population speak English, yet ninety percent of the
world's Gospel ministers are concentrated in English-
speaking areas. That leaves only ten percent of the world's
preachers to minister to the needs of the ninety percent of
the world's population which does not speak our language.
That seems so disproportionate.

Some American cities have three Christian television
stations, anywhere from five to ten Christian AM and FM
radio stations, and three to ten Christian magazines for
each believer's home. By contrast, we heard of rural
ministry in Haiti which had several ministers, but only one
Bible. The ministers ended up breaking the Bible into
smaller sections so each one could have at least a portion of
the Holy Writ. How spoiled we Americans are!

The easiest way to avoid personal glut and saturation
is to continuously pass on to others the good things the
Lord is giving us. If we will keep the stream of revealed
truth flowing out to the thirsty world, we will never
become the satisfied, jaded soul who loathes the
honeycomb. When the Lord blesses you with something
good, pass it on!

**The Lord will arise...that He may
do His work, His awesome work, and
bring to pass His act, His unusual act.
Isaiah 28:21 NKJ**

This is a promise aimed right at those of us who are proper, precise, programmed people whose lives are well-planned and carefully ordered. The prophet is not faulting us for our efforts to prepare ourselves to face challenges, to figure solutions, or to work through all the obstacles that confront us in order to see our task completed. This verse is not an indictment against ambition, aggressive action, or well-developed plans for accomplishing what the faint–hearted would never even dare to attempt.

Rather, this scripture is an encouraging promise from the Lord that we will receive an answer to our prayers — on His terms and according to His timetable. It is an assurance that our heavenly Father is going to meet our needs — as He sees fit and when He sees fit. The answer may seem to be delayed, but when it does arrive it will be awesome and unusual.

Our Father is a God of infinite variety. He has a myriad of ways to respond to our petitions and requests. I did a preliminary lexical research study on this verse and came up with the following assurance: "Your prayer has been heard; the answer is on its way. It is a most unusual answer, and it is coming from the most unexpected source."

The most exciting part of the answer is the element of surprise! We all love a pleasant surprise — and this verse promises us just that!

**Tell your children about it, let your children tell
their children, and their children another generation.**
Joel 1:3 NKJ

Here is a word covering four generations, from us to
our children, to our grandchildren, to our great-grand-
children. It is a blessed word showing how the truth of
God's Word can remain in a family for a long, long time.

In Deuteronomy 5:9, Moses stated that the sins of the
fathers would be passed down through the family to the
third and fourth generation. This verse in Joel is a positive
assurance that the blessing of the Lord will also reach to the
fourth generation.

It might be that very few people who read this
devotional are great-grandparents. (My wife and I don't
even come that close.) However, despite our age or
situation, there is a resident truth in Joel 1:3 for each of us.
The truth is that our family is included in the promises of
salvation. Again and again we read in Scripture the familiar
phrase, "you and all your household." Truth resident in
one's life has the potential for spreading through a family,
and even through a whole family tree.

If you happen to be the only one in your family serving
the Lord rejoice. The Lord has chosen you to introduce
salvation to all your loved ones. A little leaven leavens the
whole lump. (Gal. 5:9.) You will live to see your entire
family serving the Lord. It's just a matter of time!

**May I never boast except in the cross of our Lord
Jesus Christ, through which the world has been
crucified to me, and I to the world.**
Galatians 6:14 NIV

After having preached a milestone message in a
Southern California town, I was interviewed by a reporter
from a local newspaper who wrote an article claiming that I
had preached 2,500 times in ten years. That unsolicited
notoriety made me wonder: Would Paul have wanted his
ministry gloried that way? Surely not.

Some ministries publish how many countries they are
reaching, how many churches they have established, how
many missionaries they are supporting, how many buses
they run each Sunday, how many people their sanctuary
holds, how many different choirs they maintain, how many
converts they have won, and on and on.

I once knew of a ministry whose leaders boasted that
they had the largest staff of any church in the country. After
getting into financial difficulty, they called in a management
consultant team who advised them that they were greatly
overstaffed. To stay afloat, they were forced to let 200 church
workers go. Very soon afterward, those same leaders were
once again boasting: this time that they had one of the
smallest staffs in one of America's largest churches!

In an age that is impressed with success, with bigness
and with numbers, this verse reminds us of where our
priorities really are. Part of the crucifixion to the world of
which Paul is speaking here is a death to the "numbers
game." It includes pride of grace, pride of race, pride of
face, and pride of place.

Do you think we Christians will ever learn that God is
not impressed with *our* boasting?

**The beloved of the Lord shall
dwell safety by Him....
Deuteronomy 33:12 NKJ**

In a world full of evil, violence, and hatred, it is comforting to be promised *safety*. This word is vast and all-inclusive. Besides personal protection, it includes confidence, trust, security, and freedom from danger or fear. The original Hebrew word translated **safety** here is *betach (beh'–takh)*, meaning "a place of refuge." Thus this verse confidently assures us of our welfare and survival despite the vigors and uncertainties of this present unsettled age.

The beloved of the Lord includes all believers in Jesus Christ, especially those who are serving Him and doing His will. In Ephesians 1:6, the Apostle Paul declares that we believers are **...accepted in the beloved.** Acceptance by the Lord does not mean haughty exclusivism, privileged elitism, or entrance into a special inner circle. It simply makes possible that close personal relationship which exists between God and *all* those who will freely receive His gracious love.

The Bride of Christ is composed of redeemed people who are in many different stages of spiritual development. Regardless of our current level of spirituality, all of us make up the Beloved. As such, we are all promised safety, security, and confidence. We may think the Lord has "pets," "favorites," and "choice saints," those who have "an inside track" to His blessings or who enjoy a special "hot line" connection with Heaven. That is not so. We are all equal recipients of God's saving grace and therefore equal beneficiaries of His promised watchcare and safekeeping.

I will even make a road in the wilderness....
Isaiah 43:19 NKJ

You can always tell the difference between negative people and positive people. The negative have a flare for defining the problem, while the positive have a gift for pointing out the solution.

It would be easy to be a "problem definer" these days; there's plenty of material available. Our environment reminds us constantly that "it's a jungle out there." Daily we are inundated by the media with reports of human depravity, crime, and violence. And, unfortunately, the vast majority of this information is factual and valid. We do indeed live in a "wilderness."

But if we are not careful, our conversation can easily become affected by all the negatives we see and hear about us. We can begin to major on the problem instead of the solution. It really isn't very edifying to continuously talk about the wilderness, especially when the Lord has told us through His prophet that He has provided a way through this "barren wasteland."

Positive people talk more about the "road" than they do the wilderness. The Lord made that road. He has already walked it ahead of us. We know it is safe, reliable, and trustworthy. Others before us have safely traversed it from infancy to senior life. We are not consigned to groping through life trying to find our direction. The road itself is clear direction — the way to eternal and abundant life.

Take your choice: Define the problem, or declare the solution. Major in "wilderness talk" or "road talk." Talk over the woes, or talk up the way!

> **But you stand here awhile, that I**
> **may announce to you the word of God.**
> **1 Samuel 9:27 NKJ**

How do we listen and move at the same time? How do we get direction and guidance while busily engaged in our regular activities? Is it possible to hear the voice of the Lord while we're talking to other people?

This verse illustrates how to go about getting guidance in the midst of "busy-ness." As they were going down to the outskirts of a certain city, the prophet Samuel said to King Saul, "Tell your companions to go on ahead of us and you will catch up to them in a minute. Right now I want you to stand here awhile and let me give you a word from the Lord."

I believe this is a good lesson on how to go about receiving needed guidance 1) on the run, 2) when right in the midst of activity, or 3) when surrounded by people. Busy people cannot always stop everything and go off on a retreat to get a further word of direction. But they can learn to take a minute to listen to the Lord, recognize His voice, and be attuned to receive divine guidance when needed most.

The key here is **awhile**. In the original Hebrew it indicates a short space of time: "Stand still just a moment." That's all it takes to get the message. Learning how to stop long enough to receive marching orders is a vital principle in learning to be led of the Spirit. On one hand, we don't want to pack our schedules so full of activities we can't stop and get direction. On the other hand, we don't want to withdraw into such an isolation that we never accomplish anything. The solution is learning to move and listen at the same time!

Then those who feared the Lord spoke to one another, and the Lord listened and heard them; so a book of remembrance was written from Him for those who fear the Lord and who meditate on His name.
Malachi 3:16 NKJ

This verse testifies to an unusual outpouring of God's grace and favor upon a group of people who served Him with their hearts in the midst of a society inclined to rigid legal code. Three activities mentioned in this verse assure us of access to this same grace and favor: 1) speaking to one another, 2) fearing the Lord, and 3) meditating on His name.

1) *Speaking to one another*. Don't you enjoy the fellowship of other saints when the conversation is about the Lord and His doings? The Lord took notice of such conversation and rewarded it.

2) *Fearing the Lord*. This word **fear** does not refer to nervous compulsion or a guilty conscience, but to reverential awe, of being afraid of displeasing the Lord. According to Isaiah 11:2, this is one of the seven Spirits of God. It is available and desperately needed today. All we have to do is to pray and we as individuals, a family, or a church will receive this reverent Spirit.

3) *Meditating on the name of the Lord*. The powerful, majestic, glorious name of God became the object of these people's meditation.

Because they did these things, the Lord wrote a book of eternal remembrance for His people. He will do the same for us: we can make history by applying this verse.

The battle is not yours, but God's.
2 Chronicles 20:15 NKJ

We are soldiers in a fight to the finish. The final outcome of that battle has already been determined. The Lord God omnipotent reigns. (Rev. 19:6.) He is coming with ten thousands of His saints to establish His Kingdom on this earth. (Jude 14.) The government shall be upon His shoulder, and of His Kingdom there shall be no end. (Is. 9:6.) We shall reign with Him forever and ever. (Rev. 22:5.)

Ours is a warfare in which the victory has already been announced ahead of time, but we do have individual skirmishes. We have our own private battles with pride, lust, anger, fear, and a host of other opponents. Because He has overcome the flesh, the world, and the devil, the Lord Jesus assures us that we too can overcome. (Rev. 12:11.) His example motivates us to believe for total victory.

The battle is the Lord's; it is His truth against Satan's lie, His light versus the enemy's darkness. This warfare pits health against sickness, faith against fear, prosperity against poverty, and godliness against iniquity. We fight in this war, but it is the Lord Who gives the victory. At times it may seem that we Christians are outnumbered and even outmatched, but we can take courage and inspiration from the knowledge that we are on the side of ultimate triumph.

With the Lord on our side, we can say: "The battle is the Lord's; the victory is the Lord's!" Blessed assurance!

**For He Himself has said, "I will
never leave you nor forsake you.
Hebrews 13:5 NKJ**

This is a quotation from three Old Testament references:
Deuteronomy 31:6 and 31:8 and Joshua 1:5. The writer of
Hebrews simply updates these promises and gives them a
New Testament setting. The Lord Jesus is now seated on the
throne of God and is waiting for the signal from His Father
to descend into the earth's atmosphere to be joined together
physically with His waiting Church. (1 Thess. 4:16,17.)

While we who look for His appearing are going
through our preparation time in anticipation of His return,
we can be comforted in knowing that He has promised to
be with us at all times. He has assured us that wherever two
or three are gathered in His name, there He is in their midst.
(Matt. 18:20.)

Besides His presence with us as a corporate body, He
has sent the Holy Spirit to indwell our individual bodies.
The Holy Ghost always magnifies Jesus. Thus the spirit of
prophecy (words given by the Holy Spirit to individual
believers) becomes the very testimony (revelation) of Jesus
Himself.

So in the Person of the Holy Spirit, Jesus resides
continually in our tabernacles of stone (our churches) as
well as in our tabernacles of clay (our bodies). Even though
Jesus is in heaven with His Father, He has emphatically
pronounced His abiding presence with us. One Greek
scholar has translated Hebrews 13:5 with five negatives: "I
will never, never, never, never [under no circumstances, be
they ever so difficult] desert you." I believe this is a
powerful assurance for all of us.

Let God arise, let His enemies be scattered....
Psalm 68:1 NKJ

Scattering the enemy is God's plan for diffusing the malignant forces that come against the believer. Scattering the enemy breaks up his power base so that his intensity is fragmented and his designs thwarted.

When God arises in our behalf, two things happen: 1) We receive a deliverance wrought by divine intervention. God comes to our rescue and lifts us out of our adversity; 2) The enemy that posed a united threat to our progress becomes splintered and pulverized. The Lord's word of deliverance becomes a hammer to break the rock in pieces. (Jer. 23:29.) The enemy comes against us one way, but when God arises to confront him, he flees before us seven ways. (Deut. 28:7.)

Solomon tells us that a wise king scatters the wicked. (Prov. 20:26.) When you see organized opposition, collective hostility, and the enemy marshalling his forces to come against the cause of righteousness, know that God will step in and bring to naught the devices of the adversary.

Oh, blessed comfort, knowing that the Lord is looking out for our protection and preservation! Let God arise, and let our enemies be scattered. Our enemy is also His enemy. Our battles become His battles. Gloriously, His victory becomes our victory.

**If anyone speaks, let him speak
as the oracles of God....
1 Peter 4:11 NKJ**

The short word! That's what **oracles** means. In the original Greek, *logion* (*log'–ee–on*) is defined as "a brief, terse, succinct, concise, or short utterance."

It is one thing to have an answer, it is another thing to be able to give that answer without turning it into a long, drawn-out, elaborate discourse. If anyone speaks, let him speak as the *logion* of God, as one who delivers a direct and honest word.

Thayer's Greek-English lexicon tells us that all prophecies in New Testament times were brief (and to the point). In this same epistle, Peter urges us to always be ready to give an answer for the hope that is in us as believers. That answer does not need to be an hour-long dissertation. It should be the *logion* of God, a short, concise word.

I remember with painful amusement a question and answer session I participated in as a guest on CBN's 700 Club. At that time, Israel had just invaded Lebanon and the whole world was carefully watching the outcome. A lady in the studio audience asked me point blank, "Will this incident speed up the coming of the Lord?" As I look back upon the question, I realize that I could have answered it with a simple yes or no. Just that easy! Instead, I stammered around for three or four minutes and never did answer the lady's question. In that situation I certainly was not an oracle.

Let's be oracles. Let's speak as the *logion* of God. Let's make our words brief and to the point!

Give us a measure of revival in our bondage.
Ezra 9:8 NKJ

Bondage, in this verse, does not refer to the bondage of sin. We believers have been delivered from that. It does not refer to the bondage of sickness or infirmity. We have been set free from all that. This does not even refer to trying to live in the Spirit while resisting the cravings of the old Adamic nature within us — though that is a legitimate concern.

Here Ezra is asking the Lord for a measure of revival in the bondage of his *circumstances.* He is surrounded by people given over to idolatry. Seeing the gross practices of sensual people will always adversely effect those who seek to walk in the Spirit.

Bondage exists when a Spirit-minded believer has to work in an office filled with earthly-minded people who have no relish for spiritual things. Bondage exists when a Christian student finds himself surrounded by non-believers who make it clear that they neither share nor appreciate his interest in the things of God. Bondage exists when a believer's whole neighborhood majors on partying rather than on praying, when even his church is caught up in trivial social functions rather than in ministering to vital, pressing needs.

Living in this world of disbelief and unconcern can tend to stifle or suffocate us. The Lord wants to revive us so we can walk in freedom and love. If you will read the next verse (Ezra 9:9), you will see that the Lord did revive His people. He will do the same for us today!

**I am the Lord your God, who
teaches you to profit....
Isaiah 48:17 NKJ**

Profiting is more than making money. It can include
financial increase, but it has a much more blessed scope
than just material things. The Hebrew word translated
profit here is *ya'al (yaw–al')*. It has to do with climbing or
ascending, excelling, gaining around, rising above
circumstances, reaching the top or summit. *Ya'al* is also the
Hebrew word for the ibex or wild goat which was so named
because of his climbing ability.

Ya'al is used negatively throughout Scriptures to refer
to people who put value on the wrong pursuits. Israel is
often told by God that idols will not profit them. Trusting in
the military might of Egypt is unprofitable; rather, they
should trust in the Lord their God. Solomon tells us that
riches profit not in the day of wrath....(Prov.11:4). We are to
gain riches during the Gospel days and disperse them
before the coming of the Lord. Our riches can be utilized for
evangelism and missionary outreach now while producing
eternal rewards.

One generous pastor, well known for giving away
everything yet still prospering, has said: "Everything that
comes into my life is flowing out to others. I don't want $20
in my wallet when the Second Coming takes place; I don't
want to leave anything to the Antichrist!"

Satan is forever trying to demean, discourage and
destroy us. The Lord has promised to teach us to profit, to
raise our levels, to improve the quality of our lives, to help
us to ascend in life. Satan wants us to go downhill, the Lord
is taking us up to higher ground!

And I will rebuke the devourer for your sakes....
Malachi 3:11 NKJ

The **devourer** needs to be defined. The Hebrew word *akal (aw–kal')* means "to eat, consume or burn up." It was used by Bible writers to define the actions of drought, famine, war, pestilence, and plague. To "rebuke the devourer" is to check, curb and deter anything that consumes time, energy, or cash-flow.

In this verse the Lord promises to put a stop-gap on that which consumes our time. How many times have you started out a day with a plan for getting things done, only to look back at the end of the day and realize that your time had gotten away from you? The Lord has promised to rebuke the devourer of time.

The same promise applies to energy. During the average eight-hour workday, we expect to achieve a stated number of goals, to complete so many assigned tasks, to produce a certain predetermined amount of output for our efforts. It is always disconcerting to look back at the end of the day and compare how much we intended to get done with how little we actually accomplished. The Lord has promised to rebuke the devourer of energy.

This promise also applies to money. You buy tires, and they wear out too soon. You buy shoes, and they do not last. You buy groceries, and run out before the week is over. You spend money, yet have nothing to show for it. God has promised to rebuke the devourer of finances.

With God's blessings, you and I can get 60 minutes of time out of every hour, eight hours of productivity out of each working day, and a hundred pennies of value out of every dollar spent. What a blessing!

**I will...open for you the windows of
heaven and pour out for you such blessing that
there will not be room enough to receive it...
Malachi 3:10 NKJ**

Windows **of heaven!** What a beautiful, illustrious, picturesque word! Other translators use the words, "sluices," "floodgates," or "apertures." In any case, this is a promise of a deluge of blessings coming upon those who lead lives marked by generosity.

The windows of heaven are mentioned in two other places in the Bible: one is negative and the other positive. In 2 Kings 7:2 and 7:19, Elisha predicts that the famine is over and that the price of food will soon be incredibly reduced. The kings's squire responds in disbelief, "If the Lord opened windows in heaven, this thing might be." Elisha's reply is: "You will see it, but never partake of it." When the news of the miraculous turn-around hits the streets, the famished people rush out of the city to gather up the much-needed supplies. In their haste, they run over and accidentally trample to death the skeptical squire — just as the prophet had foretold.

The windows of heaven are also mentioned in Noah's day when the Lord opened the skies and deluged the earth with rain for forty days. (Gen. 7:11, 8:2.)

Thus the windows of heaven are mentioned three times in Scripture with three different applications: 1) a deluge of rain (we can compare this to revival or spiritual renewal), 2) a miraculous supply following a great famine, and 3) an overflowing provision of blessings in the lives of believers. What a promise!

A threefold cord is not quickly broken.
Ecclesiastes 4:12

One strand of cord can be easily severed. Two strands of cord can be stretched and pulled until they split. But a threefold cord is not easily broken.

The New American Standard Bible reads: ...**A cord of three strands is not quickly torn apart.** Scripture never tells us exactly what these three strands symbolize. In a case like this, there is usually much conjecture. Listed below are several suggestions for what the threefold cord represents:

1. HAM, SHEM, AND JAPHETH. *Family ties.* Man had a serious family rupture from the time of Adam to Noah. With his three sons to help him and each other, Noah (mankind) had a better chance of survival.

2. ABRAHAM, ISAAC, AND JACOB. *Covenant relationship.* Naming these three and claiming the individual blessing upon them was like having a threefold benefit.

3. THE LAW, THE PROPHETS, AND THE WRITINGS. *Three divisions of the Old Testament.* These three made up truth as revealed to Israel.

4. FATHER, SON, AND HOLY GHOST. *Threefold cord of deity.* Nothing can sever or mar the unity of God.

5. SPIRIT, SOUL AND BODY. *Triune nature of redeemed man.* All three must be integrated and functioning in harmony in order for the believer to be at his best.

6. MAN, WIFE, AND CHILD. *Basic family unit.* It has been proven that a child cements a marriage more than anything else.

7. (YOUR INTERPRETATION.) I have left this one blank so you can send me your suggestions. I would be interested in *your* response.

**I will settle you after your old estates, and will
do better unto you than at your beginnings....
Ezekiel 36:11**

Whoever heard of anyone breaking down and then
coming back better than ever? Our cynical world says
sarcastically: "One strike, and you're out!"; "Opportunity
only knocks once; if you missed it, too bad"; "If you've had
a divorce, or a stroke, or gone bankrupt, you'll never
recover completely, you'll never be the same again"; "Once
you've had it, you may as well give up!"

That is not the Lord's report. Here He is addressing a
group of dispossessed people taken captive 550 miles to the
northeast of their homeland. They were uprooted and
removed from every kind of living they had ever known.
The Lord is promising them a release, a return, a recovery,
and a restoration:

"I will bring you back to where you were before your
trouble started. I will do better to you than at your
beginning. You will not only make a comeback, you will be
better than ever."

As soon as you and I became believers in the Lord Jesus
Christ, a whole world of promises opened up to us. All
these reassuring promises tell us to expect things to get
better, that our life can be improved upon. The world
cannot promise this to us, but the Lord can and does.

Perhaps you feel as if you have lost everything, that it's
too late for you. If so, I have good news; the Lord is about to
do great things for you!

In quietness and confidence
shall be your strength.
Isaiah 30:15 NKJ

This verse assures us of quietness and confidence — in that order. Find quietness, and confidence will follow after it as a matter of course.

These two are twins — two friends to go with us on our pilgrim's journey. As the psalmist David declares in Psalm 23 that goodness and mercy shall follow him all the days of his life, so this verse proclaims that we can expect quietness and confidence to accompany us as we travel the road of life.

Quietness is not passivity, fatalism, or a state of detachment. Quietness is not resignation to a painful situation, a sort of "why try?" mindset or outlook. Quietness is a total absence of noisy distraction, tumultuous turmoil, of frantic, hectic pressure. It is God's gift of peace given right in the midst of labor and activity. Quietness is not an absence of problems or trials, it is an undisturbed calm that says in the midst of difficulty and tribulation, "It's all right; God is in control." Such calmness produces confidence.

Confidence is translated elsewhere as assurance and boldness. In the midst of quietness, confidence surfaces and emerges as a potent force.

The Lord gives quietness to the seeking, praying soul. The end result is confidence. Girded about with these two spiritual powers, we can proceed with a new strength and determination to finish the task we have been called to accomplish.

To give them beauty for ashes....
Isaiah 61:3 NKJ

Ashes are the only thing left when dreams go up in smoke.

A young woman enters marriage full of high hope and a wonderful dream. The marriage sours, the hope is shattered, the dream is gone; she is left looking at a pile of ashes.

A young man goes into business with aspirations of greatness. Errors in judgment, changing tides, wrong decision, and he goes bankrupt. Ashes!

Good health, good friendships, good plans for the future can all go up in flames overnight leaving nothing but the blackened ashes of disappointment, disillusionment, and despair.

This observation may seem gloomy and depressing, but it doesn't have to be. There is an answer. Only the Lord can turn ashes into a thing of beauty. He can take any broken situation, mend it, and make it into an object of art, a thing of beauty, a joy forever.

If you are "burned out," don't wallow in the ashes of self-pity. Let the Lord take over your life from here on. See what He will do with it. His creativity will surprise you!

Faced with ashes, we humans tend to finalize by concluding: "Well, that's it; it's all over. There's nothing left." In this verse, the Lord steps in and literally makes something out of nothing. He has the ability to take our worst losses and turn them into powerful displays of divine beauty!

You shall surround me with songs of deliverance.
Psalm 32:7 NKJ

A lady in Pasadena, California, was awakened out of a sound sleep by this word from the Lord: "Pray for Dick Mills; his life is in danger." As she interceded she began to sing confidently, "There is power, power, wonder working power, in the blood of the Lamb." She later related the incident, how peace came over her at the time the song came to her. She knew then that the danger had passed.

At precisely the same time this intercession was taking place, I was in real danger of being shot and killed by a deranged killer. I was helping one of his accomplices escape from him. In a mission meeting some time before, I had helped Jolie come back to the Lord from a backslidden condition. His prison mate heard about it, and set out for revenge. At the time of the prayer, he was following us down the street threatening our lives. His threats were not idle ones, since Jolie told me that he had seen him kill five different men.

While I was standing there on the sidewalk watching this man come toward Jolie and me, the same Holy Spirit moving on the intercessor in Pasadena began to plant the same song in my spirit. On the outside, I was shaking, but on the inside I was singing, "There's power in the blood." Same song, same time.

Suddenly, Jolie said, "Uh-oh, here he comes! We are as good as dead." That really didn't seem to me the best time for a song service, but I couldn't turn it off. We walked right past the killer unnoticed and escaped unharmed. Truly it was a song of deliverance.

**I sent you to reap that for which you
have not labored; others have labored,
and you have entered into their labors.
John 4:38 NKJ**

There are sowers and there are reapers. Preliminary work and preparation is often done by those who never get to see the result of their labors. Those who do the planting have to believe that their contribution is going to terminate in a good harvest, whether they get to experience the joy of gathering that harvest or not.

Here, however, the emphasis is reversed. The Lord Jesus tells His disciples that they are going to reap a harvest planted by someone who preceded them. He could be referring to Old Testament workers, to John the forerunner, or to Himself.

Our Lord is saying to His disciples: "I am sending you in to reap a harvest. Others ahead of you have done all the preliminary preparation. The ground work has been taken care of. All you have to do is reap the benefits of their labor."

Prophetically speaking, this verse could apply to you and me. Nearly two thousand years of planting, sowing, irrigating, weeding, hoeing, and cultivating have gone into the Gospel ministry. It is now harvest time, time to reap all the benefits and blessing that go with the worldwide harvest of souls for the kingdom. The early evangelists, intercessors, and soulwinners have done their part. Now it's our turn. Our part is to enter their labors and gather in the harvest they have made possible. The fields are white unto harvest. The time is now!

**Little by little I will drive them out from before you,
until you have increased, and you inherit the land.**
Exodus 23:30 NKJ

In this verse the Lord is assuring Israel that the
dispossession of Canaan's inhabitants will not occur all at
once, but that it will take place. In verses 28 and 29 He
explains that if these people were all driven out at once,
they would leave behind a new problem: wild, marauding
animals would multiply and become a menace. Instead the
Lord promises to remove the inhabitants little by little as
the Israelites increase enough to handle the occupation of
their inheritance.

What a message to us! God has to build us up to handle
promotion. We need to be groomed for success. Nobody
starts at the top. You don't come out of a high school
business class and begin your career as a vice-president of
the bank. No one goes directly from seminary to the
bishop's chair in one jump.

Little by little can be likened to the rings of a tree. It
takes one whole year to complete that ring. By some
people's standards, that is "too slow." But each year that
goes by, each ring is completed. The roots of that tree go
down farther into the ground, the branches reach higher
into the sky, and the tree gains additional size and strength
to withstand the storms of life which assail it.

Do you think we believers will ever learn that God's
timing is wisest for us?

**The love of God has been poured out in
our hearts by the Holy Spirit who was given to us.
Romans 5:5 NKJ**

Here is a promise of an abundance of *agape* love, the
God–like love which gives expecting nothing in return.
This promise has to do with loving the unlovely, those who
cannot, or will not, return that love. This verse means a
great deal to missionaries who give up creature comforts
and personal ease among their own people in order to take
the Gospel message to a foreign people far away who many
times neither desire nor appreciate such personal sacrifice
on their behalf.

"Yankee, go home!" is not just a political slogan. Often
it is the "buzz word" American missionaries of all
denominations and churches hear from hostile nationals
who misunderstand and resent their "intrusion" into their
everyday lives.

What would prompt a person to leave familiar and
pleasant surroundings and go hundreds, even thousands,
of miles away to invest his life in a strange, uncomfortable
and often dangerous environment? Especially when that
sacrifice seems to be neither recognized nor rewarded?
Those missionaries I talk to share how the *agape* love of God
so overwhelmed them that they had no other choice but to
respond to the call to the mission field. That love so
motivated them that they would only complain if they did
not get to go.

God's love is the greatest power in the universe. Once
people see and recognize the reality of that love
demonstrated before them, their response changes from
"Yankee, go home!" to "Friend, please stay and tell us more
about this Jesus!" That makes it all worthwhile!

Who forgives all your iniquities,
who heals all your diseases.
Psalm 103:3 NKJ

Salvation and healing are inseparable. The same Lord who forgives our sins, heals our diseases. In both the Old Testament and the New Testament, the word *salvation* is all-inclusive, including within its meaning forgiveness, reconciliation, deliverance, healing, safety, rescue, setting at liberty.

When Israel left Egypt, the sacrificial lamb slaughtered before their departure served two purposes. The blood of the lamb sprinkled on the doorposts protected the people from the judgment of sin that came that passover night. The flesh of the lamb was eaten to provide sustenance and strength for the journey ahead. The physical benefits were so great that Psalm 105:37 (NKJ) states of God's people: **...there was none feeble among His tribes.** One lamb covered both spiritual and physical needs.

Jesus went about forgiving sins and healing the sick. (Acts 10:38.) He told the twelve to do the same. He told the seventy to do the same. He could have told the five hundred to do the same. Everyone called to preach the Gospel of forgiveness of sin is also told to heal the sick. The two are inseparable.

Every time we take Communion, we are reminded of man's two areas of need: spiritual health and physical health. The cup reminds us that the blood of Jesus takes away all our sins. The wafer, or broken bread, reminds us that with His stripes we are healed. Salvation and healing come to us through the life and death of Jesus Christ. You can claim them both!

**As long as he sought the Lord,
God made him prosper.
2 Chronicles 26:5 NKJ**

All the scriptural promises of prosperity are conditional. Our hearts' response to the Lord and our desire to seek Him and to please Him assure us of His blessings of prosperity.

This verse reveals to us that King Uzziah of Judah prospered as long as he sought the Lord. The same principle applies to you and me today. By our attitude and actions, we predetermine to what extent — and for how long — the promises of prosperity are fulfilled in our lives. A lifetime of dedicated pursuit of the Lord and His righteousness and ways equals a lifetime of gifts bestowed on us by a benevolent Divine Providence.

The prophetic promise of 2 Chronicles 15:2 is addressed to you and me today just as much as it was to King Asa of Judah in ancient times: ..."**The Lord is with you while you are with Him. If you seek Him, He will be found by you; but if you forsake Him, He will forsake you**" (NKJ). As long as the king sought the Lord, he prospered. This word *prospered* has to do with advancement, promotion, gaining ground, increasing resources.

We do not seek or serve the Lord for mercenary reasons; we do so because as Creator of heaven and earth He is worthy of all our spiritual pursuit and devotion. But it is a joy to know that as we seek our heavenly Father with ardent spiritual intensity, He blesses us with all spiritual blessings. The additional benefits include physical health and financial prosperity. As children of the King, let's stop living beneath our station in life! Let's claim our inheritance, our glorious privileges! Let's seek the Lord!

**You, O God, sent a plentiful rain, whereby You
confirmed Your inheritance, when it was weary.
Psalm 68:9** NKJ

Years ago a scholar coined a phrase to describe that
state of 20th-century saints who have grown fatigued in the
march from earth to heaven. The expression he used was
"pre-millennial weariness." Not a pre-millennial rapture,
but a state of fatigue which settles in on those who have
labored long and hard for a lifetime and yet who must still
go on waiting for the Lord to return.

This verse recalls marching Israel spending forty years
on their journey to the Promised Land. The trip seemed
interminable. Weary, worn, beset with problems and
difficulties, they fretted with impatience, questioned their
leadership, complained about their surroundings. Morale
was low and even Moses could not really answer their
constant question, "How much longer?"

It was at this moment of low ebb that the Lord sent a
deluge of rain. One translator calls it "a rain of free gifts."
That's all it took to revive and refresh the souls of the weary
pilgrims.

The same principle applies to us today. The church age
has lasted nearly 2000 years now. Weary hearts are asking,
"How much longer?" The Lord's answer is an invigorating
rain of Holy Spirit blessings which the book of Acts calls
"rain from heaven and fruitful seasons." The hymnist
spoke for us as he cried out for such "seasons refreshing."
With that refreshing, we will be able to make the rest of the
journey in flying colors and full strength.

Lord, grant not just "showers of blessings," but send "a
plentiful rain!"

Established in the present truth.
2 Peter 1:12 NKJ

There seems to be a concern in some quarters of the Church today about the words **present truth**. This is an unnecessary fear, one which must be dealt with lest it deprive us of God's revelation knowledge for our time.

It seems that those who are resistant to the use of the expression "present truth" object to it on the grounds that it suggests acceptance of "a new gospel not founded on the Bible." This is a needless anxiety. There is no real danger in the Christian Church that the Bible will ever be replaced by a "revelation" given to some modern-day guru or cult leader.

The problem is a misunderstanding of the words **present truth.** In the original Greek, this was one word, *pareimi (par'–i– mee)*, meaning "the truth at hand" or "the truth for the time being." In each period revival, a new *aspect* of well-established *scriptural* truth has come to the forefront and received a Spirit-inspired focus and emphasis: In Luther's day it was "justification by faith"; in Wesley's age it was "today is the day of salvation"; during the Holiness revival period it was "without holiness no man shall see God." The Pentecostal's "present truth" is Jesus Christ, the same yesterday, today, and forever.

" ' "He who has an ear, let him hear what the Spirit *says* to the churches" ' " (Rev. 3:22 NKJ). God's Word is forever settled in heaven and will never be replaced. The Holy Spirit, however, has something to say to this age, just as He does to every age. He delivers that message by *speaking* to believers. Be listening for God's eternal, everlasting, "*present* truth"!

**While Peter was still speaking these words, the
Holy Spirit fell upon all those who heard the word.
Acts 10:44 NKJ**

Here we see portrayed a unique human-divine drama,
a picture of natural and supernatural teamwork. Peter is a
human being, using human vocal chords, phrasing human
sentences, speaking words in human language to human
listeners who understood him on human terms. That is all
natural.

The supernatural part is that while Peter was thus
functioning at the earthly, human level, the Holy Spirit fell
on all the listeners, working within their hearts what only
the Spirit can accomplish. The result of this human-divine
teamwork was a whole household of people converted to
Christ and instantly filled with the Spirit of God.

Peter spoke **words** (plural) externally, and the Holy
Spirit "co-operated" or "co-labored" with him by causing
the crowd to hear **the word** (singular) internally. The power
was not in Peter himself or even in his words, but in the
Spirit who translated words into the Word! Someone has
put it this way: "Peter was not giving a book review, a
weather report, crime statistics, or a political opinion. He
was proclaiming God's Word." That Word is the vehicle the
Lord blesses, the channel through which He moves and
acts.

As Christians, you and I can expect the same positive
response Peter received—if we do what Peter says he
always did: preach the Gospel *with the Holy Ghost sent down
from heaven.* (1 Pet. 1:12.) Let's proclaim the Word of God,
and trust Him to work with us by His Spirit to produce
miraculous results!

I free you this day from the
chains that were on your hand....
Jeremiah 40:4 NKJ

Free at last! What a word of final deliverance this is. Not only does the Lord promise through the prophet liberation and removal of all chains, He also assures that those chains will never be put back on: **...the Egyptians whom you see today, you shall see again no more forever** (Ex. 14:13,14). In other words: "The problems you have been facing up to now, you will never have to face again forever." To one who has been bound in chains, that is good news!

I had parked the car and was taking a shortcut through an alley to the church I was attending. I saw a man sitting there in the darkness. He was dejected and miserable. I recognized him as a person I had previously known. When I asked him what he was doing there in that dismal place, he showed me the needle marks in his arm.

An expensive heroin habit had done its job well, transforming a respected, productive human being into a derelict of society who could not function without a daily "fix." What had once been a free man was now a prisoner of drugs. Imagine the joy which was mine to be able to share with this one bound in darkness that Jesus breaks every chain, forever!

With the Lord in our hearts and lives, you and I never have to give up. No situation is impossible with Him on our side. This verse was given to let us know that our freedom has been purchased. Because the Deliverer has come, we can be *free at last!*

**And the Lord restored Job's losses....Indeed,
the Lord gave Job twice as much as he had before.**
Job 42:10 NKJ

What a thrilling conclusion to the book of Job! Imagine forty-one chapters describing the life of a man sorely tested and severely tried by all kinds of discouraging circumstances. The Bible tells us that Job emerged from his adversity with a double portion of blessings. Only the Lord can truly end a story with the promise of living "happily ever after." The world has no power to assure anyone that his life story will conclude on a happy note.

As a child, I was brought up on the Prince Charming story in which the hero overcomes all obstacles and defeats a fierce dragon as he battles his way to the enchanted castle to rescue Sleeping Beauty from a wicked curse. At the end, the two lovers ride off into the sunset bathed in "hearts and flowers." Solid romance!

But the story usually doesn't come out that way anymore. Today's generation is supposed to demand a more "realistic" approach, so the writer might have a terrorist group plant a bomb under Beauty's bed to blow them both to kingdom come! Another writer might suggest filling the moat with crocodiles so Prince Charming gets discouraged, gives up, and goes home to become a hairdresser! Madison Avenue would have Beauty wake up accusing the Prince of having "ring around the collar!"

Despite society's negative viewpoint, for the Christian, life doesn't have to end on a "downswing." Everything in the Bible points to an ending that is "upswing." Job ends up with twice the blessings he started out with. *That's* God's intended plan for us!

**For the children have come to birth,
but there is no strength to bring them forth.
Isaiah 37:3 NKJ**

This is a call for intercessors. The Church goes through it prenatal time of preparation for its converts. Before people can be born again, the Church has its periods of intercessory travail. Prayer, fasting, petition, and supplication are all necessary ingredients for additions to the Christian family. Isaiah's lament is due to a languishing nation. The children were ready to be born, but the spiritual vitality was so low there was not enough strength to bring forth.

Over 350,000 churches exist in the United States. Someone has estimated that one half of them do not add even one convert a year. Spiritual sluggishness and lack of spiritual strength keep the births from happening.

Healthy women have healthy babies. Vigorous women have vigorous babies. Lively women have lively babies. Healthy, vigorous lively churches will produce born-again babies in Christ who have a chance of surviving. Only a vigorous ministry of prayer for an individual or a church can turn spiritual listlessness to spiritual vitality. It is in such a setting that new births will occur.

After the fire a still small voice.
1 Kings 19:12 NKJ

The message of this verse is, "personality adjustment." In this situation, God was changing a man. In his early days, Elijah's life was stormy. He could recognize and relate to wind, earthquake, and fire. His whole prophetic career was characterized by these three qualities.

God was mellowing Elijah. By a set of circumstances and the Lord's personal dealings, the prophet ended up on the same mountain where Moses had received the Jewish law. The cave he found himself in could have been the same "cleft of the rock" in which the Lord hid Moses when His glory passed by and Moses was allowed to view God's back. (Ex. 33:20-23.)

In Moses' case, as the Lord passed by him, there was wind, earthquake, and fire. It was in this tumultuous setting that he was given the Ten Commandments. Now we read that in this same location many years later Elijah was also met by the Lord. As in Moses' case, there was wind, earthquake, and fire. But God was not in any of these violent things. Instead, the Lord came in the form of "a still small voice" — a soft, whispering stillness.

Force leaves men hard and antagonistic. The still small voice is the expression of the "more excellent way." (1 Cor. 12:31.) The gentleness of God is winning souls by grace whom might and wrath have failed to move. O Lord, give us more of Your gentleness! Elijah came out of that cave not only with restored confidence, but with a changed nature. He was a better, nobler man. David expressed this transformation succinctly when he said of God: **Your gentleness has made me great....**(Ps. 18:35 NKJ).

**The hearing ear and the seeing eye,
the Lord has made both of them.
Proverbs 20:12 NKJ**

This verse is only one of more than 17 I have counted in the Bible in which seeing and hearing are combined. It stresses that the Gospel is only complete when it is seen as well as heard. John says of Jesus that...**many believed in his name, when they *saw* the miracles which he did** (John 2:23).

For too long the Church in America has been on a "head-trip." We have placed emphasis on hearing about the faith — rather than on seeing faith in action today!

Too often Christians file out of church on Sunday morning, shake the pastor's hand and congratulate him on his good sermon, and then go their ways virtually unchanged. They may have accumulated and stored away more facts about the Gospel, but they have not really experienced the power of the Gospel. Week after week, this routine is repeated with no evidence of any real change in the lives of those who hear.

In the book of Acts, we read the Holy Ghost fell on everyone who heard the Word. (Acts 10:44.) We also read that when the disciples preached the Word, the Lord worked with them to confirm that Word with miraculous signs. (Mark 16:20.) Paul said that his speaking was accompanied by powerful spiritual demonstration. (1 Cor. 2:4.)

I believe that before the coming of the Lord, the Church will once again preach the Gospel (for hearing) with the Holy Ghost sent down from heaven (for seeing). (1 Pet. 1:12.) Lord, hasten the day when we can see the Gospel with our eyes as well as hear it with our ears!

**To those who are called, both Jews and Greeks,
Christ the power of God and the wisdom of God.
1 Corinthians 1:24 NKJ**

Power is something we can see with our eyes; wisdom is something we can hear with our ears. Jesus has both power and wisdom. He displayed His power in the miracles He performed; He demonstrated His wisdom in the words He spoke.

The Jewish people were impressed by miracles, signs, and wonders, so they sought these as proof of divine origin. The Greeks were fascinated with knowledge, wisdom and understanding, so they sought these as evidence of deity. The pursuit of the Jew was emotional, that of the Greek was intellectual.

Jesus was able to satisfy the need of both Jew and Greek. He is still able. Whatever a person's background, culture, language, race, sex, or creed, Jesus can meet him right where he lives. Our Lord adapts Himself to each individual, regardless of that person's particular situation. Jesus is the power of God for those who need might as a point of contact. Jesus is the wisdom of God for those who need reason as a point of contact.

We want to win people powerfully and to win them wisely. Sensitivity to the person and his unique personality and make-up is so vital. The Holy Spirit can help us make the right adjustment to win each individual. Jesus was so full of His Father's *love* that people were impressed with His *wisdom* and *power*. (Matthew 13:54; Mark 6:2.) As His disciples, we are indwelt by the Source of all three of these qualities of love, wisdom and power: the Holy Spirit. (John 14:12; 1 Timothy 1:7.)

**All the days of my hard service
I will wait, till my change comes.
Job 14:14 NKJ**

This verse contains the noun form of one of my favorite Hebrew verbs: *chalaph (khaw–laf')*. Here, Job is saying that despite his miserable condition, he is looking for a *change* of circumstance. E.W. Bullinger translates this phrase: "...I will wait until the time of my reviving comes." *The New International Version* renders it: "...I will wait for my renewal to come."

Unfortunately, Bible scholars have often assumed that Job was speaking of his dying. They read about death in the context and mistakenly conclude that Job's words deal with that subject. **Hard service** (or as the *King James Version* has it, "appointed time") is a military expression relating to engagement in warfare. All the time Job was waging the good fight of faith, he was not waiting for death but for a divine visitation. He was expecting a revival, a renewal, a change for the better. That change came when the Lord intervened to turn Job's captivity and reward His faithfulness with a double portion of all that he had lost in the hassle.

This can be our happy conclusion also. We too are engaged in the fight of faith. Our warfare against the powers of darkness goes on and on. We too look for a change, a renewal, a revival, a breakthrough. The Lord will intervene for us just as He did for Job.

Job expected changes in his circumstances. They came to him in double measure. We can expect the same. Get ready for dramatic changes in the whole Church world; they're coming. As the old song puts it: "There'll be some changes made today; there'll be some changes made!"

> **But those who wait on the Lord**
> **shall renew their strength....**
> **Isaiah 40:31** NKJ

As noted in yesterday's lesson, one of my favorite Hebrew words is *chalaph (khaw–laf')*. It is a word that is used in various illustrative ways to indicate personality alteration, second growth, revival, renewal, and a change for the better.

When Mohammed died, his replacement was called a *caliph*, a derivative of this word *chalaph*. There is even conjecture by some scholars that California obtained its name from this Hebrew word. In the Middles Ages a novel was written about a mythical queen named California who took a desert wasteland and turned it into a beautiful garden. The *Calif* portion of her name was supposedly traced by some to *chalaph*.

In the original Hebrew version of this verse, the word translated **renew** is *chalaph*. In this case, it is defined as "exchange." We who wait on the Lord shall *exchange* our strength. Ours for His. What a beautiful picture!

In our time of trial, we can say: "Lord I am waiting for You, and while I am waiting something is happening. An exchange is taking place. My strength is being replaced by Your strength. My limited finances are giving way to Your riches in glory. My finite wisdom is being superseded by Your wisdom from above."

You can change every area of your life right now. Quote Isaiah 40:31 and tell the Lord that you want *chalaph,* a renewal, an exchange. If you want victory in your life, trade your resources for God's!

> ### And even now the ax is laid to
> ### the root of the trees....
> ### Matthew 3:10 NKJ

Part One

Here is a verse for dealing with genetic tendencies in a family tree. It assures us that there is an "ax" which can cut the "root" of cancer, alcoholism, stroke, heart attack, emotional disorder or any other inherited negative family trait. That ax, or cutting edge, is the Word of God which is...**living and powerful, and sharper than any two-edged sword, piercing even to the division of soul and spirit, and of joints and marrow....**(Hebrews 4:12 NKJ).

According to Scripture, God's blessings are passed down through a family for a thousand generations. (Ps. 105:8.) Defective tendencies will only reach to the third and fourth generations. (Ex. 20:5.) In view of that ratio, we ought to inherit a lot more "good stuff" than "bad stuff." However, it must be admitted that there are some negative family tendencies to be dealt with.

Some families have a history of cancer, some heart problems, some strokes, some insanity. Others have a marked tendency toward chemical addiction, lust, jealously, worry, or bad temper. If there is any negative trait in your family tree, this verse is for you. Verbally state it as a confession of faith:

"Lord, Your Word is the cutting instrument. I lay the ax to the root of _____ in my family tree (fill in the word that characterizes your family tendency). *I claim freedom from the problems in my family which have been passed from one generation to the next. Thank You, Father for this deliverance. Amen!"*

> **For there is hope for a tree, if it is
> cut down, that it will sprout again, and
> that its tender shoots will not cease.**
> **Job 14:7 NKJ**

Part Two

This is a continuation of yesterday's word: "Now the ax is laid to the root of the tree." Through the eyes of faith Job sees that the purpose of God's pruning is the removal of bad roots, not the chopping down of healthy trees. If the Lord went around cutting down every life that had a defect in it, there would not be many left standing — and I'm not at all sure that I would be one of them! Neither was the psalmist, evidently, for the asked this question of His Maker: **If You, Lord, should mark iniquities, O Lord, who could stand?** (Ps. 130:3 NKJ).

Here Job is talking about replacement. He is saying that, in the process of pruning, even if a tree were completely chopped down, there would still be hope of regrowth. That tree can **sprout again**. In the original Hebrew this expression is one word, *chalaph (khaw–laf')*, the word used for the revival or renewal. Even though the ax is laid at the root of the tree, the tree itself can still revive. It can be renewed. It can come back again.

It should encourage us to know that the Lord can cut out of us every inherited genetic disturbance without destroying our lives. No matter how ingrained the cancer — the negative family trait or tendency — that root can be severed without destroying the life of the family tree. Though severely pruned, it will come back.

Tomorrow we will look at how the revived tree will be different and even better than the one it replaces.

He shall be like a tree planted
by the rivers of water....
Psalm 1:3 NKJ

Part Three

The word **planted** in this verse is the Hebrew word *shatal (shaw–thal')*. In his concordance, Dr. James Strong uses a succinct and terse expression to define this root word: *"to transplant."* Thus this verse is a description of our new status as Christians. As subjects of the kingdom of God, you and I are "transplanted" trees.

Looking back over the past three days' lessons, we read: 1) "Now is the ax laid to the root of the trees." This verse had to do with severing genetic weaknesses from our lives; 2) "If the tree is cut down, there is hope that it will sprout again." We are promised a reviving and a renewal after our family tree is pruned; 3) "He shall be like a tree planted by the rivers of water." After our pruning, we the righteous will be like transplanted trees drawing directly from the rivers of divine life.

In these verses, the Lord is telling us that as new creatures in Christ, our renewed family tree will be better than ever. It will have plenty of moisture. It will be fruitful, and its foliage will not wither away.

All of us can go through this threefold process. Let's allow the Lord to 1) cut away anything in us that is detrimental to our Christian witness, 2) renew and revive our lives, and 3) manifest the fruit of the life of Christ in us as we draw from the water of life.

Our new transplanted life will result in abundant health, happiness, and harvest.

From this day forward, I will bless you.
Haggai 2:19 NKJ

Have you seen the commercial slogan which asks the penetrating question, "Eventually, why not now?" Properly understood and applied, the message of that slogan can change our lives. There is a day of deliverance for every one of us, a day when God rends the heavens and intervenes on our behalf. According to this verse, for you and me that day is *today!*

Bringing our faith from futuristic hope and desire to present-tense "today-is-the-day!" expectation is not something you and I can do in and of ourselves. "Only believe" is only possible when we have some solid basis for belief. All our optimism, enthusiasm, cliches, "buzz words," success slogans, positive mental attitudes, and even "confession of the Word" can be helpful. But the truth is that ultimately the only way you and I can believe strongly enough to transform future hope into present assurance is by *receiving a personal word directly from the Lord to us.* This verse is that word.

"From this day forward, I will bless you!" This verse not only promises us immediate deliverance today, it is also enhances hope for tomorrow. "From this day forward" indicates that this is not a "one-time" blessing; this is a whole new way of life!

"Not only am I setting you free from all poverty, fear, sickness, trouble, and weakness," the Lord says to us, "but for the rest of your life I will continually bless you with good things." You and I have a lot to look forward to! Believe it and see!

**You shall increase my greatness,
and comfort me on every side.
Psalm 71:21 NKJ**

In the original Hebrew version, the word translated
comfort is *nacham (naw–kham')*. It describes God's response
to our trying circumstances.

One definition of *nacham* is "to sigh." The prophet
Isaiah says of God and His people: **In all their afflictions,
he was afflicted....**(Is. 63:9). The writer of Hebrews tells us
that we have a High Priest Who is touched with the feelings
of our infirmities. (Heb. 4:15.) So when circumstances cause
us to sigh, the Lord sighs with us. But, He does infinitely
more than that.

Another definition of *nacham* is "to breathe strongly" or
"to draw breath forcibly." We do this in times of strong
physical or emotional stress. We breathe hard when excited,
when forced to move rapidly, or when the pace of our lives
is drastically speeded up. When the Lord says through the
psalmist that He will comfort us, He is saying that He will
be right by our side. Our eagerness, excitement and
enthusiasm become His eagerness, excitement and
enthusiasm. In stressing that the spirit (Spirit) is *willing*, the
Bible uses a word that describes ardent eagerness. Our God
is just as eager for our victory as we are.

Another definition of *nacham* is "to pity," implying
feeling such sorrow for a person as to step in and avenge
him against his adversary. Gesenius, the grammarian, says
of *nacham*: "It includes the notion of God putting forth help
and taking vengeance."

Our God does much more than console us in battles;
He takes our side with us against our enemy!

Hope does not disappoint....
Romans 5:5 NKJ

You have always known that God was going to answer your prayers. When you were unmarried, you knew that one day the Lord would bless you with a spouse and children. When your family members were still unsaved, you knew that someday they would all come to know the Lord. When your church was in need of revival, you knew that if you prayed with faith and patience, sooner or later that revival would break forth. You even knew that you would eventually get that much needed and deserved promotion and raise at work. You waited patiently to see these things (and other prayer requests) come to pass, because you had *hope* as an anchor for your soul. (Heb. 6:19).

Hope is a good ingredient to have in our Christian character because it motivates us to keep going. When my wife and I accidentally drove our car off a hill and landed at the bottom of a ravine, it was the walk back up the side of that hill that told me how strong hope really is. I kept telling my wife while we were climbing, "Cars are only metal, glass, and rubber. We can always get another car, or even do without one if we have to. But there is one thing we have that no one can take from us, and that is our hope and desire to go into all the world and preach the Gospel to every creature."

Hope keeps spiritual desire alive. It motivates us every day to get up and give life another try. It keeps us going when circumstances are screaming at us: "Give up! You'll never make it, why try any longer?"

Hope does not disappoint because it brings us to the point of our deliverance. The psalmist exhorts: **Be of good courage, and He shall strengthen your heart, all you who hope in the Lord** (Ps. 31:24 NKJ). Never give up!

**Return to the stronghold, you prisoners of hope.
Even today I declare that I will restore double to you.
Zechariah 9:12 NKJ**

Prisoners of hope is an expression used to describe those who have waited a long, long time for a specific prayer to be answered.

Actually, the expression is a bit misleading. In reality, it is hope which is the prisoner. We lock it up in our hearts and refuse to allow it to escape. The word **prisoners** in this verse is a translation of a Hebrew word whose verb form means "to tie down, to hold down, to bind in order to keep in one place." Applied to a person or thing, our modern-day equivalent might be "to put on hold." Hope is a very good thing for us to "put on hold" in our hearts.

Hope deferred makes the heart sick, but when the desire comes, it is a tree of life (Prov. 13:12 NKJ). What wise Solomon meant here was that sometimes hope is not easy to hold because it seems to cause us misery — until it is fulfilled!

An airline attendant recognized me on a flight and told me that eight years earlier in church I had given her a Scriptural promise from the Lord that her husband would be saved. She had locked that verse up in her heart and kept it. Her husband's actions and lifestyle did not encourage her, so she was tempted to give up. But she kept holding on to the promise as a prisoner of hope. Later her husband was not only saved, he began family devotions in the home, and enrolled in a local Bible-study group. Her hope resulted in a double portion: Salvation of her mate and a future as the wife of a minister of the Gospel!

By pride comes only contention....
Proverbs 13:10 NKJ

Much of earth's strife, conflict, turmoil, and war can be traced back to pride. It was a heart lifted up with pride that provoked the first war in all recorded history when Lucifer and his followers tried to overthrow the throne of the Most High. (Rev. 12:7; Ezek. 28:17)

Pride always exalts self above true relationship to God. Contention results when pride drives a person furiously to "make it," even if it means crawling over others and clawing his way to the top.

Pride is behind virtually all misunderstandings, disagreements, differences, church squabbles, matrimonial friction, and family turmoil. The answer to pride is a healthy spirit of humility.

The word *humility* is always associated with lowliness. **...with the lowly is wisdom,** wrote the author of Proverbs 11:2...**Mind not high things, but condescend to men of low estate...**,counsels the great Apostle Paul in Romans 12:6. **Let the brother of low degree rejoice in that he is exalted,** says James in chapter one, verse nine, of the epistle by his name.

You and I can avoid the "hassle" of strife and conflict by heeding the words of wise Solomon: **Better it is to be of an humble spirit with the lowly, than to divide the spoil with the proud** (Prov. 16:19).

A truly humble person cannot be humiliated. How can you put down someone who is already low and sitting at the feet of Jesus?

**The more you are enriched the more scope
will there be for generous giving....
2 Corinthians 9:11 Phillips**

Two things go with the Christian territory: gratitude and generosity.

Let's consider ourselves before our conversion. You and I were not born naturally grateful or generous. It was not our inherent nature either to esteem or praise others more than ourselves or to really enjoy giving away to others anything of real value to us. We weren't totally selfish, but then again we weren't totally unselfish either. We were just *self-centered*.

But then we were converted. To convert means "to turn around and go in the opposite direction." Now that we are heading in the opposite way, we have a new nature. Now that we are *Christ-centered*, we find it easy to give praise to God for His goodness and mercy to us and to praise other people for their efforts on our behalf. Likewise, we find it easy to give away material things. That giving starts a cycle of receiving which enables us to give even more. While we don't "give to get" (for ourselves), we do *give to get more to give.*

This verse assures us that the more we are enriched, the more scope we will have for generosity. Prosperity makes sense when it is motivated, not by selfishness, but by a sincere desire to bless others. The basic rule is: "Give, and it shall be given to you in return — and in abundance — so you will have more to give next time."

I believe that in the future we will see surface a large group of dedicated and committed believers who have a pronounced ministry of giving. I am convinced that Christians will become conspicuous by their generosity. Overflowing — *out*flowing — prosperity is on its way!

Feed me with the food You prescribe for me.
Proverbs 30:8 NKJ

This is the Old Testament equivalent of "Give us this day our daily bread." With this verse from Proverbs, I was able to lose twenty pounds.

As a result of spending a month in a very expensive facility (paid for by an appreciative church group) and dining on the tempting gourmet dishes provided me there, I found myself overweight. More than that, I discovered that indulging my appetite had let it get totally out of control. I knew I had to do something. Then I recalled this verse from a previous weight-loss experience.

The *King James Version* reads:...**feed me food convenient for me.** In this version the writer asks God for the food which He prescribes. The Hebrew word translated **prescribe** here is *choq (khoke).* It is defined as "an appointment combining time, labor, and usage." Elsewhere it is translated "daily portion" or "daily bread."

The amount and type of food you and I need for the average day depends upon the schedule and demands of that particular day. I found that I could determine that amount by a sensitivity to the promptings of the Holy Spirit. Listening to the still small voice within enabled me to recognize my daily need. Relying on the power of the Holy Spirit strengthened me to consume only what was necessary to fulfill that need. No more, no less. Such commitment requires self-disciple, but the reward is well worth the effort. When all the "fad diets" have failed, try the Lord's prescribed plan: our daily bread.

**The blessing of the Lord makes one
rich, and He adds no sorrow with it.
Proverbs 10:22 NKJ**

Here is an encouraging word from the Lord. It is an assurance that the good and beneficial blessings our Father bestows upon us will enrich our lives. In addition, He promises us help in avoiding the sorrow that often goes with earthly increase and promotion.

In the original version, the Hebrew word translated **sorrow** is *'etseb (eh'tseb)* and is defined as "physical toil, emotional pain and anguish, mental fatigue and discomfort." On the human level, advancement often leads to problems. In our world, the higher a person climbs up the ladder of success, the more risks he encounters. Many time, the inner price of outer success is a heavy one indeed.

In this verse, wise Solomon assures us that it is not so in the kingdom of God. Our loving Father blesses and enriches His children while at the same time deflecting any grief that might tend to accompany and spoil the joy of His benedictions.

It is as though the Lord is saying to us: "My blessings are not sweet and sour. I am not going to make you both happy and miserable. I do not open My hand to pour out blessing and sorrow at the same time."

One scholar has written concerning this verse: Whatever we receive in the way of providential benefits has God's blessing in it and will do us good. Cares, troubles, and difficulties come with all property not acquired in this way. God's blessing gives simple enjoyment and levies no taxes upon the comfort we receive."

Do not lie in wait, O wicked man,
against the dwelling of the righteous;
do not plunder his resting place.
Proverbs 24:15 NKJ

This verse speaks directly to those who break into people's homes to steal and vandalize. It warns them against trespassing on the premises of the righteous.

Law enforcement agencies claim that one out of seven homes in the United States will be broken into this year. The media tells us that in New York City, the most common "status symbol" is an elaborate security system consisting of seven chains, locks, bars, dead-bolts, barriers, and door restrainers. One writer here reported pathetically that it takes him nearly fifteen minutes to disengage his anti-burglar system so he can open his front door.

As believers, this verse is given to assure that there is something better than all that protective paraphernalia. Our trust in God Almighty provides us a peace and assurance unknown to those outside the Lord.

The Bible tells us that the angel of the Lord encamps about those who reverence and respect Him. (Ps. 34:7.) For us Christians, there is a better way. Our protection is not physical, but spiritual. We could call it "the celestial security system"! Try it, it works!

**Let us continually offer the sacrifice
of praise to God, that is, the fruit of our
lips, giving thanks to His name.
Hebrews 13:15 NKJ**

A sacrifice is something of value which is freely given
up by one person in order to please, enhance, or benefit
another. Jesus' death on the cross is an example of the
supreme sacrifice. He freely offered up His life for us
human beings in order to accomplish for us what we could
never do for ourselves: pay the full price of our redemption
from our sins.

The sacrifice of praise is something we offer up to our
Lord. A sacrifice requires self-denial. Just as Jesus
voluntarily gave us His life for our sakes, though He
despised the cross, so we give Him the praise and
thanksgiving due Him, though we may not always feel like
doing so.

If ours is to be a true sacrifice, we cannot wait for
favorable circumstances before we offer it. We are to offer
up praise and thanks continually. Such praise is not always
a sincere expression of the heart. Sometimes the fruit of our
lips can be the most shallow effort imaginable. Phonetically,
all the lips can do is enunciate sounds. Those sounds alone
do not necessarily constitute true praise. It is when the lips
overflow with that which is welling up in our innermost
being that we produce the real fruit of praise.

However, even if our praise does seem superficial and
shallow, it is still highly acceptable as a sacrifice to the Lord.
God does not require us to feel, only to acknowledge: **Let
every thing that hath breath praise the Lord** (Ps. 150:6).

Instead of the thorn shall come up the fir tree, and instead of the brier shall come up the myrtle tree....
Isaiah 55:13

This is one of those before and after verses. It describes you and me before and after our conversion. It stresses the difference between life without the Spirit and life filled with the Spirit.

The thorn describes the unregenerate man. A thorn tree grows like a weed without cultivation; it has no utility, no beauty or redeeming features. A thorn punctures and irritates. Thorns go with the wasteland, this wilderness we call the world.

The fir tree, on the other hand, is a picture of the regenerated man. It is an evergreen. Green is the color of eternal life. Thus the evergreen is symbolic of salvation. The fir does not fade; all year long its needles and branches point right up toward heaven. Instead of being thorn trees in the wilderness, you and I are living fir trees, perpetually straight and green and lively.

The brier represents the dead and barren life without the Spirit. The brier is a good picture of the self-life: uncrucified, unruly, undisciplined.

The myrtle represents life with the Spirit. The myrtle is known for its aroma. The fragrance of righteousness, love, and eternal life replaces the stench of worldliness, selfishness, and death.

All this life, beauty, and fragrance is worth receiving!

**Judah shall again take root
downward, and bear fruit upward.
Isaiah 37:31 NKJ**

A tree grows in three directions: downward, upward, and outward. This verse promises growth and expansion in two of the three directions, both down and up at the same time. The message is that our growth as Christians is recognizable by ourselves, by the Lord's angelic host, and by others as well.

Taking root downward is progress known only to us. The root system is below the surface and not visible to anyone. In the course of a year, there is growth, but it is undetected. You and I are not the same people we were a year ago. Perhaps others cannot see the deepening process at work, but we know it is there.

Bearing fruit upward has visible results. Fruit bearing is an activity that is open and apparent to any observer. Fruit is the end result of a year's special effort. It is for all to see and enjoy.

Bearing fruit is also another word for productivity. When Jesus said that we would be able to judge a tree by its fruit, He was telling us to be observant of our own lives, as well as others', because we show what we are by what we produce.

The ring on the inside of a tree may be minuscule and totally hidden from human view. But year in and year out, it records a message: this tree is growing and producing fruit. Visible and invisible growth is taking place.

You and I should be encouraged! The Lord has promised us continuous and on-going growth!

**I have been crucified with Christ; it is no
longer I who live, but Christ lives in me....
Galatians 2:20 NKJ**

The usual Greek word translated **crucified** is *stauroo
(stow– ro'–o)* meaning "to impale on a cross." Here in this
verse, Paul uses the Greek word *sustauroo (soo–tow–ro'–o)*,
"to impale in company with," referring to a co-crucifixion.
This is the word used for the two thieves who were crucified
along with Jesus.

Paul stresses that he was also impaled on the cross with
Jesus. When Christ died, Paul died with Him. But like
Christ, Paul did not stay dead. If Paul was crucified and
buried with Christ, he was also raised to new life with
Christ. The remainder of this verse declares: **"...and the life
which I now live in the flesh I live by faith...."** The apostle
understood that his old life *"of the flesh"* was gone and the
life he now lived *"in the flesh"* was a spiritual one.

Paul's new life was totally different from that which he
had lived before the crucifixion of his "old man." The same
is true of you and me. We too were crucified, dead and
buried with our Lord. We too were raised to new life in
Christ. Christ is seated in the heavenlies, and Paul tells us
that we are seated there with Him. (Eph. 1:3.) If that is so, if
we are new spiritual beings, what kind of life should we
now live?

Men have spent centuries focusing on our need to be
crucified with Christ, to nail our "old man" to the cross. But
the co-crucifixion is not the end, the ultimate achievement,
or the final goal. It is simply God's ordained method for
getting us into *resurrection life.* As Paul said of himself, you
and I can say of ourselves: we are *dead to sin, but alive in
Christ!*

They willingly received Him into the boat,
and immediately the boat was at the
land where they were going.
John 6:21 NKJ

Two things happen at once when Jesus stepped on
board the disciples' boat: 1) the storm ceased, and 2) the
boat landed at the shore to which the disciples were
headed.

There is a very important message for all of us in this
story. The Lake of Galilee is six to eight miles across.
Having been born and reared in this area, no doubt the
disciples were in familiar territory. They had set out from
the eastern side of the lake at about 6 p.m., intending to
cross over to the western shore.

As they made the crossing, suddenly a storm came up
and their passage became extremely difficult. They rowed
until 3 a.m. and had only been able to cover three or four
miles. That is when they saw Jesus coming toward them,
walking on the water.

After six to nine hours of exhaustive toil, they were
only halfway across the lake. In the midst of the storm, in
the middle of the lake, Jesus stepped on board their ship.
When His feet touched the deck, immediately the storm
was calmed and the boat landed on the other shore.

This may be a picture of your life right now. It may
seem that you have been rowing forever, and yet are still far
from shore. In the midst of your storms and toil, invite Jesus
to come aboard. He will still the storm and get you to your
destination far quicker than you could ever imagine!

> **Now in the morning, as He returned to the city,**
> **He was hungry. And seeing a fig tree by the road,**
> **He came to it and found nothing on it but leaves,**
> **and said to it, "Let no fruit grow on you ever**
> **again." And immediately the fig tree withered away.**
> **Matthew 21:18,19 NKJ**

During their travels, Jesus and his disciples, looking for nourishment, came to a fig tree. To their disappointment, the tree had leaves but no fruit. Jesus spoke to the tree, and it died and withered away.

Some critical writers feel that Jesus' cursing the tree is out of character. Their rationale is: "Jesus went about doing good. Why does He now reverse field and go in an opposite direction? Why cursing instead of blessing?"

Utility is the word. In the economy of God, all living organisms function to produce and reproduce. This tree was occupying space in an already crowded world. Its roots were taking valuable nutrients out of the soil. Its branches were soaking up sunshine. Its leaves were drinking in rain. The tree was taking in but not giving out. It was serving no purpose, yet was draining resources. So the Creator removed it by speaking to it directly.

Fear, poverty, insecurity, bodily ailments — anything negative or debilitating, anything that takes up time, space, or energy without producing positive results — can be removed from our lives. Our Lord has promised to prune us, to cut away everything from us which has no utility, purpose, or benefit. (John 15:2.) With this assurance, we can concentrate more fully on the areas of our life that are fruitful and productive.

**The God of peace will crush Satan
under your feet shortly....
Romans 16:20 NKJ**

The two key words here are: **crush** and **shortly.** One tells how thoroughly powerless our enemy has been made since his defeat at Calvary; **crush** indicates total destruction. The other tells us how soon we can expect to see this destruction; **shortly** indicates that we do not have long to wait.

In the original Greek text, the word translated **crush** (**bruise** in the *King James Version*) is *suntribo (soon–tree'bo),* which is a verb meaning "to crush completely; to shatter; to break in pieces; to pulverize, disintegrate, torpedo, annihilate." The word represents an image of all the works of the enemy being thoroughly taken apart. What a promise of victory for the Christian.

In the original, **shortly** is an expression made up of two Greek words: *en (en)* and *tachos (tahk'–os).* It is defined as "in haste, as soon as possible, without delay, suddenly, swiftly, with all speed." This too is encouraging to the believer.

Do you have problems? Quote this verse as a confession of faith: "The God of peace is going to shatter the enemy under my feet without delay. In Luke 10:19 my Lord has promised that I will tread on Satan and his demons. My feet are shod with the gospel of peace. I am ready for the imminent victory — right now in Jesus' name!"

> **There is one who speaks like the piercing of a sword, but the tongue of the wise promotes health.**
> **Proverbs 12:18 NKJ**

I meet people everywhere I go who were raised in a climate of sarcasm. All they ever heard were cutting, belittling, abrasive words. On the outside, such people may appear unharmed, but inside they are still bruised, cut, and bleeding. Unless they find healing, that invisible hurt will usually make its presence known and felt in one negative way or another.

We Christians must be on our guard against sarcasm. Because of its powerful negative effect, this word is worth examining. According to *Webster's New Twentieth Century Dictionary*, it comes from the Greek word *sarcasmos*, which is a derivative of *sarkazein*, meaning "to tear flesh like dogs."

This verse tells us that sarcastic speech pierces like a sword. Sarcastic people can cut you to pieces with their tongues. Their words tear to shreds, wounding the "flesh" — especially the *spirit* — of their victims.

But the verse ends on a positive note: **the tongue of the wise promotes health.** Our words can cut or they can mend. They can wound, or they can heal. They can tear down or build up. We have a choice: we can pierce with sarcasm, or we can heal with words of wisdom.

Luke tells us that the people were astonished at the gracious words that came out of Jesus' mouth. (Luke 4:22.) What a role model He was! Following our Lord's example, we can always speak healing words. Let's do it!

**The mountains and hills will burst
into song before you, and all the trees of
the field will clap their hands.**
Isaiah 55:12 NIV

We know that the earth we live in can respond to the kind of treatment we give it. In Genesis 4:10, the blood of Abel (recently murdered) cried out from the ground on which it had been spilled. The Red Sea parted to allow the children of Israel to march through to safety. When Solomon was dedicated and anointed king, the very ground on which he was standing shook by reason of the occasion.

In Revelation 12:16 we read in symbolic language that during future times, the earth will help the woman and will swallow the flood of persecution that comes forth from the mouth of the dragon. Scripture also tells us that the earth is affected by the sin and depravity of humanity. Paul writes that the whole creation groans and travails under the burden of mankind's fallen state. (Rom. 8:21,22.)

In this verse, the prophet says that mountains and hills will "break forth into singing" and the trees of the field will "clap their hands." The earth responds favorably to the proclamation of the Good News. Mountains and hills are symbolic of permanence and strength. All of life is not quicksand, barren wilderness, or dry desert; some of it is tree covered. Trees represent growth, beauty, and fruitfulness. Even the mountains and trees will rejoice at our coming to announce the Good News of Jesus Christ.

Can you imagine what kind of desolate wasteland this world would be without the Gospel or its messengers?

> **For you shall go out with joy,**
> **and be led out with peace....**
> **Isaiah 55:12** NKJ

The first time this verse ever came to me was in a moment of great need. I had just graduated from a Bible school with an evangelistic call on my life. Only one door was opened to my wife and me. An invitation came to hold several meetings, but there were problems.

We had a small, light, ten-year-old car, which was totally incapable of making the long trip from California to the Colorado mountain town to which we had been invited. In order to accept the invitation, we knew that we would have to sell our old car and purchase a newer one and a travel trailer. Realizing we needed divine help, we parked the car by an open field in the San Fernando Valley and prayed to the Lord for guidance, direction, and assistance. A peaceful calm filled the car and this verse came to us: **"...you shall go out with joy, and be led out with peace...."** Immediately our outlook changed from reticent uncertainty to confident assurance.

In the next 90 days the Lord restructured our transportation system by supplying us with a newer, heavier car and a travel trailer. He also sent us the cash we needed for travel expenses. We made the trip and arrived safe and sound and ready for revival. The joy and peace that accompanied us was very real.

This verse knows no geographical limitation, time restriction, financial hindrance, physical confinement, or legal blockage. It applies equally to everyone who is working for the Lord and doing His will. It is a word just for *you!*

**For you shall not go out with haste,
nor go by flight....
Isaiah 52:12 NKJ**

The two key words here are **haste** and **flight**. They need to be defined because both words speak volumes to us in understanding the Lord's leadings and dealings with us.

Haste is a word which implies compulsive action. It suggests being on the run due to guilt, fear, or anxiety. A verse that describes the impulsiveness and impetuousness inherent in those who act hastily is Proverbs 28:1: **The wicked flee when no one pursues....**(NKJ*).*

You and I, being led by the Spirit of the Lord, never have to make decisions or take actions motivated by guilt or fear. The way our loving Father leads us is by the reassuring words from His book and by the calm and encouraging workings of the Holy Spirit.

Flight is easily understood by adding a "y" and changing it into *flighty.* Webster defines this word as "given to flights or sallies of fancy, caprice, etc.; volatile; frivolous; slightly delirious; light-headed; mildly crazy." A flighty person is unstable, always trying to escape reality by trips into the world of the imagination or wishful thinking.

Led by the Lord, you and I will never have to go anywhere motivated by guilt, fear, or nervous unrest. Isaiah tells us that we will go out with joy and be led forth with peace. (Is. 55:12.) What a difference there is between going with fear, anxiety, or capriciousness and going forth with joy and peace. Our choice is the latter! I know it's your choice too!

**For the Lord will go before you, and
the God of Israel will be your rear guard.
Isaiah 52:12b NKJ**

Every group of travelers has two kinds of people: fast
movers and slow movers. Fast movers are aggressive,
ambitious, alert, and highly motivated to move out and get
on with the journey. Slow movers tend to dawdle, waver,
hesitate, to be unsure, reticent, or indecisive. It is very
difficult to lead any group of people when part of them are
forever rushing ahead while another part is always lagging
behind.

This verse says that the Lord is out in front of the self-
motivated marchers, and He is also following up at the rear
of the stragglers. David calls attention to the fact that the
Lord both goes ahead and follows up when he says of Him,
You have hedged me behind and before....(Ps. 139:5).

It is a comfort to know that our God is present in both
areas of our lives. He is "proceeding" out in front of us
leading the way, and He is our rear guard protecting us
from being picked off by the enemy.

The *King James Version* used an archaic word for rear
guard. *Rereward*, a holdover from antiquity, is derived from
a word meaning "to gather together." No matter where we
are positioned in the army of the Lord — front line or rear
echelon — we are safe. The Lord is in both areas watching
over us!

**The Lord has made bare His holy arm in the
eyes of all the nations; and all the ends of the
earth shall see the salvation of our God.**
Isaiah 52:10 NKJ

This verse combines the past and the future. The Lord
has bared His arm and the earth *shall* see His salvation.

The baring of the arm of the Lord took place at the
crucifixion of Christ. The ends of the earth began to see the
salvation of the Lord at the resurrection of Jesus and will
continue to witness the ongoing of that salvation until it is
complete. The baring of God's arm has been accomplished,
but the vision of His salvation is not yet totally realized.

At the crucifixion of Jesus, the world was represented.
People from over 70 nations were present in Jerusalem
because of the Jewish passover feast. The ruling
government of Rome set the stage. The Greek culture
provided the language used by the principal players. The
Hebrew religionists were present to act out their parts. The
drama unfolded, as the arm of the Lord was made bare.

You and I enter into this, the greatest drama of human
history, by volunteering to take the Good News of man's
redemption to the very ends of the earth. That Good News
has not thoroughly penetrated every corner of the globe,
but it will. We all have a role to play in the thrilling
fulfillment of this verse. Each of us must do our part to see
to is that...**all the ends of the earth shall see the salvation
of our God!**

> **Although your beginning may seem small,**
> **He will make your later years very great.**
> **Job 8:7 MLB**

This verse promises us a good, vigorous, productive, fruitful, and expanding future. It is an assurance that God can do great things with our lives no matter how insignificant our beginnings. History records the success of many famous people who began life in the most humble of settings. One of these is the Lord Jesus Christ.

There is something about life that challenges people to raise their level of desire and expectation. The story of our own Christian lives actually begins with us deep in sin. Then salvation lifts us up out of the muck and sets our feet on the firm rock of the Son of God. Sanctification replaces our filthy garments of pride and self-righteousness with the dazzling white robes of His righteousness. The Holy Spirit gives us the power to run the race of life that is set before us and to gain the victory in the good fight of faith. At the close of the battle, we are each given a wedding garment. The story ends with us — the Bride of Christ — being enthroned with Him next to the Father. (Rev. 3:21.)

Our beginning can be compared to a mustard seed — small and insignificant. Our ending is centered in the universal acclaim of Jesus as Lord of the whole creation.

Christians have so much to look forward to. Our best days are yet to come!

My cup runneth over.
Psalm 23:5

In Psalm 66:12, David writes of His God: **...thou broughtest us out into a wealthy place.** The Hebrew word translated **wealthy** in that context is the same Hebrew word translated **runneth over** in this verse. The word is *revayah (rev–aw–yah')* which has to do with an abundance of moisture. This abundance is so overflowing its satisfies all thirst so that the person becomes saturated or satiated.

In Psalm 66:12, David notes that after having been submerged (inundated) by men, fire, and flood, the people of Israel had been brought by their God to a place of overflowing *(rev–aw–yah')* abundance and blessing. The psalmist exults in the Lord's tender loving shepherd's care for him and his people. His cup is saturated to overflowing *(revayah)*. He is experiencing more than a sufficiency of God's wonderful blessings in his life.

Do you think it is possible to live this way today? We hear people say, "I'm just hanging in there," or, "If I can just make it to payday," or, "I'm just getting by, just holding on!" Do such statements reveal the presence of an overflowing abundance in these people's lives?

Revayah indicates living in a realm of abundant blessing. It suggests having not only a cup of your own, but having that cup full to overflowing. The overflow always becomes a surplus to share with others.

Deliver us, Lord, from all the restrictions we put on Your bountifulness!

Go in this thy might...: have not I sent thee?
Judges 6:14

God's commands are also His enablements. When He says to do something, He imparts the ability to do it. In this verse, He is telling Gideon to go, and to expect unusual things to happen as he does.

The Lord is not saying, "Go, just to be doing something. Keep busy and you'll stay out of trouble." Rather, He is ordering Gideon out on the cutting edge of the unusual. The unexpected and the extraordinary are embodied in this little word *go*.

"Go in this thy *might*". In the original Hebrew from which this text was translated, this word is quite unusual. *Kowach (ko'–akh)* is defined as "capacity, means, substance, wealth, or ability." So what the Lord was telling Gideon was, "Go in your ability; I am well aware it is not sufficient for the task I am sending you to accomplish, but don't worry about that because I am going with you to see that it gets done!"

As Christians, our function in life is very similar to that of Gideon. We too have a special touch of God on our lives. We are not here to duplicate, imitate, or copy anyone else in this world. By doing God's will, following His leadings, obeying His voice, like Gideon of old we too are assured of having all the power and resources of heaven behind us. To go is to be guaranteed the glorious presence of the Lord with us. When God goes into operation, phenomenal things begin to happen!

"Take what you have and go where I send you, because as you go I will go with you!" (Matt. 28:20; Mark 16:20.)

**And when the Chief Shepherd appears, you will
receive the crown of glory that will never fade away.
1 Peter 5:4 NIV**

The title Chief Shepherd is a very interesting
description of Jesus. *Archipoimen (ar–khee–poy'–mane)*
compounds two Greek words: *arche (ar–khay')*, meaning
"commencement, first, beginning, author, principle;" and
poimen (poy–mane'), meaning "pastor, shepherd."

Jesus is our Chief (Primary) Shepherd. All other church
leaders are under-shepherds who lead us to Christ, the
Head of the Church. Under-shepherds also lead us in behalf
of Christ as His appointed representatives. Thus, our
pastors lead us *to* Christ, and they also lead us *for* Christ.

Jesus is Chief Shepherd because He originated our
faith. He authorized it and perfects it. (Heb. 12:2 NIV.)

Jesus is Chief Shepherd because He lead us to God, to
salvation and eternal life. (John 14:6; John 10:7–18.) By
clearing the road, He insures all of us that once we have
begun the journey of faith, we can be assured of reaching
our final destination safely.

Jesus is also Chief Shepherd because by His atoning
death and triumphant resurrection, He earned the right to
be Head of the Church. (Phil. 2:9–11; Eph. 5:23.)

Jesus is the power-center of the universe. He is also the
role model we can safely look to and follow. He chose
twelve champions who were willing to give up their lives
to follow a Super-Champion. He puts shepherds in each
congregation to lead the flock to the Chief Shepherd so He
can lead us home!

Although your beginning may seem small,
He will make your later years very great.
Job 8:7 MLB

We have already looked at this verse on another day.
There is one word in it, however, that needs to be scruti-
nized. The *King James Version* reads: **...thy latter days** (the
last years of your life) **should greatly increase.** In the
original Hebrew text, the word translated **greatly** is *me'od*
(meh–ode') and has a certain intensity about it. *Me'od* means
"vehemence, speedily, with rapid acceleration."

Look at an airplane going down the runway. For a time
it looks as though it is barely moving. Then it begins to pick
up speed. The really exciting part of the takeoff is the
moment of liftoff. The plane leaves the ground and rapidly
begins its ascent into the sky. *Me'od* is the word that the
ancient Hebrews would have used to describe the
acceleration and liftoff of a modern-day jetliner.

For a long time now you have been in motion. For all
your efforts, it doesn't seem that you have gone anywhere.
Despite your lack of progress, you have kept trying. You
haven't quit. You have kept on "giving it your best shot."
Very soon now, a new acceleration and thrust is going to
take over. Before you know it, you are going to be off and
climbing, soaring to worlds unknown. All this is promised
you in this verse.

Paraphrased, it comes out: "Your start may seem to you
quite small and insignificant. But very soon now, and very
suddenly, you will be propelled by the Lord into a larger
and greater sphere of influence."

The literal Hebrew reads: "Your start was small, your
future shall rapidly increase." Praise the Lord!

**You number my wanderings; put my tears
into Your bottle; are they not in Your book?
Psalm 56:8 NKJ**

God keeps very accurate records. Not only does He record our thoughts, words, and deeds, He also keeps account of our tears. This verse tells us that they are all recorded, stored up, and filed away in heaven's treasury. Two types of tears are especially dear to God:

TEARS OF INTERCESSION. Jesus wept over Jerusalem. John Knox shed tears over his beloved Scotland. Evan Roberts interceded for Wales with tears. Charles Finney shed tears for the dreadful plight of Colonial America. All tears shed in intercession are kept for a memorial.

TEARS OF JOY. Whenever a prodigal returns home, a loved one is born again, a lost sheep is found, it is quite natural for tears of joy to well up and flow out. These tears are also kept for a memorial.

A man once came to our town who was billed as "the man who can neither smile nor cry." A reward was offered to anyone who could bring a smile to his face or tears to his eyes. No one collected. It was sad in a way to see people follow him around, trying in vain to make him respond. There was no reward for their efforts but a lonely vacant look in his eyes.

Tears are an indication of a tender heart. Hard-hearted people cannot weep. It is a spiritual distinctive to be so sensitive, so tender, that you can rejoice with those who rejoice and weep with those who weep. (Rom. 12:15.)

All our tears are kept as a memorial for us. They are not gone, we will meet them again. One day we will be rewarded by them and for them. O blessed day!

May my prayer be counted as incense
before Thee....
Psalm 141:2 NASB

Here is a verse that speaks to people who are unable to go to the Lord's house for worship due to unfavorable circumstances. The psalmist David was fleeing from King Saul and could not go to the synagogue or temple for regular worship. These words in Psalm 141 express his desire to be a worshipper even though deprived of entrance into the house of the Lord.

During World War II, our military base was put on a three-to-four-month alert. From 6 a.m. to 6 p.m., seven days a week, we were busy preparing for the North African invasion. The first thing I missed was worship in the house of the Lord and the fellowship of the saints. Necessity brought a few brothers in the Lord together for prayer and fellowship. Since then I have had a real compassion for people who are unable to go church.

In his commentary on the Bible, Adam Clarke comments on this verse: "The psalmist appears to have been at this time at a distance from the sanctuary, and therefore could not perform the Divine worship in the way prescribed by the law. What could he do? Why, as he could not worship God according to the letter of the law, he will worship God according to the spirit; then prayer is accepted in the place of incense; and the lifting up of his hands, in gratitude and self-dedication to God, is accepted in the place of the evening minchah or oblation."

The lesson is: If you cannot go to the sanctuary, you can still offer up the sacrifice of praise and the incense of prayer.

**The owner of a house....brings out of
his storeroom new treasures as well as old.**
Matthew 13:52 NIV

Part One

This is a balance verse. It tells us that we do not have to choose between old and new. We can have both. In a world given to choosing up sides, it is good to know that we can reap the benefits of both sides. The kingdom of God is not an either/or proposition. It is both old and new.

Old is a good word because it means "time-honored, time-tested, time-proven." In this setting, *old* doesn't denote that which is obsolete, archaic, or worn out. Rather, it suggests paths that are well trodden; truths that have stood the test of time; ways, customs and traditions that are familiar, meaningful, dependable.

A geyser is called "Old Faithful." A dog lover calls his faithful pet "Old Shep." A proud nation symbolically calls its flag "Old Glory."

The householder, representing the Christian, brings out of his pantry old, basic, reliable staples for his menu. The Lord does the same for us: the blood of Jesus, the name of the Lord, the power of the Holy Spirit, the effectiveness of prayer, the preciousness of worship, the warmth of fellowship.

If fasting and prayer brought revival 150 years ago, they will do the same today. If songs of praise produced the presence of the Lord in the Welsh revival of 1904, they will do that for us today. The message of this verse is: "Don't discard the old in order to be ready for the new. God's treasures are like new edifices laid on the old foundations!"

The owner of a house...brings out of his storeroom new treasures as well as old.

Part Two

Yesterday's article spoke of the value of the "old" treasures. In addition to time-honored and trustworthy truths, the Lord has some "new" truths for us. In the Old Testament, the word *new* has the connotation of something fresh, exhilarating, invigorating. One translation of it is "fresh and green." "Having life," "being supple and vibrant," and "having a growth potential" all describe this word *new*.

Changes do not come easy to the church world, yet it must change in order to keep up with the Holy Spirit. Changes do not come easy to individuals, yet the Lord wants us to be receptive to all the new things He offers:

NEW WINE: Predictable Christianity reduces our service to the Lord to sameness, tameness, and lameness. New wine gladdens the heart. It brings new life, spontaneity, and the release of God's creativity.

NEW ANOINTING: In Psalm 92:10 David writes: ...I **shall be anointed with fresh** ("new") **oil.** The Lord has a new touch of His Spirit to place in our lives.

NEW HEART: God has promised to replace our calloused, stony heart with a new heart of flesh. (Ezek. 36:26.) You will always know when you have a new heart by the attitude change that comes to you.

We have been promised a new name, a new strength, new tongues, new direction, new blessings, a new heaven, and a new earth. Let's retain and esteem the old things of God, but let's also be open to all the new things the Lord has prepared for us.

The owner of a house...brings out of
his storeroom new treasures as well as old.
Matthew 13:52 NIV

Part Three

An old song was sung about "Poor Johnny One-Note."
He had a great voice, but he could only produce one note.
Every time he got up to sing, out came that one sound. It
wasn't long before everyone became tired of continuously
hearing Johnny's one musical repertoire.

In the church world, it is common for an evangelist, a
pastor, or a teacher to become a "Johnny One-Note." It is so
easy to find a favorite subject or a pet theme and ride it to
death.

Early in his Christian life, the new believer begins to
discover that there is a whole new world of spiritual
knowledge available to him. As he listens, reads, meditates,
and studies, the Holy Spirit reveals to him many wonderful,
exciting truths about God's nature and man's potential. The
problem develops when the believer settles down and begins
to major on one particular truth to the exclusion of all others.

Ours is a God of infinite variety. His wisdom is many-
hued and multi-faceted. He wants you and me to be open to
ever new manifestations of His glory and power. In 1707
A.D., in his expository notes on the New Testament,
William Burkett, commenting on this verse, noted that "A
household steward must provide (food) for the household
both with plenty and with variety. He brings out of the
treasury in plenty ...*Things new and old,* for their Variety. He
must be prudent, in bringing things new, as well as old;
...lest the Household by always feeding upon the same
dish, do nauseate it, instead of being nourished by it."

Let's balance our lives with new as well as old.

> **Are the consolations of God too small for you,
> and the word spoken gently with you?**
> **Job 15:11 NKJ**

God's gentle nature never changes. His patient attributes are immutable, His kindly ways past finding out. In the process of time, His gentle words sensitize us into recognizing His patient dealings with us.

We may be expecting a more harsh, severe response when we fail our Lord, but He is working on our development. His plan is to improve us by working out our carnality and working in His spiritually. **The word *spoken* gently** will tug at our heart strings and produce a Christ-like response in us.

To my great regret, I once used the name of the Lord in an outburst of profanity. I was 16 at the time and tried to impress a group of guys by using coarse language. Not only were the guys not impressed, the Lord spoke gently to me and said, "You have hurt Me." That gentle word broke me up so much that I vowed never again to use God's name in vain or profanely.

In other situations I have made snap judgments, or acted impulsively, impatiently, or impetuously. Instead of "raking me over the coal of His righteous indignation," the Lord would simply speak a gentle word of reproof. He would let me know that such behavior was offensive to Him. He would show me what I had done wrong. Then He would give me godly sorrow for my sins, lead me to a heart-felt confession of my wrongdoing, and restore me to fellowship by His reconciliation.

God's gentleness is a salve or precious ointment to be applied to our spiritual man when we are hurting because of mistakes we have made.

**You did not choose Me, but I
chose you and appointed you....
John 15:16 NKJ**

This verse can be a great source of encouragement to each of us. God, at the beginning of creation, looked down the telescope of time and saw every person who would ever exist. For His own purposes, and for His own honor, He selected those who would bring glory to His name. These He set aside for Himself, calling them vessels of honor.

As Christians, children of God, beloved of the Father, each of us has been individually chosen and appointed as ....a vessel for honor (2 Tim. 2:21 NKJ).

In Deuteronomy 18:4,5, the Lord told the children of Israel why He had selected them as His people. It was not because of their size; the other nations around them were much larger in territory and number. Nor was His choice based on any goodness or excellence on their part; in their wilderness rebellions they constantly provoked Him to the point of totally destroying them. God did not choose Israel because of their good looks, wealth, achievement, or intelligence. He chose them because He had given His word of covenant to Abraham, Isaac, and Jacob. Why He chose Abraham (and us) on whom to bestow His promise or blessing is still a mystery to us.

For us to attempt to itemize all the reasons why the Lord might have chosen us would be to miss completely the message of this verse and all those which speak of our election. Such verses are recorded to give us "humble boldness." Boldness to know that we are included in the number of God's redeemed. Humility to know that it was not we who chose Him, but He who loved us, knew us, and chose us — from the foundation of the world. (Eph. 1:4.)

**If you abide in Me, and My words abide in you, you
will ask what you desire, and it shall be done for you.
John 15:7 NKJ**

Part One

This verse points out the benefits of abiding in the Lord
and of His words abiding in us. This word **abide** suggests
taking up residence in a place for the purpose of making it a
permanent home. As believers, our true homeland is the
kingdom of God, which is spiritual, not material. The
kingdom is *within us.* (Luke 17:21.)

We abide in the Lord by believing, serving, obeying,
submitting to and following after *Him* — the Person, the
Sovereign, the King. The idea is that as children of the
Living Lord, we have a new family, location, sphere of
influence, and Source: "If you will settle down in *Me,* and
all that I represent, and if you will allow *My words* to settle
down in you, then you will be able to ask what you will in
confident assurance that it will be granted."

The Lord's **words** which are to abide in us, in addition
to written Scriptures, are His *rhema (rhay'–ma),* His *utterance,*
His spoken words to us personally and individually.
Hearing these words spoken directly to us into our own
ears by the Spirit of God is the basis for guidance and
confident assurance in our praying. *The key to answered
prayer is knowing what to ask for!* That knowledge comes
from *hearing* the *rhema* (the Voice) of God personally,
speaking the Word to us by His Spirit. (Rom. 10:17.)

This verse challenges us: 1) to settle down in the
kingdom, and 2) to allow God's word *to* us to settle down
and take root *in* us. Then, and only then, are we ready to
start making requests of the reigning Monarch.

If you abide in Me, and My words abide in you, you will ask what you desire, and it shall be done for you.
John 15:7 NKJ

Part Two

The word **ask** in this verse is an interesting one. In the original Greek, it is *aiteo (ahee–teh'–o)* meaning to "ask, beg, call for, crave, desire, require." Because of its usage in Matthew 5:42, some Bible scholars have interpreted it to mean to "demand." In that verse, the Lord Jesus was emphasizing that a rude, insensitive, boorish person can ask a favor of us in an insolent manner making us unwilling to comply with his request. He did not mean to imply that we are to ask in this way.

G. Campbell Morgan, a great Congregational minister of yesteryear, commented on John 15:7: "When we abide in Christ and His words abide in us, we can literally demand what we will and it shall be granted." The word *demand* here needs some clarification.

Aiteo (or ask) can have the connotation of putting in a requisition. Picture a large supply depot with all kinds of items in storage. As part of the organization, you find yourself in need of a particular item in stock. You obtain a requisition slip, have it signed by the properly authorized person, and send it through channels. In a sense, your requisition is a "demand" in that it places a "demand" upon the existing supply. However, that "demand" or request is in no way arrogant or authoritarian. It is simply a request for supplies.

Here Jesus tells us that we can "requisition" from heaven's warehouse, knowing that when duly authorized by His signature (His name), our request will be honored and our need met. Let's ask largely and receive largely.

Your words have kept men on their feet, the weak–kneed you have nerved.
Job 4:4 MOF

Here Eliphaz is reminding his friend Job of how he has ministered to others in the past. In verse three Eliphaz remembers how Job **...set right, and put strength into feeble souls** (*Mof*). Then in verse four he states that Job has given people words that have kept them on their feet.

This ability and capacity should be desired by all of us. In our speech, we can major on ministry. We can learn to use words that have a beneficial and supportive effect upon people. Our words can put people down or stand them up. Words can hurt or heal, blister or bless, destroy or deliver, tear down or build up. Job's words were so encouraging, they kept men on their feet and gave strength to the weak.

Some church groups and ministries which are now moving into prophecy (giving people words from the Lord) need to learn to put the emphasis on the positive promises of God. Before presuming to issue words of rebuke from the Lord, they first need to learn to speak forth His words of encouragement. The Lord tells us to edify or build people up. This does not refer to flattery, insincere praise, or "buttering up" people. It means giving people the words they need to keep them on their feet, determined to keep marching on to victory.

Make it a practice to speak wholesome, edifying, upbuilding words to friends, relatives, co-workers, and fellow Christians. Your words will keep many people on their feet in times of difficulty and will come back to you loaded down with many blessings. Start today!

**Don't let the world around you squeeze you into
its own mould, but let God re-make you....
Romans 12:2 Phillips**

Part One

The ancient Greek had two special words to describe a
thing or a person. The words are *schema (skhay'–mah)* and
morphe (mor–fay'). We can relate easily to these words
because of English derivations. *Schema* becomes scheme in
English. *Morphe* is recognized in the word *metamorphosis,*
used to describe the change of a larva into a butterfly or a
polliwog (tadpole) into a frog.

Schema has to do with externals — outward
appearance, shell, visible form or fashion, something
molded into a certain shape or fixture. The "scheme of
things" thus refers to the visible pattern of things.

Morphe has to with internals — the inner nature of a
thing, situation, or person. In Christians, it points to their
character, integrity, and basic decency because of the
presence of the Christ-nature within them.

Schema can be transient and *morphe* can be quite
permanent. When Paul says in the *King James Version,*...**be
not conformed to this world: but be ye transformed,**....the
first verb is derived from *schema,* the second from *morphe.*

J.B. Phillips translates this verse with a touch of elegant
humor: **Don't let the world around you squeeze you into
its own mould, but let God re-make you....** The whole
world system is transient, not permanent. It is unreal, since
God's kingdom is the only ultimate reality. According to
this word from the Lord, we do not need to lose a lot of
sleep worrying about how the world looks to us or at us!

**Don't let the world around you squeeze you into
its own mould, but let God re-make you....
Romans 12:2 Phillips**

Part Two

The *King James Version* says: ...**be not conformed
(*schema*) to this world: but be ye transformed (*morphe*) by
the renewing of your mind....** Renewal of the mind is an
integrated part and natural consequence of the New Birth.

One language expert has defined this transformation
as "undergoing a complete change which, under the power
of God, will find expression in character and conduct.
Morphe lays stress on the inward change, while *schema* lays
stress on the outward."

Today we are considered "real squares" if we don't
keep up with current trends. Yet to truly "keep up" with all
the latest and ever-changing fads, fashions, styles, and hit
songs would require a 24-hour-a-day concentration.

Paul implies here that there is a certain amount of
phoniness in the whole world system. He declares that
conforming to the world's transient patterns is not for the
Christian. Instead, the believer is to be transformed. To be
transformed is to be "turned on to the Lord," lit up with His
light, joy, glory, and honor. To be transformed is to
unashamedly yet unpretentiously love the Lord with all
one's heart, soul, mind, and strength. The transformed
Christian is not overly concerned about the world's opinion
of him because he knows that this world will soon pass
away. Linked to eternity, he has been translated into a new
dimension of living with a new priority list and a new value
system. What a change!

> **But that the world may know that I love the Father,**
> **and as the Father gave Me commandment, so do I.**
> **Arise, let us go from here.**
> **John 14:31** NKJ

Jesus is our role model. The word *Christian* means "a diminutive Christ." It implies a person who thinks, acts, talks, serves, and speaks like Jesus. This verse shows us four outstanding qualities Jesus exhibited which can be strong motivation for us:

1. SACRIFICIAL LIFE: The very next day after this discourse, Jesus died on the cross. His words at that time all point to the fact that He came into the world for this one purpose — to give His life as a sacrifice for us so our sins could be forgiven. The Righteous One gave Himself for the unrighteous. The Just died for the unjust.

2. LOVE: Jesus' death on the cross was motivated by love for mankind. In the crucifixion, God's love for man was demonstrated to the whole world.

3. OBEDIENCE: Jesus' earthly life was lived in perfect obedience to the divine will of the Father. The will of God dominated and determined His whole existence.

4. COURAGE: Jesus did all this with an unshaken courage: "Arise, let us go from here" is an expression of great bravery in the face of imminent death.

In 1825, Adam Clarke, a great commentator, stated: "All our actions should be formed on this example and plan. We should have the love of God and man for our principle and motive; God's glory for our end; His will for our rule. He who lives and acts thus shall live forever." This verse reveals a sacrificial nature, a motivating love, an obedient will, and an unflinching courage. May it describe us as well as it does our Lord.

**I will no longer talk much with you, for the ruler of
this world is coming, and he has nothing in Me.**
John 14:30 NKJ

Here the Lord Jesus is talking to His disciples about the
enemy, Satan...**he has nothing in Me,** He tells them. No
power, no dominion, no mastery, no control, no handle,
nothing to grasp on to — all these thoughts are expressed in
this statement. Other translations of this phrase read: "...he
has no hold over Me," "...he has no rights over Me," "...he
has no sins to work on," "...he has no claims on Me," and
"...he has nothing in common with Me."

It is as though the Lord is saying: "I am so completely
covered by the Father's protection that there are no handles
on Me for the enemy to grab hold of. Nothing about Me is
available for his grasp."

The Lord has made it possible for all Christians to be
completely covered by His righteousness and divine
protection so that when the tempter comes to grapple with
us, he can get no hold on us. The shield of faith is given to
us against the fiery darts of the wicked one. This shield
covers our total personality.

Every area of our life can be protected from Satanic
assault. Our thoughts, words, imaginations, actions, will,
work, recreation, social activities — all can be covered by
the shield of faith. When Satan comes around to assail us,
we will be able to say, "The ruler of this world is coming,
but he has nothing in me. Nothing is exposed for his
exploitation."

John says that the evil one cannot touch us. (1 John
5:18.) Praise God for His covering and protection.

**Having mind of him wherever you may
go, and he will clear the road for you.**
Proverbs 3:6 MOF

Do you recall what automobile travel was like in the days before the development of modern highways? Most roads were narrow and winding as they followed the natural contour of the land. Traffic was slow and visibility limited. Motoring was dangerous and tiring. It seemed to take forever to get anywhere.

Now, by way of contrast, picture a modern interstate highway as it is laid out across the landscape. Today, rather than allowing the terrain to dictate the shape of the road, skilled engineers using heavy-duty equipment, huge earth–moving vehicles, and blasting powder, cut a wide, straight swath through every kind of natural obstacle and barrier. As a result, land travel has become so much easier, quicker, and safer. Due to carefully banked curves, graduated ascents, and increased visibility, traffic now glides safely and smoothly.

That is what this verse promises us. Bring the Lord into all your plans, and He will clear the road for you. Another version reads: "...he will direct your paths." *Direct* can mean "lead," "guide," or "show the way." It is also used as an adjective to indicate the shortest route between two points, as the most direct route from one city to another.

The Lord's guidance will always keep us from having to follow a round-about path. He will clear the road ahead of us and get us to our destination by the safest, straightest route possible. No back roads, no detours, no roadblocks, no lost time. Just straight ahead and on the right track!

I have been anointed with fresh oil.
Psalm 92:10 NKJ

Part One

In the Old Testament, kings, priests, and prophets were anointed with oil. Revelation 1:6 tells us that Jesus has made us believers kings and priests. We are also told that He has imparted prophecy to us. His three leadership functions have thus been translated to us.

The Hebrew word translated **anointed** here is *balal (baw–lal')* and refers to mixing and mingling since the anointing oil was prepared by mixing together different ingredients.

In the nine gifts of the Holy Spirit (1 Cor. 12:8-10), three kinds of anointings can be seen:

The KINGLY anointing is evident in the word of wisdom, the word of knowledge, and the discerning of spirits. Proverbs 16:10 say: **Inspired decisions are on the lips of a king....**(RSV).

The PRIESTLY anointing is evidenced in faith, miracles, and gifts of healing. Many times when Jesus healed the people, He sent them to the priests who were responsible for ministering to the sick and declaring them recovered.

The PROPHETIC anointing is represented by tongues, interpretation of tongues, and prophecy because these are vocal gifts.

Christians are anointed with the fresh oil of the Holy Spirit for kingly, priestly, and prophetic functions. All three anointings mingled together constitute the "fullness of God." (Eph. 3:19.) That fulness is ours for the asking.

I have been anointed with fresh oil
Psalm 92:10 NKJ

Part Two

A key word here is **fresh.** In Hebrew it is *ra'anan (rah–an– awn')* which is defined as: "flourishing, green, happy, cheerful, bright, new, luxuriant, prosperous." Besides indicating an anointing to set apart for service and to empower for spiritual ministry, this word embodies some additional features that can help us become better stewards of the Lord.

There is a refreshment implied in the word *ra'anan. The Bible In Basic English* translates this phrase,...**the best oil is flowing on my head,** while *The New International Version* renders it,...**fine oils have been poured upon me.** Moffat's version reads,...**thou dost revive my failing strength.** All three indicate a before-and-after situation. Before anointing, we see a picture of a sun-baked desert traveler with dry skin, chapped lips, and languishing spirits. The anointing with fresh oil changes all that to a picture of vitality, exhilaration, and renewed vigor.

There is also an in-strengthening suggested here. One grammarian has defined *ra'anan* in these terse words: "The anointing in Psalm 92:10 seems also to imply a penetrating power." A fresh anointing can turn spiritual weariness into spiritual energy and revived strength.

Also in this word *ra'anan* is an association with hospitality, with the proper way an honored guest should be treated. (John 11:2; Luke 7:46; Psalm 23:5.) The compassionate Savior sees us journeying through the wilderness-world and bids us stop along our weary way to enjoy His hospitality, refreshment, and renewal.

August 13

My elect shall long enjoy the work of their hands.
Isaiah 65:22 NKJ

Part One

One sector of the Christian Church has outlawed any kind of enjoyment. Their worship is icily cold. Their lifestyle is somber. Their conversation is solemn. Their daily existence is joyless. Such legalistic believers cannot smile because they do not have anything to smile about. By way of contrast, this verse promises an inward happiness of long duration.

It is sad that man's religion has taken the joy out of living. Some people cannot enjoy music, art, poetry, humor, possessions, or relationships. One lady feared enjoying her children too much lest the Lord should take them away. One man commented, "I just adore my wife and am greatly in love with her. Do you think Jesus will become jealous because I love my wife so much?" The answer came back, "No. Jesus would be jealous of His reputation for bringing happiness to a marriage if you did NOT love your wife."

Examine your heart and ask yourself the searching question: Am I able to enjoy my church? my family? my home? my work? my friends?

Satan wants to rob Christians of everything that could make for happiness in life. Our heavenly Father, because He loves us so dearly, wants us to enjoy life in all its fullness and abundance. (John 10:10.) His blessings upon us are expressions of His love for us. The way to enjoy all the good things the Lord gives us and does for us is simply to remember to keep Him in the center of our existence. When God is central, joy is universal.

My elect shall long enjoy the work of their hands.
Isaiah 65:22 NKJ

Part Two

When I was preparing for the ministry, I was part of a religious group with a rigid caste system. A person's rank was reflected by the type of car he drove. The top executive leaders of the church drove luxury cars. People in a supervisory capacity drove top-of-the-line-cars. Pastors with ten to twenty years seniority drove medium-sized cars. Those just starting out drove modest cars. Students fell into a category of wrecks, old bombs, junkers, and high-mileage used cars. This unofficial "pecking order" was not written anywhere in a manual, but eyebrows were raised if anyone dared to "get out of line." To do so was supposed to indicate pride — a deadly sin. To the hapless offender, the message was loud and clear: "Stay in your realm!"

On the very bottom rung of this organizational ladder, I as a Bible school student was put into a top-of-the-line luxury car by an interested friend. When I saw the negative reaction caused by my "impertinence" and "conceit," I purposed to sell the offending vehicle and settle for something more "becoming my low estate."

On my way down to automobile row, the Lord gave me this verse and this message: "I gave you this car to use and enjoy. Don't let man's opinion dictate to you or man's traditions dominate you. You will be doing a lot of driving. I want you to arrive at your destination safe and rested. Keep this car. Drive it. Enjoy it!"

I did just that. This verse became to me a promise of long-term duration. I had a good car plus a precious promise from a loving, caring, heavenly Father.

My elect shall long enjoy the work of their hands.
Isaiah 65:22 NKJ

Part Three

The Hebrew word translated **long enjoy** is very unusual. In the original text it is *balah (baw–law')* which is used 16 times in the Old Testament. Except for this verse and Job 21:13, *balah* always has to do with erosion, consuming, wearing out, or wasting away.

Scholars are at a loss to reconcile long enjoyment with a word used to describe the wearing down of life by the aging process. When she heard the angel's message that she would bear a son to Abraham in her old age, Sarah responded by laughing in derision. In her reply to the message, she used *balah* to describe herself: **After I have grown old** *(balah)* **shall I have pleasure?...** (Gen. 18:12 NKJ). The answer was yes!

Bible words are so full of meaning and so rife with possibilities. Fourteen times *balah* is used to indicate wearing out through time. Twice it is used to refer to the utilization of time for long-range benefits: "...My elect (the followers of Christ) shall long enjoy the work of their hands. Making full utilization of all the good things that go with eternal life, My people shall last until time itself has come to an end. Instead of wearing out, they will fully enjoy all of Calvary's benefits and blessings."

Pleasures in the worldly scheme are short-lived. Momentary thrills lead to a lifetime of remorse and regret. Not so with the kingdom of God. Till the end of this age, believers can see the work of their hands outlast and survive the fatigue and destruction that go with the passage of time.

**Great peace have those who love Your law,
and nothing causes them to stumble.
Psalm 119:165** NKJ

In the path of every forward-marching believer, there are booby traps, land mines, and obstacles. Satan's strategy is to keep us from reaching our appointed destination. In this verse, the psalmist assures us that by loving God's "law" we can get past all the hurdles, barriers, and stumbling blocks placed in our path. The filling of our hearts with the Word of God is the only sure way of overcoming the enemy's ambushes.

This **great peace** promised those who love and trust the Lord is so profound that with it in our hearts we can be assured of passing safely through all the danger zones that lie between us and our ultimate destination.

Nothing causes them to stumble. The psalmist also assures us that those who know and keep the commandments of the Lord will never stumble, falter, or fall by the wayside. Rooted and grounded in the will, the Word, and the love of God, they shall overcome.

Jesus said, **"blessed is he who is not offended because of Me"** (Luke 7:23 NKJ). If we are not ashamed of our Lord, if we are determined to trust and serve Him without doubting or complaining — even when we don't understand His dealings with us — then we can come through to victory regardless of circumstances.

Armed with this verse, you and I can daily overcome the sensual world, the carnal flesh, and the malignant devil. "Great peace without stumbling." What a word of assurance in a world full of tension, stress, and failure. Come what may, you and I can walk in confidence and *great* peace — 24 hours a day!

A man of understanding has a cool spirit.
Proverbs 17:27 AMP

In our day, the word "cool" has taken on a new significance. Among our youth, it is often considered the height of sophistication to be thought of as "cool." An individual who is "cool" is "street wise, "mod," "chick," "avant-garde," "hip." A "cool dude" is one who has "got it all together" — he's in control of his own life and destiny. Everything about him is "cool, man, cool." He listens to "cool music," drives a "cool machine," is always seen in the company of "cool chicks."

Thus, the word *cool* is something of a "buzz word" to indicate those who are "on to something" or who "have something" that the rest of dull society is missing.

As far as we know, Solomon was the first man to use the word *cool* when he wrote: **...a man of understanding has a cool spirit.** Wise Solomon was not "trendy." His primary interest was not popularity or "peer group acceptance." He didn't follow fads or conform to the latest fashions — especially not in spiritual matters. Neither will a man (or woman) of understanding. The truly spiritual person is "cool" because he is disciplined and even-tempered. He doesn't "blow up," lose control, give vent to emotional outbursts, show temperament, or give in to moods.

In the original Hebrew, the word translated *cool* is *qar (kar)* and is defined as "quiet, calm, composed." The person with a "cool" spirit is self-possessed, free of anger, passion, or resentment. He is what every Christian should be. One writer has stated it well: "The ideal for all of us is to have a cool head and a warm heart." Let's be "cool" the Bible way!

**He chose for himself five smooth
stones from the brook....
1 Samuel 17:40 NKJ**

Why did David put five stones in his pouch when he only needed one to kill the giant?

Some scholars see a symbol of the five-fold ministry in this verse. (Eph. 4:11.) Others see a picture of the parable of the five wise virgins who had oil in their lamps and were ready for the arrival of the bridegroom. (Matt. 25:1-13.) Still others think the five stones represent the five books of Moses which make up the Jewish law. One scholar has suggested that the brook represents the Holy Spirit flowing continuously out of lives in power and wisdom.

Other experts hold that the five stones represent the law of God, or the Word of the Lord. The Word and the Spirit together provide the balance needed for victorious Christian living. Being full of the Word and Spirit of God is all that the believer needs to rid himself of the giants which would invade and conquer his personal Promised Land.

I would like to add another option to the list of possible meanings of the five stones. Some scholars believe that Goliath had four sons whom David ultimately faced and overcame. If the four sons mentioned in 2 Samuel 21:22 were the sons of Goliath, we can well understand why David chose five stones. His action was in preparation for overcoming the giant and his offspring. Instead of just barely getting by Goliath, David was ready for total and final victory.

God help us to use wisdom and foresight in all our planning. Amen!

He who exalts his gate seeks destruction.
Proverbs 17:19 NKJ

Here is a call for modesty. It says to us: Don't build for arrogant ostentation, materialistic display, or as a demonstration of wealth.

The Hebrew word translated **gate** here is *pethach* (*peh'–thak*) and is defined as "an opening, a doorway, or an entrance." In ancient times, for the purpose of utility and protection, people of modest means would build the entrance to their homes low to the ground, not more than three feet high. Thus marauders and thieves would not be able to ride their horses into the courts of the lower-income people to rob or attack them.

"Exalting the gate" (increasing the height and size of the entrance) was a symbol of increased affluence, prestige, and status. In contrast to the lower echelons, the wealthy would have high and wide gates to their estates so honored guests could ride on horseback or in carriages right up to the house. In a society composed of two economic extremes ("the haves" and "the have nots"), this architectural difference could easily incite ambition to become a "high-gater."

When invading Israel, Nebuchadnezzar honored the "low-gaters" by allowing them to choose whether they wanted to go away into captivity in Babylon or to remain in their homes. The "high-gaters" were given no such choice. They were carried away against their will and their homes burned to the ground. (2 Kings 25:9-12.)

Approximately 400 years earlier, Solomon might have foreseen all this and prophesied of it when he wrote that he who exalts his gate is asking for destruction. Some of us would be much better off staying low to the ground.

**Surely I have calmed and quieted my soul,
like a weaned child with his mother; like
a weaned child is my soul within me.**
Psalm 131:2 NKJ

This verse shows us how to progress from an attitude of getting things from the Lord to a desire to simply be near Him for the sheer pleasure of His presence. A weaned child takes nothing from his mother, yet he still seeks the comfort of being near her loving heart.

The Apostle Peter spoke of us as new-born babes. (1 Pet. 2:2.) He admonishes us to desire the sincere milk of the Word of God. The writer of Hebrews goes on to describe the difference between babes in Christ who feed on milk and those mature saints who feed on the solid food of the meat of the Word. (Heb. 5:12-14.)

The weaning process occurs when the child is no longer sufficiently nourished by the mother's milk. He is then given food that must be chewed. Mastication (chewing) is part of the growing up process and has spiritual significance.

The psalmist is saying to us here: "As a baby, I wanted to be close to my mother because she nursed me. As I grew, however, I learned to eat for myself. I still wanted to be close to my mother, but not for what she could provide for me materially."

"In the same way, as a spiritual baby I once sought the Lord for what He could give me. Now I seek Him for no other reason than to be close to Him, to be in His blessed presence. My happiness in the Lord is not dependent upon what He gives or does for me; rather, my contentment comes from being near Him like a weaned child resting on his mother's comforting bosom."

> **He shall not come into this city, nor shoot**
> **an arrow there....By the way that he came,**
> **by the same way shall he return....**
> **Isaiah 37:33,34** NKJ

This verse can be used to keep your thought life undisturbed and in complete tranquility, serenity, and composure.

Satan uses thoughts like flaming arrows to lodge in our minds and arouse us to anxiety, fear, insecurity, anger, or lust. The Greek word for *devil (diabolos)* is composed of two words: *dia (dee–ah')*, "through," and *ballo (bal'–lo)*, "to throw." Thus, it is Satan's strategy to attempt to "throw" (shoot) arrows "through" (at) the believer to ignite trouble within him. (Eph. 6:16.)

In this passage, the Lord is speaking through the prophet Isaiah, telling the people of Israel that their enemy is coming against them but that he will not be able so much as to shoot an arrow into their city. As Christians, we can have the same protection. Our minds can be so fortified with the Word of God, our hearts so filled with His Spirit, our walk of faith so undergirded with His divine presence and support, that the enemy will have to flee the same way he came against us.

Lately, I have been verbalizing a confession of faith to contradict negative mental suggestions. I say: "That is not my thought; I don't think that way. Lord, it's not Your thought either, because it does not agree with Your written Word." Then I quote a positive scripture in opposition to that negative thought. Peace descends, and I can get on with serving the Lord.

You can do the same. Resist the devil with the Word!

And Saul also went home to Gibeah; and valiant
men went with him, whose hearts God had touched.
1 Samuel 10:26 NKJ

Here is a word about teamwork. It might be important
to you, when planning your future, to consider the type of
people with whom you will be working. In the Old
Testament, God touched the hearts of valiant men and
caused them to be willing to go with King Saul of Israel.

If you are obedient to His call upon your life, the Lord
will move other people to want to assist you in
accomplishing your God-given task. However, you must
also do your part. Your gift will open the right doors for
you, but it takes personal integrity and consistent character
to continue to elicit support from others.

Our society fosters "Lone Rangers," superstars, and
prima donnas. The Lord calls for teamwork and
cooperation. Paul said it tersely in 1 Corinthians 3:6: one
plants, another waters, and God gives the increase.

No one is a law unto himself. No one can finish the task
alone. We need each other. Someone has said, "You are only
as good as the people surrounding you." With this in mind,
determine to: 1) be open to the teamwork concept, 2) expect
quality people to want to join team, 3) reject all concern
about who will get the credit for a job well done, 4)
concentrate on doing your best, and 5) work for God's glory
and honor, not yours or someone else's.

Nothing else matters. As the Lord opens doors for you,
look for the right people to work with you. Just as He has
prepared you, so also He has prepared them. Together you
make an unbeatable team — you, your "valiant men" (and
women), and the Lord your God!

**Because you would forget your misery, and
remember it as waters that have passed away.
Job 11:16 NKJ**

Here is a precious promise for us for the dislodging of
every unpleasant memory we retain.

There is an ocean called the Sea of God's Forgetfulness.
There is a river that washes away all our transgressions.
There is a fountain for sin and for uncleanness. (Zech. 13:1.)

All these images are given to us as a means of
describing the current of cleansing water which washes
away all our past sins, mistakes, traumas, and defeats. The
tide carries them out and they are buried in the bottom of
the ocean.

In Micah 7:19 (NKJ), the prophet says of his God: **...you
will cast all our sins into the depths of the sea.** A famous
evangelist of yesteryear stated, "When God cast all our sins
into the bottom of the ocean, He put up a sign saying, 'No
fishing allowed'!"

You and I can forget our past failures, past traumas,
past sins and mistakes. This verse assures us that they can
be put out of sight and out of mind. The Lord promises us
here to take the lid off our minds and to remove all the
painful residue from our past life. Good thoughts can then
replace miserable ones.

Serving the Lord offers us many benefits. Not the least
of these is a peaceful mind to replace a troubled one.

We should not trust in ourselves, but in
God who raises the dead, who delivered us
from so great a death, and does deliver us;
in whom we trust that He will still deliver us.
2 Corinthians 1:10 NKJ

Here is a line from the past to the future: God has delivered us in the past, does deliver us in the present, and will deliver us in the future. This statement makes our confession of faith and our Christian witnessing simply a matter of declaring what the Lord has done, what He is doing, and what He is going to do.

Sometimes, fear suppresses our outward profession because we are hesitant to make any verbal pronouncement about the future. Uncertainty and insecurity tend to shut down our own interior faith and to quell our exterior Christian witness to others.

When some skeptic asks you, "How do you know God is going to heal you (or prosper you, or answer your prayer)?" how do you answer? Do you mouth vague expressions of wishful thinking? Do you make excuses for your own lack of firm assurance? Do you have any basis for expectation that God *will* intervene on your behalf?

Paul did. He would have answered that question like this: "I know that God is going to heal (prosper, answer) me because He has delivered me in the past and is delivering me in the present. Therefore, I am trusting Him to do the same in the future."

Since Jesus is the same yesterday, today, and forever (Heb. 13:8), and since our God has said, **"...I am the Lord, I do not change..."** (Mal. 3:6 NKJ), why not put your whole trust in Him for deliverance? Remember, Paul says that it is not ourselves that we trust, but God — the same Person Who delivered Christ (and us) from death.

**Wherein I suffer trouble, as an evil doer, even
unto bonds; but the word of God is not bound.
2 Timothy 2:9**

The big word here is **bound**. In Greek it is *deo (deh'-o)*, a
primitive verb root meaning "to chain, shackle, put in
fetters, imprison."

Here Paul refers to his own prison confinement. He is
suffering hardship and being treated like a common
criminal. His ankles are in stocks and his wrists in irons. Yet
joyfully he bursts forth with this praise report: "I am
suffering imprisonment as though I were a criminal, but the
Word of God is not bound."

Paul is telling us that although circumstances may try
to limit, restrict, or bind us, we should always praise God
that His promises can never be confined.

This verse reminds me of the story of the man who had
gone grocery shopping for his family. On his way home, he
was held up and robbed of all his food supplies. Still he
came home brightly whistling a song of praise. His family
couldn't understand how he could be so cheerful when he
had just lost all their food. His reply was, "Oh, that man
may have stolen our food, but we still have our appetite! He
didn't get that!"

Paul could rejoice in the fact that even though he sat
chained in a dark, dismal cell, the Word of God was out
criss-crossing Asia Minor and turning people by the
thousands to the Lord.

"I am limited in what I am able to do and where I can
go," Paul admits. "But the promises of God know no
limitations. He is still sending His Word and healing people
everywhere!" (Ps. 107:20.)

His commandments are not grievous.
1 John 5:3

When Jesus came to earth preaching the good news of God's love, the whole world was in a state of religious bondage. Even in Israel among God's own chosen people, the religious leaders of the day had imposed a harsh and burdensome legalistic code.

In Matthew 23:4 (NKJ), Jesus spoke to the multitudes about the scribes and Pharisees: **"For they bind heavy burdens, hard to bear, and lay them on men's shoulders; but they themselves will not move them with one of their fingers."** Our Lord was pointing out the tendency of religious people everywhere to impose upon others a dogmatic and tiresome system of doctrines, creeds, rituals, ceremonies, holy days, taboos, religious practices, formulas, confessions, and prescribed forms of worship and praise.

The Apostle John contrasts this kind of works program with what the Lord really desires: **"For this is the love of God, that we keep His commandments. And His commandments are not burdensome"** (1 John 5:3 NKJ). Another translation of this last phrase reads, "...His commandments are not irksome." Another renders it, "...His commandments are not hard to keep."

The Greek word translated **grievous** is *barus (bar–ooce')* which comes from a root word meaning "to overload." The Gospel liberates us from a rigid legalistic code of do's and don'ts. We find from experience that the Lord's yoke is easy and His burden light. Do you remember the heavy bondage you were in before your conversion to Christ? Now you are free!

For God so loved the world that He gave His only begotten Son....
John 3:16 NKJ

God so loved that He gave. Giving is the normal expression of love. When you love someone, you want to express that love by giving something of yourself.

Love prompts action. That action always originates from the lover and moves toward the person loved. In our case, it was God Who loved; we were the objects of that love which was expressed in Jesus Christ.

Our loving heavenly Father demonstrated His love for us, His creation, by giving His Son to redeem us when we had gone astray. By so doing, He ran the risk of having that love thwarted, misunderstood, and rejected. But God loved anyway, because love is His very nature.

Love not only gives, it gives the best. God gave His best when He gave His Son. This is another proof of God's love for us. Those who love want the one loved to have the very best.

Love not only gives the best, it gives it sacrificially. God revealed the unselfish nature of His love by freely sacrificing His own Son for our sakes.

Love not only gives the best, and sacrificially, it also gives generously and equally. God's love is so vast that each one of the 5 billion people on the earth today (as well as each of those who have ever lived or ever will live) is loved personally and individually by His Maker. God loves all of us completely and equally.

Because He loves, God gives. We, in turn, respond. Someone has said it succinctly: "Salvation is not an escape from the flames of hell, though those flames do exist. Salvation is a surrender to the love of God."

Come aside by yourselves...
and rest a while....
Mark 6:31 NKJ

In Mark 6, we read how Jesus and the disciples could not function properly because the crowds kept coming and going, disrupting their normal eating and sleeping routines. Finally, the pressure of ministry became so great Jesus announced that it was time to draw aside and rest a while.

The key word here is **rest**. In the original Greek text, it is *anapau (an–ap–ow'–o)*. This word has three possibilities that speak to us today in our pressure-laden, stress-filled world:

Anapauo is the word used to describe an intermission in a play, an opera, a concert, or a stage production. This cessation is not only to give the audience a break in the action, but also so the artists and performers can have a moment to recuperate.

Anapauo also indicates recreation. This word can also be spelled re-creation. God created us originally, but from time to time we need to be physically, spiritually, mentally, and emotionally *re*-created. This can be accomplished through leisure-time activities such as fishing, camping, golfing, hiking, or picnicking — anything, in fact, that is totally different from our usual daily routine.

Anapauo also refers to refreshment. The Lord wanted the disciples to have a break in the action, to take some physical and spiritual refreshment, and then to go back to ministry with renewed strength and courage.

Anapauo. This could be a real word for us today: "Come aside by yourself...and rest a while. Then go back again rested, re-created, refreshed, and renewed."

God wrought special miracles
by the hands of Paul.
Acts 19:11

A miracle is always special, so what does Luke mean here when he speaks of **special** miracles? Other versions of the Bible translate this word as "unusual," "extraordinary," or "uncommon." Since by definition a miracle is always something unusual, extraordinary, or uncommon, this verse is almost a play on words: "God wrought 'special specials,' 'extraordinary extraordinaries,' 'unusual unusuals' by the hands of Paul."

The thing that made these particular miracles so "special" was the geographical location in which Paul was ministering when they were performed. In New Testament days, the two cities most widely known for their total degeneracy and depravity were Corinth and Ephesus. Biblical scholars tells us that these two towns were open sewers of dissolution and debauchery. Yet they were the very areas God chose in which to perform the greatest miracles recorded in the books of Acts. Why?

There is a spiritual isometric that states, **...where sin abounded, grace did much more abound** (Rom. 5:20). Paul could well have been speaking of these two cities when he made that statement. The greater the sin, the greater the need of a Savior. The greater the presence of darkness, the greater the provision — and the power — of God's redeeming light.

That should encourage us today. Perhaps none of our modern-day cities compare in wickedness with Corinth and Ephesus, but God still has "special" miracles for each of them. Claim the "special" miracles of divine deliverance the Lord has for you and your hometown!

**I will restore health to you and heal
you of your wounds, says the Lord, because
they called you an outcast....
Jeremiah 30:17 NKJ**

There are definite compensations for patiently suffering resentment, rejection, and ridicule for the sake of the Gospel and of Jesus Christ. (Matt. 5:11.) In my life, the miraculous power and mighty presence of the Lord were the most conspicuous when I stood alone in the midst of persecution because of my Christian belief, lifestyle, and witness.

In one place I worked, I found myself facing a constant barrage of hostile, cutting words from antagonistic associates who seemed to take delight in trying to discredit all Christians and Christianity in general. Since it was obvious that I was a believer, these people made the most of every opportunity to "put me down." They did everything in their power to make it appear that I was physically weak, intellectually inferior, mentally deficient, emotionally unstable, and socially unacceptable.

As painful as their constant harassment was, it did have one positive result. In the midst of it, I became aware that the Lord was doing a beautiful work of grace inside of me. I realized that I was being sustained inwardly by a divine power whose holy presence more than made up for what I was suffering outwardly. (1 John 4:4.)

No one enjoys being an outcast. But it is encouraging to remember that our patient endurance of shabby treatment on the Lord's behalf kindles a positive response from Him on our behalf that causes many good things to come our way!

Teach me Your way, O Lord;
...unite my heart to fear Your name.
Psalm 86:11 NKJ

Have you heard of the person who finally "got it all together," and then forgot where he put it?

In this verse, the psalmist prays for wisdom to know how to take all the different areas of his life and weave them together into a single strand of unity and strength. This passage has done a great deal to help me learn to bring my total being into harmony with itself, with the Holy Spirit, and with the rest of the Body of Christ.

In the original Hebrew text, the word translated **unite** in this verse is *yachad (yaw–khad')*. Grammarians define this word as "to join together, to become *one*." A genuine Christian is not a divided personality. Although comprised of different "parts," he is not really a *"triune* being"; rather, he is a *unified* being. His tangible and intangible bodies are inextricably interwoven together with each other and with the Spirit of his Maker. He is one with himself and his God.

The next step is to recognize that he is also one with his brothers and sisters in Christ. In such a fusion, there are no divisions, no separations, no barriers, no cross purposes, no conflicts of interest.

When believers truly become one Body, with Christ as Head, instead of going off in hundreds of different directions, we will finally be able to give total concentration to the one thing we are all called to do: worship the Lord and be witnesses to Him in all the world!

This verse is a good prayer, "Unite my heart to fear Your name."

When a man's ways please the Lord,
He makes even his enemies to be at peace with him.
Proverbs 16:7 NKJ

This verse is a great help to those who work alongside others who are hostile, perverse, sarcastic, antagonistic, or demonized. It is an assurance that one can get on with his job and his responsibilities without continuous friction or daily hassle.

In the Greek language Bible (LXX) the word translated **enemy** is *echthros (ekh–thros')*. When the Bible speaks of our enemy, it is referring to anyone who is opposed to our forward progress or who stands against us as a foe or adversary. Our enemy is one who hates us or is hostile to us. This word is used mainly as a reference to Satan, but also includes his human subjects who have nothing in common with the subjects of Christ.

When you as a Christian go to work on a job with non-believers, there is immediately produced a friction or a conflict because there can be no natural harmony between light and darkness, truth and error, purity and impurity, love and hate, good and evil. But despite this situation, according to this verse it is possible to have perfect peace in the midst of such potential turmoil.

I have worked on jobs where other employees lied, cheated, stole tools, drank on the job, and were very lustful and profanely vulgar. This verse helped me to do my job, keep my mind on my work and my heart tender toward the Lord. It helped me to remain peaceful in an unfriendly atmosphere. When we read this passage, it is as though the Lord is saying to us, "Since you please Me, I will cause your enemies to leave you alone." Try it; it works!

**Your people shall be volunteers
In the day of Your power...
Psalm 110:3 NKJ**

What a wonderful promise for these last days prior to the return of the Lord Jesus — a host of people volunteering their services in the day of the Lord's power. We have not yet seen this response in full expression, but it is starting to happen.

In the original Hebrew **the day of Your power** reads "the day you muster up your army," referring to the day the Lord goes to war. This moment is the time just prior to the Second Coming when the Lord arises and all His enemies are scattered. We find a reference to this day in Zephaniah 3:8: **"Therefore wait for Me," says the Lord, "Until the day I rise up for plunder...."** (NKJ).

We know that when God goes forth to do battle against the hosts of hell, His people will respond spontaneously. Some translations of this verse read: "Your people will offer themselves as free-will gifts." Others read: "In the day you muster up your army and go forth to war, your people will volunteer themselves freely for your service."

I believe that day has arrived! Do not give up on your loved ones who at present seem indifferent. Perhaps the right kind of challenge has not yet come their way. I predict that many believers who now seem uninterested in spiritual things will be the first ones to volunteer when the Lord pours out His Spirit. It is the driest land which responds most to the rain.

In the beauties of holiness...
Psalm 110:3b NKJ

Before we accepted the Lord and became believers, sin had left us deformed and lacking in any spiritual beauty. When we invited Jesus into our hearts and lives, He came in bringing a total transformation.

We are now arrayed in a robe of His righteousness and an adornment which this verse calls **the beauties of holiness.** In the original Hebrew this word **beauties** is *hadar (haw–dawr')*. It is defined as "a glorious majesty, an ornament of splendor, magnificent decoration." In Isaiah 63:1 the root word from which *hadar* is derived is translated **glorious**. The Lord is said to be **glorious in his apparel,** or clothed with holy ornament.

If you are a Christian, you are wearing this apparel 24 hours a day. It goes with conversion and becomes the clothing of the redeemed.

In Hebrew **holiness** is *godesh (ko'–desh)* and is defined as "ceremonially pure or morally clean." It is the word used to pronounce a person or object purified, consecrated, dedicated, and set apart for sacred purposes. *Godesh* is used of any person who devotes himself to the Lord.

Psalm 110:3 describes a group of volunteers who are free-will gifts in the military service of the Lord. Their distinctive feature is their holy adornment. For God's glory and to contrast His beauty with the ugliness of sin, these people are arrayed in beautiful holy garments. Each believer is dressed as one who performs a priestly function.

Did anyone ever tell you that you are beautiful? This verse says you are!

From the womb of the morning,
You have the dew of Your youth.
Psalm 110:3 NKJ

After the world sleeps through its long night of darkness, an unusual phenomenon occurs with the coming of the dawn. As the sun prepares to rise and light up the dark sleeping world, dew begins to form on the ground. Millions of dewdrops cover the vegetation giving everything an appearance of abundant freshness, vigorous renewal, and a vitality with splendor.

This verse gives us a word picture of the people of God staying young in heart, fresh and energetic and as pure as the morning dew. C.H. Spurgeon has remarked: "How wonderful is the eternal youth of the Christian church. Since Jesus ever lives, so shall His church ever flourish. His strength never fails so shall our vigour be renewed day by day."

Since dew falls fresh on the ground daily, we can expect a perpetual succession of converts. In Acts 2:47 we read that **...the Lord added to the church** *daily* **those who were being saved** (NKJ).

Prior to conversion, our soul is in a long dull night of ignorance. The light of the Gospel shines bright as the morning sun. An innumerable host come to the Lord as soon as His love and warmth is received. The numberless multitude are spread all over the landscape just like the pearly drops of morning dew.

I believe heaven will be fully populated with a multitude glittering as the morning dew. No church should be tired and fatigued. No Christian should be weary or worn out. The promise of this verse assures us of a daily freshness. It is ours for the asking.

**I counsel you to buy from Me gold refined
in the fire, that you may be rich...
Revelation 3:18 NKJ**

Laodicea was an unusually privileged town. The tax base was so strong and dependable there that the Roman emperor had exempted the city from a decree he had issued halting the flow of gold from Asia Minor to Jerusalem to support the Jewish temple.

Naturally the Laodiceans felt privileged to be the only town the Roman government allowed to send gold out of the country. As a result of their privileged status, the townspeople of Laodicea smugly acted superior to the citizens of other towns. They began to say, "Look at us. We are wealthy. We are rich. We really do not need anything from anyone."

This superiority complex also affected the 7,500 Jewish people who lived in Laodicea. It is bad enough for a town to feel itself superior to others, but when the church begins to reflect the thinking of the town, then the Lord steps in and gives His evaluation of the situation.

In scripture, gold has been likened to wisdom. Some scholars believe it signifies purity and righteousness. Some writers equate pure gold with pure motives. Since Nebuchadnezzar's image had a head of gold, some feel that gold is likened in the Bible to an intelligence that demonstrates godly leadership. Some feel that gold is kingly. In the words *gold, silver,* and *precious jewels* some see the Father, the Son, and the Holy Ghost.

Gold tried by fire is God's antidote for spiritual poverty. It is an antidote which we can all obtain!

**If anyone enters by Me, he will be saved,
and will go in and out and find pasture.**
John 10:9 NKJ

Go in and go out! What a beautiful balance between being a true worshipper and a faithful witness. As the children of God, we go in to be with the Lord, to worship Him, learn of Him, and establish a relationship with Him. True worshippers relish any opportunity to go in and intimately commune with their heavenly Father. Going in is an expression of a soul that desires to love the Lord with all the heart, mind and strength.

Going out is our service. We go in and discover truths, to get our marching orders, and to understand what the Lord is really saying to us. Then we go out to share with the world the things He has shared with us.

I have paraphrased the words of the Lord in Matthew 10:27 like this: "You came in and waited before Me. I spoke to you in secret. Now you go out and speak in public. What you have heard in privacy, proclaim publicly."

Just as a door swings both ways, so the Lord invites us to a two–way lifestyle. He beckons us to come in and be alone in true worship to Him. Then He sends us out to proclaim good news to a waiting, needy world.

If we just go in and stay in, we will fail to reach the world. If we only go out without first going in and establishing a daily relationship with our Father, we will end up running till we burn ourselves out.

Going in — going out. What a practical balance!

Filled with the Holy Spirit,...they spoke the
word of God with boldness.
Acts 4:31 NKJ

Boldness is one of the Apostle Paul's favorite words. In Greek it is *parrhesia (par–rhay–see'–ah)* which is defined as "freedom of speech, unreserved utterance, an all outspokenness with confidence and plainness." This kind of boldness gives the Christian the ability to express himself freely and graciously in the teeth of secular humanism, radical philosophies, arrogant unbelief, and hostile opponents of Christianity. It was when the disciples were filled with the Holy Spirit that they had *parrhesia*, this boldness with words.

It is a sad thing to me to meet from time to time good Christian people who are locked up verbally. Many times such people are victims of some childhood trauma. Some critical, judgmental, legalistic, opinionated, and overbearing relative or friend put fear into them and took away their ability to express themselves freely. Having experienced this sort of thing in a mild way myself, I can truly empathize with anyone who does not find it easy to express himself with words.

The thing which freed me from this verbal bondage was a gracious visitation from the Lord when I was between the ages of sixteen and seventeen. I was fulfilled by the Holy Spirit, found a new freedom of expression, and words flowed out of me in praise and adoration to the Lord. Acts 1:8, 2:4, and 13:52 all promise this same release to anyone who will open himself to the infilling of the Holy Spirit. The result of this glorious and gracious infilling is always the same: boldness and freedom of speech.

> **Only do not...fear the people of the land...;**
> **their protection has departed form them....**
> **Numbers 14:9 NKJ**

In this passage, Joshua and Caleb are exhorting the Children of Israel to have confidence enough to go into the Promised Land and possess their inheritance. Because the ten other spies had come back telling about the giants in the land, a great fear possessed the people. In this verse the two men of God are urging them to overcome their fears and insecurities because the protection of their enemy is gone.

In the original Hebrew the word translated here as **protection** is *tsel (tsale)*. It is defined as "a shade, a shadow, a cloud cover, or a defense like a roof affording protection." *The Amplified Bible* translates this verse: **...the shadow [of protection] is removed from over them, but the Lord is with us; fear them not.**

Shadow is the Bible word for protection. The Prophet Isaiah says of the Lord, **For thou hast been a...refuge from the storm, a shadow from the heat....**(Is. 25:4). He likens God to...**the shadow of a great rock in a weary land** (Is. 32:2). The Lord declares to His people through the prophet,...**I have covered thee in the shadow of mine hand....**(Is. 51:16).

This shadow is important. It encourages us when we are faced with all kinds of opposition and seemingly insurmountable obstacles. In the New Testament, Peter's shadow fell on people and they were healed. (Acts 5:15.) In the Old Testament, Solomon said of His God:...**I sat down under his shadow with great delight, and his fruit was sweet to my taste** (Song of Sol. 2:3). While under the shadow of the Almighty, we are safely covered while our enemy will end up getting "Son–stroke!"

> **But when a stronger than he comes upon him
> and overcomes him, he takes from him all his
> armor in which he trusted, and divides his spoils.**
> **Luke 11:22 NKJ**

In this verse Jesus describes the god of this world who guards his palace and keeps his realm in undisturbed control. Then our Lord draws a word picture of Himself as the Stronger One Who invades that spiritual domain, binds the strong man, scatters his goods, and takes away all the instruments in which he trusted.

I would like to enumerate some of the strategems the enemy of our souls has used to keep the world in bondage. I also want to show how Jesus replaced these strategems and rendered the enemy powerless.

Satan kept the world in spiritual ignorance. He trusted that ignorance would hold his subjects under his control. Jesus came, bringing knowledge of the truth, and that truth broke the yoke of ignorance.

The enemy trusted in fear to keep his subjects under his sway. Jesus gave faith in God and it broke the power of fear.

The adversary trusted in sickness; Jesus gave health. Our opponent used poverty; Jesus liberated us with His prosperity. Satan relied upon hate to keep his followers under his thumb; Jesus broke the power of hate by giving us love.

Every device the enemy relied upon — ignorance, fear, sickness, poverty, hate — has been destroyed by the Lord and replaced by His abundant life. Everything the strong man trusted in has been overcome by the Stronger One — Jesus Christ — and now we are free!

> For if we would judge ourselves,
> we would not be judged.
> 1 Corinthians 11:31 NKJ

This verse encourages a self-examination and self-discipline that can prove very beneficial. The whole world system is centered on self-indulgence and self-gratification. The Christian is one who has turned around and is going the other way. The Christian's lifestyle is one of self-control and self-discipline.

This verse speaks volumes about the Christian's efforts to walk in the Spirit and deny the tendencies of his inherited Adamic nature. Simply stated, the rule is: *Judge yourself, and you will not be judged.*

The scriptures tell us elsewhere to humble ourselves and the Lord will not have to humble us. (James 4:6,10; 1 Pet. 5:5,6.) After studying the Bible, I believe that if we will chasten ourselves (this refers to self-*discipline*, not self-*punishment*), then we will not have to be chastened by the Lord. As we willingly accept self–restraints, the Lord does not have to impose restraints on our tendencies to follow our senses rather than the leading of the Holy Spirit.

Many petty, chafing, irritating, and vexing situations could be avoided in our lives if we Christians would only learn to judge ourselves. The way we judge ourselves is by comparing our individual lifestyle to the standard of the Word of God. When the Holy Spirit, through the Word, reveals and illuminates an area of our personality that needs readjusting, we need to immediately surrender that area to the Lord. Discontinuing any activity which the Lord reveals to us is displeasing to Him is one important part of judging ourselves.

> My son, do not despise the chastening
> of the Lord, nor be discouraged when you are
> rebuked by Him.
> **Hebrews 12:5 NKJ**

The word *chastening* has a lot more going for it than we see at first glance. It is an educational word that describes the Christian discipline and training we go through as we grow up in the faith.

In the original Greek, the word translated in English as **chasten** is *paideuo (pahee–dyoo'–o)*. From this word we derive our English words *pediatrician* and *pedagogue*. Originally a pedagogue was one who simply accompanied a child to school. Later on, the word came to be applied to the instructor, the teacher, or the school master. Thus, *paideuo* evolved from simple direction to instruction. It came to be identified with the educational process and training of a child.

Whom the Lord loves, He educates or trains. Sometimes people say the Lord is "chastening" them, meaning He is "spanking" them. The only time I spanked my children was when they were rebellious or unruly. The Lord can and does "spank" His children, but in general His chastening involves the whole educational process. **Take my yoke upon you, and *learn* of me....**(Matt. 11:29) is the Lord's invitation to growth and maturity.

We can make it a lot easier on ourselves by asking the Lord to educate us in holiness, righteousness and faith. As we submit ourselves and our future willingly to Him, He will remove from us all the unchristlike characteristics. Our submitting to His chastening process keeps the Lord from having to deal with us harshly. Submitting to God is much easier — and much wiser — than having to be rebuked by Him!

They...consulted against thy hidden ones.
Psalm 83:3

The hidden ones (in our times) are believers who make up the bride of Christ. This verse refers to more than concealment. It has to do with watchful care and protection. This word **hidden** in the original Hebrew is *tsaphan (tsaw-fan')*. It computes as: "protected, covered over, secretly hidden." It indicates those who are made inaccessible by the protection of God, those guarded and defended by the Lord.

It is the Lord's personal love for us that qualifies us to be His *tsaphan*. It is because we are dear to Him and considered precious by Him (Is. 43:4) that He hides us from the assaults of our enemy. One time during a period of fasting and prayer, the Lord gave me an overview of a great fortification. Inside, we Christians were safe and secure. (Prov. 18:10.) Outside, the devil was viciously raging, ranting, and roaring — threatening to destroy anyone who ventured out.

The Lord reassured me that my life was hid with Christ in God and that He was my place of refuge. The encouraging thing about his word *tsaphan* is that it is a term of endearment. The *New International Version* of this verse indicates that we are the ones God *cherishes*. The *New American Standard Bible* says we are His **treasured ones**. *The New King James version* refers to us as the **sheltered ones**.

To the Lord we are of value. To the enemy we are inaccessible and off limits. In prayer, put a "Do Not Disturb" sign on your soul and enjoy seclusion with the Lord.

You have circled this mountain long enough.
Now turn north.
Deuteronomy 2:3 NASB

Have you ever felt that you were going around in circles really getting nowhere? How would you feel discovering that you were leading two million people in forty laps around the same mountain? This was the case with Moses. In His mercy, God intervened and told the people following Moses to stop their incessant circling and move onward.

Can you imagine some of the people actually enjoying the circuit? Through the years the path they took had become well marked and easily recognized. The predictability and familiarity made it easy for them to make another go-around. I can ever hear some of them saying, "I like this mountain. I know what to avoid, what to look forward to, and what to expect. I have made friends all around this mountain and I am looking forward to seeing them again."

One thing was wrong with the forty laps the people were making: they were not getting anywhere! The Lord ended the predictable routine by stating: "You have circled this mountain long enough; turn and go in another direction."

It is time for you to break out of your rut. It is time to break the bubble. It is time for new dynamics, new dimensions, and new directions. You have been going around in circles long enough!

Men prepare a meal for enjoyment....
Ecclesiastes 10:19 NASB

One day I counted up how many times it is recorded in the Bible that Jesus sat down at a table and had a meal with people. As best as I can remember, it was something like 14 times that scripture records our Lord's mealtime activities. Some of His most profound and penetrating truths were declared in a setting of food preparation and consumption.

Legalistic, ascetic people look suspiciously at the enjoyment of food as though eating is a lust of the flesh or a sin against God. Others deplore it because the "eat, drink and be merry philosophy" has programmed them to automatically view the table as an open invitation to immorality. Jesus' warning about overemphasis on food (eating and drinking) in Noah's day also causes some sincere persons to prefer fasting to eating. And old religious war cry was, "God give us people given to fasting and praying instead of feasting and playing." This philosophy could put guilt on people who have a normal approach to food.

I predict that in days to come Christians moving in the reverential joy of the Lord will have more enjoyable meals and hearty fellowship together. God's blessed people will experience a "good time" with each other and their Lord, knowing full well that this is a type and shadow of a greater banquet that is coming: the wedding supper of the Lamb. (Rev. 19:7.)

**He who believes in Me, the works that I do he
will do also; and greater works than these he will do,
because I go to My Father.**
John 14:12 NKJ

There is a kind of false humility that surfaces when this verse is discussed by Bible commentators. The thinking is, "How could anyone ever imagine he could do anything greater than Jesus? It would have to be vain conceit or spiritual arrogance to even *want* to do greater things than our Lord."

Jesus did not speak this word and then step back and threaten us with an "I dare you to even try it." He spoke this word as an assured fact to be incorporated unto the functioning of His Church. Can we really expect to do greater things than Jesus did? Let us look at some possibilities.

Jesus' earthly ministry lasted between 36 and 42 months. He worked within a three-year span of time. His Church is now headed toward its two-thousand-year birthday. Contrasting three years of ministry with 2000 years of Christianity gives us one view of greater things: works done in a greatly expanded time frame.

Jesus ministered within a 100-mile radius. The Church has now gone around the world with the Gospel. His followers have done greater works by doing them on a wider scale.

Jesus spoke these words while functioning in His earthly sphere. His glory has been restored since the ascension with the descent of the Holy Spirit. We now have a better covenant based on better promises. (Heb. 8:6.) We are now fully endowed to go forth in the power of the Holy Spirit and work the greater works that Jesus promised His Church. Let us get on with it!

Before Him went pestilence,
And fever followed at His feet.
Habbakuk 3:5 NKJ

This verse links the ministry of the Word and the ministry of the Spirit. **Pestilence** can be traced back to the Hebrew root word *dabar (daw–bar')* used figuratively to refer to the Word of God. In the LXX or Greek Old Testament this verse reads, "Before Him went the *logos*" (the Word). In the *King James Version* this word **fever** is rendered **burning coals.** The Hebrew indicates they are the result of fire or being inflamed.

This verse assures us that if we will take the Word of God with us and make it known everywhere, the Lord will back up that Word with the fire of the Holy Spirit. In Mark 16:20 we read that the disciples went everywhere preaching and proclaiming the Word of God, and the Lord worked with them,....**confirming the word with signs following.**

The pattern is very clear. The Word goes first, then the Holy Spirit has material to work on. Acts 10:44 tells us that while Peter spoke the Word, the Holy Spirit fell on everyone who heard it. Later Peter declared, "We are preaching the Gospel with the Holy Ghost sent down from heaven." (1 Pet. 1:12.)

My witness needed a lot of improvement. Then I discovered in Habbakuk 3:5 that the Word comes first, the fire follows after. I reversed the order of my presentation and began simply giving the people the Word of God. The Holy Spirit authenticated and confirmed the Word preached with the supernatural evidences I had always desired to see. Before Him goes the *logos* (or Word). After Him comes the fire of the Holy Spirit.

**Anoint your eyes with eye salve,
that you may see.
Revelation 3:18 NKJ**

These are the words of the Lord Jesus addressed to the Laodicean church. Laodicea was world famous during Bible days for its manufacture of an eye powder which could cure weak eyes. Workmen would make cylindrical tubes of this substance in a form called collyrium. It was in great demand as an export item. One medical writer listed five different kinds of eye trouble that was helped by application of the Laodicean eye powder or eye salve.

There is such a thing as the eyes of the soul. Laodicea could cure defects of physical sight and yet be blinded to spiritual insights. David prayed when reading the Word of God for the ability to see the truths that were in the scriptures. (Ps. 119:18.)

Elisha prayed for the Lord to open the eyes of his servant who was frightened by a pursuing host coming to capture him and the prophet of God. Second Kings 6:17 tells us that the young man's eyes were opened and he saw the mountain full of angelic protection.

The regular word for *anoint* is *chrio (khree'–o)* meaning "smearing, rubbing or superficially touching a surface lightly with a substance such as oil." In this verse, John compounds the word making it *egchrio (eng–khree'–o)* which is more thorough than *chrio.* The Lord is thus saying that instead of merely going over the surface lightly, we are to rub carefully and deeply: "Do a thorough job of rubbing in the ointment or eye salve of truth," He tells us, "so you will have lasting results!"

Draw me, we will run after thee....
Song of Solomon 1:4

Part One

We are told in the New Testament to draw nigh to God and He will draw nigh to us. (James 4:8.) In this verse, the bride (a symbol of the Church) says to the bridegroom, "You do the drawing, and we will respond." This attitude is one of compliant submission to the actions of the bridegroom as a forerunner.

In Jeremiah 31:3 the Lord expresses His love for us in these words:...**with lovingkindness have I drawn thee.** In Hosea 11:4 He speaks of His children, saying: **I drew them with cords of a man, with bands of love....**

"Draw me" can be a statement of total dependence upon the Lord. It implies a looking to God for all our needed help. David says in Psalm 25:15: **Mine eyes are ever toward the Lord....**Later he pleads to the Lord: "Send out Your light and Your truth. Let them lead me." (Ps. 43:3.)

Jesus told us that He was going to be lifted up (referring to the crucifixion) and that He would draw all men to Himself. (John 12:32.) He also stated that no man could come to Him except His Father drew him. (John 6:44.) This prayer in Song of Solomon 1:4 is a good prayer to pray: "Draw me, Lord, and we will run after You."

I do believe there is a restlessness expressed in this statement. It comes from a soul that does not want too great a distance between itself and the Lord. It is the expression of an earnest desire we all should have for closer communion with our Lord. David said it for each of us in Psalm 73:28:...**it is good for me to draw near to God....**

Draw me, we will run after thee....
Song of Solomon 1:4

Part Two

We will run after thee expresses something of the energetic spirit Peter showed in John 21:7 when the Lord appeared to the disciples while they were out on the lake fishing. As soon as Peter heard that it was the Lord, he cast himself into the sea. It was as though he could not get to Jesus fast enough. "Draw us, Lord, and we will run after You."

Jesus is the forerunner. He has left us an example. We can follow His steps. (1 Pet. 2:21.) It is always best for Jesus to assume the lead and for us to follow after.

We can easily complicate things by getting ahead of the Lord and marking out for ourselves a way of our own. "When He puts forth His own sheep, He goes before them. The sheep follow Him." (John 10:4,5.)

This wonderful promise assures us two things:) the Lord is drawing us toward Himself, and, 2) we are following Him or running after Him. He draws and we run. In Psalm 119:32, David said of the Lord: **I will run the way of thy commandments, when thou shalt enlarge my heart.** In verse 60 he writes: **I made haste, and delayed not....**

It takes a lot of stamina to run after the Lord. In Isaiah He has promised the needed stamina to those who wait on Him:...**they shall run, and not be weary....**(Is. 40:31).

**For we do not have a High Priest who cannot
sympathize with our weaknesses, but was in all
points tempted as we are, yet without sin.
Hebrews 4:15 NKJ**

If anybody can relate to us in all our circumstances and
fully empathize with us in every situation, it is the Lord
Jesus. He grew up in a family with brothers and sisters. He
learned a trade, carpentry. Around age seventeen, He lost
His earthy father, Joseph. By choice He remained
unmarried. He cared and provided for His mother and
unmarried sisters for thirteen years.

At age thirty He left home and began a public ministry
which lasted from three to three and one-half years.

He knew what it was to be followed by crowds of
people, and He also knew what it was to suffer loneliness.
In His short lifetime He encountered both love and hate,
acceptance and rejection, belief and unbelief. He personally
experienced the whole range of human response, including
laughter and tears. He lived with people who understood
Him and with those who misunderstood Him.

Our Lord knows how to relate to you in your situation
because He has been there. A thirteen-year-old girl was
praying and telling Jesus all her troubles. Finally she said in
desperation, "But why am I telling You all this, Jesus? You
don't know how a thirteen-year-old feels."

"Yes, I do," He whispered to her. "I was thirteen once! I
understand!"

**Master, we have toiled all night and
caught nothing; nevertheless at Your word
I will let down the net.
Luke 5:5 NKJ**

Here is a *rhema* promise for everyone who has read the manual, followed all the rules and still not attained the desired results. One leader complained, "I went to a church growth seminar. While I was away some of the folks in the church got discouraged and quit. When I got back home from learning how to help the church grow, I had fewer people than when I went away. I must be doing something wrong."

If anyone knew how to fish, it was Peter. Prior to meeting Jesus, Peter had been a professional fisherman. He knew about fish. He knew their feeding habits, when and where to go looking for them, and how to catch them.

Peter had fished right the evening before. He knew that the fish fed at night up close to the shore, so that's where he fished for them. Yet he had caught nothing. Then along comes Jesus, a carpenter, who tells him to do two things, both contrary to all the rules of good fishing practice. First, He asks him to fish at the brightest time of the day. (Any lake fisherman knows that when the sun is on the water, the fish all go to the bottom of the lake.) Secondly, Jesus asks Peter to reverse his direction and fish out in the center of the lake rather than along the shore.

Peter knew the habits of fish. But he also knew the power of Jesus' Word. His response to these seemingly contradictory directions was, "Master, we have done it right, but have had no results. However, at Your *rhema* (Word), we will try it again Your way." The Lord's way worked! His way and His Word will work for us, too!

Why do you cry to Me?
Tell the children of Israel to go forward.
Exodus 14:15 NKJ

The parting of the Red Sea depended upon and coincided with the children of Israel's willingness to move forward. The way wasn't opened to them until they took the first step.

We have a tendency to wait for someone to clear a path for us. Then we want someone else to pave that path and add lights along it to illuminate the way. Then we want some brave soul to try out the new route and report back to us that it is all right for traveling. We want to be assured that the road we are about to embark on is reliable, safe, and trustworthy. It takes some doing for the Lord to get some of us to risk following paths no one has ever blazed before.

This is one of the solid support systems the Word of God provides for us. When the Lord says, "Don't come crying to Me; tell the people to go forward, " He is giving us a *rhema* word with His backing. His Word is all we need.

You are not alone. God is there with you. His Word is all you need to see you through. In the Old Testament God's spokesman asks: "Has the Lord said, and will he not do it? Has He spoken, and will He not make it good?" (Num. 23:19.) Exodus 33:14 assures us of God's presence going with us. It also assures us of inward peace:....**My presence shall go with thee, and I will give thee rest.**

Forward is a motion word. It is on-going. It is goal-oriented. It is directional. With this word spoken to us, we inwardly know we are on time with God's timetable for our life.

**I have found David, the son of Jesse, a man
after My own heart, who will do all My will.**
Acts 13:22 NKJ

This is one of those verses which reads the same in the Old Testament (1 Sam. 13:14) as in the New Testament. When the Lord states that David is a man after His own heart what He is saying is: "David is My kind of man! I can count on him to do all My will without any reluctance or hesitation."

Twice in the Psalms, David discusses his willingness to do the Lord's will. In Psalm 40:8 he declares: **"I delight to do Your will, O my God. And Your law is within my heart"** (NKJ). Then in Psalm 143:10 he requests the Lord's help in this area: **Teach me to do Your will....**(NKJ). This desire to do the Lord's will was pleasing to God.

David had another characteristic that qualified him to be a man after God's own heart. It was a quickness to acknowledge wrongdoing when he was confronted with it. David was quick to repent. He did not hide his sins. He did not carry grudges, hatred, unforgiveness, or resentment in his heart.

He always hurried to the place of forgiveness and reconciliation. How many hours, days, weeks, months, and years have we wasted by not coming to grips with unconfessed sin? David was so sensitive about displeasing the Lord that he was quick to make amends and be restored to loving fellowship. He did not lose any time clearing away the debris in his life. It was this quality that caused him to be a man after God's own heart.

Noah found grace in the eyes of the Lord.
Genesis 6:8 NKJ

The ancient Hebrew language was written by symbolizing only the consonant sounds. Vowel symbols were not developed and added to the writing system until about 700 A.D. Prior to that time, only the consonant sounds of the spoken language were recorded in writing.

In the original Hebrew the word *Noah* was a combination of sounds rendered *Noach (no'–akh)*. This word would come out nch or N-h in writing depending upon how the word was pronounced orally. The word *grace* in Hebrew was made up of two letters pronounced *chen ((K)hane)*. Thus, in the ancient Hebrew parchments this verse would be recorded, "N-*h* found *h-n* in the eyes of the Lord."

We do not often find two words which can be reversed and still read the same ("*n-h* found *h-n*"). This is significant. Our English word *conversion* describes a "turn-around." Before our conversion to Christ, we were on a downhill path to destruction. Then we met Christ and changed directions. Now we are on an uphill path to eternal glory. This "turn-around" is called *conversion*.

In conversion, the Lord can change our name, our nature, our outlook and attitude, and our direction. In Noah's case, N-*h* became *h-n*. The grace of God turned things around for Noah. The same grace turns things around for us, too.

The word *evil* turned around becomes *live*. The assurance the Lord offers us by asking us to come to Him is that He will redirect our lives from *evil* to *live*. Only the Lord can work this transformation fully and thoroughly.

There was the hiding of his power.
Habakkuk 3:4

Jesus did not work miracles on demand. When the Pharisees demanded a sign from Him, He refused them. I have often wondered, if Jesus were here today, would He be featured on the TV newscast? Would He be front-page news? Would He be visible for the whole world to see?

Miracles have two kinds of effects on observers. For those who love the light and the truth, those who have a heart inclined toward the Lord, miracles are a great source of encouragement and wonder.

For those who hate the light and the truth, those whose hearts are hard, miracles are a source of skepticism and antagonism. When Jesus raised Lazarus from the dead, those who had talked of killing Jesus now added Lazarus to their hate list. (John 12:10.)

The same sun that melts wax, hardens clay. Jesus conceals His power and hides it from the view of the bored, the disinterested, the unbelieving, and the skeptical. His power is available only to those who believe:....**these signs shall follow them that believe....**(Mark 16:17).

Do not equate miracles with crowds. You can have a power ministry and still be concealed from public view. God may release through you all the miracles in the sign-gift ministries and yet choose to keep you hidden from the media. There is the hiding of His power.

> **For you died, and your life is**
> **hidden with Christ in God.**
> **Colossians 3:3** NKJ

To be **hidden with Christ** has many different meanings. The English word *hidden* carries the connotation of concealment. We Christians are hidden from the judgment of God which is coming upon the earth. Isaiah 26:20,21 tells us of a time when the Lord will come forth out of His place to punish the inhabitants of the earth for their iniquity. The word to the believer in this passage (v.20) is:....**enter your chambers, and shut your doors behind you; hide yourself, as it were, for a little moment until the indignation is past** (NKJ).

In one of the parables regarding the discovery of a treasure in a field, our Lord says that the man who found the treasure hid it again until he could go and raise enough money to purchase the field for himself. (Matt. 13:44.) As believers we are hidden by the Lord for safekeeping to be united with Him at His Second Coming.

Sometimes we are hidden by the obscurity of our station in life. Not many Christians are prominent or conspicuous in our society. We are known to the Lord even though we are unknown to the world.

Some are hidden by a reticent disposition. Joseph of Arimathaea and Nicodemus each came to Jesus secretly and by night to avoid open criticism. They ultimately overcame their fears, but for them their initial inquiry into the Christian walk was a day of small beginnings.

We are hidden from any evil devisings of our adversaries. In Psalm 27:5 David says of the Lord: **For in the time of trouble he shall hide me in his pavilion....** Our being hidden in Christ is our protection from the evil one. Oh, safe retreat!

He that raised up Christ from the dead
shall also quicken your mortal bodies by his
Spirit that dwelleth in you.
Romans 8:11

Quicken is a beautiful word that is full of life. It is not used in our modern vernacular as it was a hundred years ago, but it is a word which still retains dignity, beauty, and potential.

The Bible speaks of **the quick and the dead** (1 Pet. 4:5). (One person thought this was a description of Southern California pedestrians; out there when crossing busy streets and thoroughfares on foot, a person is either "quick" or he's "dead.") When used in this Biblical context, this word has nothing to do with speed. Rather it refers to life and the living.

The dentist when drilling your tooth slips and hits a tender spot. "I'm sorry," he apologizes as he peels you off the ceiling. "I guess I touched the 'quick'." He is referring to the live flesh which has not been deadened by numbing the tooth. Aunt Hulda is crying because Cousin Mathilda criticized her and hurt her "to the quick." She means, of course, that Cousin Mathilda said something that hurt her feelings.

To quicken means "to have or restore life." According to the Apostle Paul, the same Spirit which raised Christ from the dead dwells in us. This Spirit will give life to our mortal bodies. Note that Paul does not say that the Spirit of God will give life to our *im*mortal bodies in *eternity,* but will give life to our *mortal* bodies in *this world*.

Are you living in the fullness of this promise? If not, you can start today!

> When Jesus saw her weeping,
> and the Jews who came with her weeping,
> He groaned in the spirit and was troubled.
> John 11:33 NKJ

The basic Greek word *embrimaomai (em–brim–ah'–om–ahee)*, translated **groaned** in this verse, only appears five times in the New Testament. Two of those times are found in this passage. (John 11:33,38.) It is a very difficult word to pronounce, but interesting in its definition.

In the original New Testament, the word has to do with anger and indignation.

Jesus was angry that Satan had stolen Lazarus away by death. He counteracted the theft of this life by crying out with a loud voice, ..."**Lazarus, come forth!**" (v. 43 NKJ). He was not going to allow the enemy to get away with this murder of one of His closest friends.

Jesus was angry that sickness could strike a person with such malignant force that he would die a horrible death. The groan of our Lord is an indicator of how He feels about sickness. To Jesus, disease is no friend, it is a malignant foe.

Jesus was also filled with indignation when He met with hypocrisy. Some of the people who came out of Jerusalem to weep and mourn with Mary and Martha went back into town and turned Him in to the Pharisees. Their hypocrisy hade Him indignant.

I also believe Jesus in His humanity groaned because of the *phileo* love He had for Lazarus. He really cared for him as a friend. He cares for us the same way.

He delivered me because He delighted in me.
Psalm 18:19 NKJ

Out of the Dark Ages came a concept of God that is very terrifying. He was pictured as angry, full of wrath, and looking for an opportunity to strike people down at the slightest provocation. The idea was: "If you step out of line for a second, the Lord is going to get you!" Unfortunately, this idea still exists today.

It is the goodness of God that leads people to repentance. God's goodness is extended to us daily in many varied ways. This verse says that He actually finds pleasure in us and delivers us because of His great love for us.

One day while working for a boss who was impossible to please, I began to pray for grace sufficient to function adequately in such a deplorable situation. As I prayed, the Lord revealed to me an area of wounded pride that I had to surrender. He also showed me how resistant I was at that time to an authority figure. Again I surrendered. Then He showed me how to please a fellow human who was very insecure. Finally, He revealed to me how delighted He is in His redeemed.

We are very precious to the Lord. Why the God of the universe should delight Himself in us mortals is a question which cannot be answered. It is a mystery which angels cannot solve. That He does delight in us is certain. The benefits of that favor are numerous.

I benefited from my surrender to the Lord. Not only was I enriched by seeking the Lord for help, I also discovered a new way to get along with an impossible boss. Best of all, because of this situation I learned how much the Lord delighted in me.

Your gentleness has made me great.
Psalm 18:35 NKJ

Part One

As used here in this verse, the word **gentleness** has a variety of definitions all with great possibilities of application. In the original Hebrew, the word translated **gentleness** is *anavah (an–aw–vaw')*. Its definitions are:

Condescension; God stoops to view the skies and bows to see what angels are doing. David ascribes all his own greatness to the condescending goodness and graciousness of his Father in heaven.

Correction: The Anglican *Book of Common Prayer* renders this verse: "...Your loving correction shall make me great." Our Lord's fatherly discipline is designed to better our lot in life.

Help: "...Your help makes me great." This interpretation stresses God's providential care for His own. Providence is a firm ally of the saint, helping them in their service of the Lord.

Goodness: David experienced many deliverances as a result of God's goodness to him. He always ascribed goodness, not to himself, but to the Lord God.

Lowliness: "...Your humility has made me great." To see Jesus is to see the Father. Since Jesus was meek and lowly (not arrogant or conceited), we can know that the Father is also lenient, gentle, and condescending. It is this patience, forbearance, clemency, and condescension of God that makes good men into great men.

Enlightenment: The Chaldee language version of this verse reads: "...Your word has increased me." It is the entrance of God's Word into our inner man that illumines to us all the benevolent and gentle attributes of our Creator.

Your gentleness has made me great.
Psalm 18:35 NKJ

Part Two

There are two main words for *great* in the Old Testament. One has to do with greatness in the eyes of man. The other speaks of greatness in the eyes of the Lord. One indicates an undesirable motive of self-gratification. The other expresses a desirable motive, the glorification of God.

In Jeremiah 45:5 the Lord asks: **"And do you seek great things for yourself? Do not seek them...."** (NKJ). The Hebrew word translated **great** in this verse is *gadol* *(gaw–dole')*. It has a connotation of pride or boasting. It is used to refer to the seeking of estates, status, position, and earthly honors. In many verses in the Bible, *gadol* has a tinge of insolence and is used to describe people who hold others in contempt. Having *gadol* is defined as suffering from delusions of grandeur or "making it into the big-time."

In this verse from Psalms, David uses a different word entirely to express the idea of greatness. Here the word translated great is *rabah (raw–baw')* which has to do with the normal increase which comes when God's blessing is on a person, a city, a church, or a nation. It expresses the idea of a wholesome increase, of making numerous, of adding to one's life.

David could have said:"...Your gentleness has made me numerous." We Christians are a myriad people because of God's blessing. We should be mindful of the lesson of Paul who taught us that one plants, one waters, and God gives the increase. (1 Cor. 3:6.) It is the Lord's graciousness and kindly gentleness that has given us our increase or, as the text implies, our numerical greatness.

My soul followeth hard after thee....
Psalm 63:8

The Septuagint Greek Old Testament renders this verse: "My soul has been glued to you..." The verb in this sentence is a word which has to do with adhesive qualities. When we say we are going to "stick" with someone, we are very close to the meaning of "following hard" after the Lord.

The original Hebrew word translated **followeth hard** in this verse is *dabaq (daw–bak')*. It is defined as "to cling to, to adhere to firmly as if with glue." It also is used in a loving and devoted way to mean "to be attached to someone or something by the heart strings."

Dabaq also can be defined as "clinging to someone in affection or loyalty." It carries with it the idea of keeping very close to someone. This is what the psalmist is referring to when he says, "Lord, my soul follows hard after You." It is the same word as used in Genesis to describe what happens in marriage: A man shall leave his father and mother and shall "cleave" to his wife. (Gen. 2:24.) In this verse the word **cleave** is *dabaq*. It expresses the concept of "staying real close to someone."

When you love, respect, and admire someone, you want to be as near that person as possible. The psalmist wanted to be close to the Lord. He told Him so. He was a worshipper who did not want to be at a distance from his God. He wanted to cling to Him like an adhesive. Because of his desire, David was increased greatly.

We can have the same spiritual desire with the same spiritual results. I think this is a good desire, don't you?

**So the Spirit lifted me up and took me away,
and I went in bitterness, in the heat of my spirit;
but the hand of the Lord was strong upon me.**
Ezekiel 3:14 NKJ

This verse is an unusual blend of divine action and human response. Ezekiel was in captivity with the rest of the displaced tribes of Israel. He was known by many and had a lot of friends. Then he received an unusual visitation from the Lord that set him apart to be a prophet to the Jewish people in exile.

Ezekiel's call was great. He was given a scroll to eat (the Word of God) which was as sweet as honey in his mouth. (vv. 1–3.) The Spirit of the Lord then lifted him up and gave him ecstatic revelations of God's glory. He received a direct commission to go and deliver God's message to his people. This is the glorious side of his calling. But there is another side, and that is how Ezekiel as a human being responded to that call.

In Revelation 10:10, John took the book that was presented to him and ate it. It, too, was as sweet as honey in his mouth, but when it hit his stomach it became bitter. Ezekiel had a beautiful relationship with the Lord, but had a difficult time speaking His message to a people who did not really want to hear what he had to say. The bitterness of the message, the resistance of the suffering exiles, the difficulty of the task, and the drastic change it brought in the life of the prophet all took their toll.

An overpowering anointing gave Ezekiel the ability to go and speak. You have that same anointing upon your life. You are capable of doing the work of the Lord even though your soul and body may rebel at the idea.

**Jesus therefore when he saw her weeping,
and the Jews who were with her weeping,
he groaned in spirit, and troubled himself.**
John 11:33 IGENT

Jesus...troubled himself. The force of this word appears to be that the Lord related humanly as well as divinely to the bereavement, the sorrow of the loss of a friend, and the weeping of the family. He outwardly manifested His feelings when he "troubled" Himself. He Himself wept. He groaned twice. He cried with a loud voice when He called Lazarus forth. This is Jesus' involvement at the natural level.

Jesus...troubled himself is another way of saying that He participated as a friend of the family. The verb in this phrase is reflexive which means that He made this choice Himself and then acted upon it. As the divine Son of God, Jesus knew by omniscience that Lazarus was going to get sick, that He himself would delay coming to him, that Lazarus would die and then be brought back to life. Verses 40, 41 and 42 all imply Jesus' foreknowledge of these events.

One of the remarkable things about John 11 is the ideal blend of humanity and deity portrayed in it. This is one of the great chapters in the Gospels for revealing Jesus' omniscience and omnipotence. His divine attributes are all brought into sharp focus. But His humanity is also presented in great contrast.

Jesus wept as a human. He raised Lazarus from the dead as God. At the moment you read these words, Jesus is still participating in our life as an intercessor seated at the right hand of the Father. He is willing to "trouble" Himself for us! All we have to do is call upon Him. (Ps. 50:15.) Call upon the Lord; He will respond!

**Be my strong habitation,
To which I may resort continually....
Psalm 71:3 NKJ**

This word **resort** is an interesting one. Embodied in it is the idea of a place where we can get away from the daily hassle of life. One translation of this verse says: "You are a great protecting rock where I am always welcome." Another speaks of "A place of security and strength." Our English word *resort* is usually associated with a place of rest and amusement. It carries with it the idea of vacation, a change of pace, of recreation, refreshment, renewal, and revival.

My concern is for busy, active, responsible people who need to "continually" resort to the Lord just as David did. How does a mother with growing children find time to resort? She may not be able to get away physically or geographically; however, there is the opportunity spiritually for her to commune with the Lord in the midst of all her family responsibilities. An executive, a mill worker, a student, or a traveler can each have his or her own private "resort."

I once worked in an office with eight people who were all vocally clamoring for recognition. As non-believers their conversations were not always very "edifying." I prayed David's prayer for a place of resort. The water cooler was a busy spot and so was the bathroom. I finally put a small painting of Jesus in my desk drawer and several times a day would pull the drawer open and gaze on the face of my Savior. In a busy office filled with a lot of noisy activity, I had a few moments of being alone with the Lord. Without any verbal expression, I found a place of resort where I could commune with Jesus. It was a source of strength.

**The rain is over and gone.
...The time of singing has come....
Song of Solomon 2:11,12 NKJ**

The original *King James Version* reads:...**the time of the singing** *of birds* **has come....** The phrase *"of birds"* is italicized to indicate that these words were not in the Hebrew but were added by the translators to give meaning and continuity to the sentence. After consulting numerous translations and commentaries, I have learned that many Bible scholars feel that the reference to birds is warranted by its contextual setting.

Where I live we recently went through a week of heavy rain which resulted in serious flooding. For days skies were oppressively overcast and clouds covered the nearby mountains obstructing their majestic view. After days of such gloomy weather, one begins to look forward to the return of sunshine and warm clear days. Can you imagine the joy we felt upon waking up and hearing birds singing their song of praise to the Lord? The sun was sending forth rays of warmth and cheer that made the awakening process quite pleasant. The sound of birdsong made the experience even more enriching.

One writer has said: "The little birds, which all winter lie hid in their retirements and scarcely live, when the spring returns forget all the calamities of the winter. To the best of their capacities they chant forth the praises of their creator." I see renewal in these words. The winter is past. The Church has gone through its cold spell, revival has come like a spring shower, the earth is warming up, and soon blossoms will turn into fruit. The singing of the birds is like the joyful sounds of revived and refreshed believers!

Cast your burden on the Lord, and He shall sustain you; He shall never permit the righteous to be moved.
Psalm 55:22 NKJ

This verse has a lot to say to us about personal challenge and encouragement. Its three main power words are: 1) **cast,** 2) **burden,** and 3) **sustain.**

Cast means "to throw, hurl, abandon, or toss away as no longer needed or wanted." It also means "to dispense with something in such a way as to have nothing more to do with it." Our cares and our burdens are to be thrown away, abandoned into God's care, dispensed with so that we have nothing more to do with them.

Burden is a word used to describe a load of anxiety that weighs a person down. It has to do with one's lot in life, his particular sphere of influence, his daily duties and responsibilities. Various Bible scholars have defined this expression **your burden** in the following ways: "God's gift to you," "your hope," (LXX) "your allotment," "your portion" and "your cares, travails, and troubles that go with your business or your occupation."

Sustain is a good word. It has to do with upholding, feeding, nourishing, supporting, and taking care of. God gives us a life to live and then invites us to turn over to Him the weight of it all so He can carry us and the load.

Incidentally, Peter, quoting from the Septuagint Old Testament, gave us the same words in the New Testament setting: **casting all your care upon Him, for He cares for you** (1 Pet. 5:7 NKJ). God cares for you. Shift the load from you to Him. He knows what to do with it!

**Jesus answered, "A person who has had a bath needs
only to wash his feet; his whole body is clean...."
John 13:10 NIV**

During the time I was growing up, my family attended
a church that could be called "the guilt center." The
unconscious thinking seemed to be, "One strike and you're
out!" Every Sunday evening we had a ritual we secretly
called "the charge." At the end of the service we would all
"charge" down to the altar and confess all the sins we had
committed that week. Our Christian walk was a precarious
balance between trusting God for His keeping power and
our efforts and struggles to keep from failing the Lord and
grieving Him by falling into sin.

When it becomes a matter of losing your salvation, the
whole question of sin makes the Christian life a constant
struggle with guilt, fear, condemnation, and insecurity. In
this verse Jesus is compassionately showing the difference
between initial conversion and walking through this
polluted world to the other world.

In the original Greek version, two words are used in
contrast. The word translated **bath** is *louo (loo'–o)*, the word
used to describe bathing the whole body. **Wash**, the word
Jesus used when speaking of the feet, is *nipto, (nip'–to)*,
which refers to washing some part of the body such as the
face, hands, or feet.

After you have bathed and are heading home, you only
need to have your feet washed to clean away the dust of the
road. To all of us this footwashing is a reminder of our need
for cleansing from daily pollution. We do not need a new
salvation (a new "bath") every day, but we do need a
cleansing ("washing") to rid us of the dust of the road we
have picked up in our travels. This is what the footwashing
represents — a removal of road dust.

**Your teeth are life a flock of shorn sheep
Which have come up from the washing....
Song of Solomon 4:2 NKJ**

"Sheep which have come up from the washing." What a beautiful picture of the Christian Church. Jesus is the Chief Shepherd. We are the sheep who follow the Shepherd. This verse calls the sheep a flock, the very word Jesus used when He said to His disciples: **Fear not, little flock....**(Luke 12:32).

This word **washing** is so descriptive of our salvation. The world of sin in which we lived prior to conversion is a polluted place. We became soiled and stained just walking through it. Our garments became spotted, we were left defiled and unclean.

The Lord has opened a fountain in Jerusalem for sin and uncleanness. (Zech. 13:1.) Now He challenges us: **"Wash yourselves, make yourselves clean...."** (Is. 1:16 NKJ). John says of the redeemed:...**These are they which came out of great tribulation, and have washed their robes, and made them white in the blood of the Lamb** (Rev. 7:14). Christ laid down His Life for the Church that He might sanctify and cleanse it with the washing of water by the Word. (Eph. 5:26.) Now we are urged to draw near with a true heart in full assurance of faith, having our hearts sprinkled from an evil conscience and our bodies washed with pure water. (Heb. 10:22.)

There is a good feeling when you have showered and bathed and know you are clean. There is a greater feeling knowing your sins have been washed away. Jesus told His disciples: **Now ye are *clean* through the word which I have spoken....**(John 15:3). What a privilege to be truly *clean*!

Praise the comely for the upright.
Psalm 33:1

Two old English words which sound alike present a real study in contrast: *homely* and *comely.*

Homely, unfortunately, has in our day taken on the meaning of "unattractive, dowdy, lacking in beauty." Originally, however, *homely* simply meant "proper or suitable to the home or ordinary life." For example, Cinderella could be said to have worn "homely" clothes when she did the cleaning and scrubbing around the house. In fact, her whole everyday setting could be described as "homely" or "domestic."

Comely, on the other hand, meant "pleasing in appearance; fair; proper, seeming; becoming." It would describe Cinderella when she was dressed in her finest apparel to attend the ball at the palace of the prince. That setting was not domestic, but royal.

In the original Hebrew, the word translated **comely** is *na'veh (naw–veh').* It is defined as "fitting, appropriate, suitable." In Isaiah 63:3 the prophet speaks of the "garment of praise." Thus, the psalmist is telling us here that praise is the proper adornment for the believer when in the presence of royalty.

When invited to a royal function (as Cinderella was), one is expected to dress appropriately. Everyday activities may allow for "homely" apparel, but spiritual worship calls for "comely" attire. When entering into the Holy of Holies for an audience with the King of Kings, we should be properly clothed. That's why we are exhorted to enter His gates with thanksgiving and to come into His courts with praise. Praise is our comely adornment for a visit with His Majesty the King.

**Your teeth are as a flock of ewes ready for
the shearing, all fresh from their washing.
they are in pairs, not one of them is missing.
Song of Solomon 4:2 MLB**

The Bible frequently mentions various parts of the body such as eyes, ears, hands, feet, knees, bones, heart, etc., but it does not say a great deal about the teeth. One prophet did foretell a cleanness of teeth due to scarcity of food. (Amos 4:6.) In Proverbs 25:19 Solomon likens confidence in an unfaithful person to the pain of a broken tooth. In Ecclesiastes 12:4 he describes a slowdown of the body when the grinding of teeth is not vigorous. (*AMP*). (See Adam Clarke's Bible Commentary, pp. 337, 836.) In this verse he speaks of the bride's teeth as having great beauty.

Up until a few years ago, I wore braces on my teeth, but not just to improve my looks. The orthodontist explained to me that braces represent more than dental cosmetics. One of their chief purposes is to restore "bite" to the teeth. I was surprised to find out that many people do not have a proper bite because their upper and lower teeth do not meet as they should.

Bible scholars feel that teeth are a type or symbol of faith, sound teeth representing the ability to chew on the meat of the Word. A baby without teeth is fed milk and soft food. As soon as teeth are developed, he can start in on solid food. Here the bridegroom is symbolically complimenting the bride for: 1) having a relish for the Word of God, 2) eating the Word, and 3) having the strength to act on it. Our teeth are reminders of Job 23:12: **I have esteemed...the words of His mouth more than my necessary food** (AMP).

> **For the weapons of our warfare are not carnal**
> **but mighty in God for pulling down strongholds.**
> **2 Corinthians 10:4** NKJ

Part One

SPIRITUAL WEAPONS

It takes spiritual weapons to be able to engage in spiritual warfare. God has no place for spiritual pacifists. Personally, you may be a peace-loving person, but the fact is you have an enemy whose hatred for truth and righteousness knows no bounds. David described this adversary well when he said of his companions: **I am for peace; but when I speak, they are for war** (Ps. 120:7.) He also urged all those who love the Lord to hate (resist) evil. (Ps. 97:10.)

Someone once said that we Christians were born for battle. Someone else has urged us to get out of the "romper room" and into the trenches. One speaker I heard told all the believers within the sound of his voice to get off the charismatic love boat where it had been all fun and games and get onto the Christian battleship and start shelling Satan's strongholds.

We are not going to a religious playground or a sports arena. This is not an Olympic tournament we are engaged in. It is a grim, bloody, no-holds-barred conflict that pits light against darkness, truth against error, good against evil, the forces of God against the minions of Satan. Since we are on the Lord's side, our triumph is assured. Our victory is past, present, and future: We have won, we are winning, and we will yet win. (2 Cor. 1:10.)

This lesson is one of six in which we will examine what this conflict is all about, name the weapons God has placed at our disposal, and claim the assurance of our total victory in the final outcome.

**For the weapons of our warfare are not carnal
but mighty in God for pulling down strongholds.
2 Corinthians 10:4 NKJ**

Part Two

THE GOOD FIGHT OF FAITH

The victorious Christian life is called the good fight of faith. (1 Tim. 6:12.) We are told to endure hardness as a good soldier of the Lord. (2 Tim. 2:3.) We are also instructed to put on the whole armor of God in order to stand our ground. (Eph. 6:11.) The whole tone is militant. As believers, our theme song is "Onward Christian Soldiers"; our password is "Victory!"

I am so glad the last two decades of the contemplative sixties and the introspective seventies are over and gone. For too long the focus was on me, my, mine — on looking inward, on pulse-taking to find out if the real person on the inside could or would be able to stand. Now a survival mentality has set in. A new "get–tough" vocabulary is surfacing. Once again songs about spiritual warfare are being written and sung.

We have, as victorious believers, a "killer" instinct. Ours is not a defensive stance, we are taking the initiative. We do not simply resist doubt, we *vanquish* doubt. We do not repel fear, we *conquer* fear. We do not reject poverty, we *defeat* poverty. We do not renounce sin, we *subdue* sin. Armed with our spiritual weapons, we *overcome* the flesh, the world and the devil, pulling down his strongholds and demolishing his fortresses.

We believers are called to have a winner's attitude. No general ever sends his troops into battle planning to lose. We who are on the side of truth are destined for the winner's circle. A winning attitude is vital in spiritual warfare.

**For the weapons of our warfare are not carnal
but mighty in God for pulling down strongholds.
2 Corinthians 10:4 NKJ**

Part Three

THE BLOOD OF JESUS

One of the greatest weapons we have for winning great victories is the blood of Jesus. There is prevailing power in the mention of Jesus' blood. Revelation 12:10 says that we can overcome all evil and gain mastery over Satan by the blood of the Lamb and by the word of our testimony.

According to medical authorities, it is safe to say that Jesus had four to five quarts of blood in His body when He sacrificed His life on the cross. Jesus, born of the virgin Mary, had no earthly father's blood in His veins because the Holy Spirit instigated His birth process. Formed in the womb, our Lord came into the world having a blood which contained none of man's sins, imperfections, defects, or human frailties.

Only a perfect sacrifice could accomplish our personal salvation. The sacrifice on the cross of Calvary *was* perfect. The shed blood was so pure that offending man and an offended God were completely reconciled.

Because of Jesus' sinless life and death, all the powers of hell are broken. When Jesus arose from the dead, He held in His hands the keys to death, hell, and the grave. He then gave us, His disciples, authority to bind and loose, authority to cast out demons. His blood is so powerful that to mention it in prayer is the equivalent of placing dynamite under Satan's fortifications and blasting them to pieces. What a weapon!

> **For the weapons of our warfare are not carnal
> but mighty in God for pulling down strongholds.**
> **2 Corinthians 10:4 NKJ**

Part Four

THE NAME OF JESUS

Another great and powerful weapon is the name of Jesus. "In My name, you will cast out (or expel) demons," He told His disciples. (Mark 16:17.) Paul tells us of a day when universally all creation, including heaven, earth, and hell, will acknowledge the name of Jesus and bow to Him in confession of His total lordship. (Phil. 2:5-10.)

The name of Jesus personifies Him; when spoken in prayer and deliverance, it invokes all His majesty, authority, power, rank, character, and excellence. His name embodies all that He Himself is and has. The name of Jesus is not a magic formula; it cannot be thought of as an amulet or a good-luck charm. Rather, it is a base of power for demolishing the strongholds of the enemy.

If you will read carefully Philippians 2:5-11, you will discover that ultimately every knee shall bow and every tongue confess that Jesus is Lord. The day is coming when Satan and all his impious hosts will be forced to bow in total humiliation before the King of Kings and Lord of Lords and acknowledge to Him personally, "You won, we lost!"

Every time you face demons or even the devil himself, if you will mention the name of Jesus you will be reminding the enemy of his three-dimensional defeat: he was defeated at the cross, he is defeated right now by the resurrection, and he will yet be defeated on the day of judgment. What a powerful weapon we have: the name of the Lord!

> **For the weapons of our warfare are not carnal**
> **but mighty in God for pulling down strongholds.**
> **2 Corinthians 10:4** NKJ

Part Five

THE WORD OF GOD

Another great weapon for winning spiritual victories is the Word of God. It has been likened to a sharp two-edged sword. (Heb. 4:12.) In Ephesians 6:13-17 where he describes the armor of God, the Apostle Paul calls the Word of God "the sword of the Spirit." The other pieces of the armor of God — the helmet, shield, breastplate, etc. — are all defensive elements; they help to protect the Christian against the fiery darts of the enemy. The sword of the Spirit — the Word of God — is the only offensive weapon at the disposal of the believer. With it he can put the enemy on the run.

In Psalm 119:89 we read that the Word of God is forever settled in heaven, God's final court of appeals. When Jesus quoted scriptures three times during His wilderness temptation, the devil left Him alone. (Luke 4:13.) There was nothing left for Satan to say; he had no recourse but to go away. When we stand on the scriptures as our basis of faith, we disarm the enemy.

There is no power in the universe that can come against the Word of God with any hope of prevailing. The Word is spoken as a fire, a hammer, a sword, and a weapon. I would urge you to familiarize yourself with as many of the promises found in it as you can. In coming days, a working knowledge of powerful promises from the Lord will be the best weapon you could ever have.

Other books are written for our information. The Bible was written for our transformation and preservation. Oh, precious book!

For the weapons of our warfare are not carnal
but mighty in God for pulling down strongholds.
2 Corinthians 10:4 NKJ

Part Six

PRAISE AS A WEAPON

We have already looked at the blood of Jesus, the name of Jesus, and the Word of God as powerful weapons to be used in spiritual warfare. Now we are adding another weapon: praise.

According to the Bible, it was while they were praying and singing praises unto God that an earthquake occurred which released Paul and Silas from jail. (Acts 16:25.) The very next day the two disciples were able to plant the gospel in Europe. Up to that time, no one had preached the gospel there. Imagine, if you will, Paul and Silas singing and praising at midnight and the song breaking open a whole continent for the gospel!

We also find in Psalm 149:5-9 all kinds of mighty victories promised to those who sing praises to the Lord. The whole passage is one continual assurance of dominion and authority over all obstructions and hindrances that come against any believer.

In 2 Chronicles 20:22, it was when the people of Judah began to sing and praise the Lord that God smote their enemies. Praise not only makes the powers of darkness highly nervous, it also causes them to flee. The old hymn says it best: "At the sign of triumph Satan's host doth flee; On, then, Christian soldiers, On to victory! Hell's foundations *quiver* At the *shout* of praise; Brothers, lift your voices, Loud your anthems raise!" Praise is a powerful weapon. Use it and win the victory!

> **For the wages of sin is death, but the gift of
> God is eternal life in Christ Jesus our Lord.**
> **Romans 6:23** NKJ

What a study in contrasts! Wages and gift. These two words are so opposite in meaning that we could easily overlook the full import of their significance.

The Greek word translated **wages** is *opsonion (op–so'–nee–on)*. It is the word for subsistence or salary. It involves the concept of a reward of recompense for services rendered. Thus "the wages of sin" refers to the payoff which comes as a result of serving Satan. The deceptive thing about sin is that it so often comes disguised as pleasure and fulfillment. Here, Paul is saying that the devil is a deceiver who lures people into a life of sin by promising them all kinds of future bliss. However, the real payoff for all their hard work (yes, sinners work real hard at sinning!) is disintegration, destruction, and death.

The *gift* of God. What a beautiful contrast to the wages of sin. The original Greek word for **gift** is *charisma (khar'–is–mah)*, meaning "an endowment, something given freely." God freely bestows grace (unmerited favor) on those who call upon His name. Blessings, benefits, and bestowments all come to us from a loving, heavenly Father Who gives, and gives, and keeps on giving — because it is His nature to give.

The wages of death is earned. The gift of life is freely received. Before a conversion we were on Satan's payroll, now we are on God's gift list! Satan's final payoff is death, but God's ultimate gift is eternal life. Which do you prefer: death or life? wages or gift?

You do not have because you do not ask.
James 4:2 NKJ

I learned to appreciate the full extent of this verse as a result of a personal experience earlier in my life. Preparing for a career in nationwide evangelism, I felt the need of acquiring a trombone and learning to play it as the musical portion of my planned evangelistic services. The more I thought about it, the more I was convinced I needed a trombone.

My faith was too weak to ask the Lord for such a mundane thing as a musical instrument. In this sense, my thinking was typically immature. "What if I ask for a horn and the Lord doesn't give me one?" I asked myself. "I wouldn't want to embarrass the Lord by asking Him to do something that might not be His will. After all, He knows where I live and what I need, " I rationalized fatalistically, "So if He wants me to have a trombone, He can send it to me." As a result of my fuzzy thinking, my prayers were vague, general and ambiguous. It soon became evident, however, that they weren't producing anything.

In His usual merciful way of dealing with His children, the Lord led me to this verse:...**you do not have because you do not ask.** He showed me how pathetic, anemic, and unscriptural my prayers were. I learned that weak faith produces weak prayers.

The Lord dealt with me about asking specifically for a trombone: "If you want a trombone, ask for it, and I will give it to you." I did, and He did! From that experience I learned a valuable lesson about praying. I learned to change my prayers from general, vapory wishes to specific, concrete requests.

**And the earth was without form, and void; and
darkness covered the face of the deep. And the
Spirit of God moved upon the face of the waters.
Genesis 1:2**

Moved is a word that is picturesque and rife with
meaning. In the original Hebrew the word translated
moved in this verse is the root word *rachaph (raw–khaf')*
meaning "to brood." One grammarian has defined it as "to
hover with a gentle wavering or fluttering motion as a bird
broods over her young."

Rachaph has also been defined as "to express a feeling
of tender or cherishing love, as a mother soothing her
child." The Spirit of God brooded over the shapeless mass
of the earth, cherishing and imparting warmth, love,
energy, and life to a world which was then chaotic.

This verse is a beautiful picture of our new creation.
Like the discordant elements of the primeval earth, because
of our sin we, too, were without form, and void, and
darkness covered us completely.

Then the Holy Spirit lovingly and tenderly began to
flutter over us. Warmly He hovered over our hearts and
began to draw us with God's love. Our discordant life took
on form, shape, symmetry, and beauty.

Just as God created the earth out of nothing, so also He
created us out of nothing. His Spirit took us when we had
no beauty or form and lovingly transformed us into a new
creation. Thank God for His love, patience, and design.

Whoso breaketh an hedge,
a serpent shall bite him.
Ecclesiastes 10:8

This verse speaks to husbands who are the priests and spiritual defenders of their families. The word *husband* comes from an Old English word meaning "house-bond" or "house-covenant." It expresses the idea that the man roamed at will while single, but now that he has entered a covenant with his wife, he will stay home to love and protect those in his care. The true husband accepts the role and responsibilities which go with being a "house-bond."

In the Bible the word *hedge* is used to indicate any enclosure placed around something to protect it. In the Old Testament, Satan complained to God that He had put a hedge around Job so he was untouchable. (Job 1:10.) In the book of Ezekiel, the nation of Israel was so spiritually unprotected that God was looking for a man to make up the hedge and stand in the gap. (Ezek. 22:30.) He found none.

My concern is that Christian husbands make sure that they do not break down the spiritual hedge that surround their homes and family. A broken hedge weakens the moral stamina of the family and allows the serpent to gain entrance. Adam had a spiritual enclosure in the Garden of Eden. His job was to be fruitful, multiply, replenish, and subdue. One act of rebellious disobedience on his part and the serpent was able to get in and infect the whole human race with the venom of sin and death.

Christian man, be the "house-bond," the husband who prays for, encourages, praises, and inspires his family members. If you will keep your home in spiritual purity and strength, you will keep the serpent out.

Greet Andronicus and Junia, my kinsmen...,
who also were in Christ before me.
Romans 16:7 NKJ

Three times in this chapter Paul makes mention of his relatives. In this verse it is Andronicus and Junia (most likely a husband-and-wife team in ministry). In verse 11, it is Herodian. In verse 21, it is Sosipater. In addition to these personal references, in Acts 23:16 we read where Luke spoke of the son of Paul's sister. These are the only references in the New Testament which indicate that Paul had any living relatives.

In this verse Paul mentions the fact that Andronicus and Junia were converted to Christ before he was. Paul himself was born again early in the Christian era. Some scholars believe Andronicus and Junia were converted either when Jesus sent out the seventy or on the day of Pentecost.

Can you imagine what it must have been like for these two to try to witness to Paul while he was still Saul, the persecutor of the Christians? Can you picture how unreceptive and hostile he must have been whenever these two kinsmen of his were around him?

You may have loved ones who are as violently opposed to you and your witness to them as Paul was to Andronicus and Junia. In spite of his animosity, I believe Paul's kinsmen planted a seed within his heart which took root and prepared him for his eventual conversion experience.

Do not give up on your relatives. You may have another Apostle Paul in your family. God's mercy touched a murderer and made him a messenger. Don't give up!

But without faith it is impossible to please Him,...
Hebrews 11:6a NKJ

What is faith? It is a combination of several things:

TRUST: Faith enables us to approach the Lord in trust. It causes us to say by our actions: "Lord, I trust You. Your Word says You can be trusted and I believe it." Faith in God is trust in God.

CONFIDENCE: Faith enables us to approach the Lord with confidence. Our confidence is not in the abilities, cleverness or ingenuity of man — but of God. Faith is confidence that God will keep His promises.

ASSURANCE: Assurance tells us that God is everything His Word says He is. It tells us that He is intervening on our behalf and for our deliverance. Faith is assurance.

COURAGE: Faith is the courage needed to approach God with a long list of needs and know He hears our prayers and answers them for His glory and honor. It is the courage to look to the Lord in any time of need and not allow our circumstances to intimidate us or dictate to us.

ACTION: Faith has a passive side. It can be received as a gift from God. It also has an active side. Faith prompts action. Hebrews 11:33 tells us that faith *subdued*, faith *worked*, faith *obtained*, and faith even *stopped the mouth of lions*.

One scholar has stated: "Faith's inner conviction about God is always translated into action and results in a lifestyle through which the reality of faith is expressed."

**For he who comes to God must believe
that He is, and that He is a rewarder of
those who diligently seek Him.
Hebrews 11:6b** NKJ

This phrase **diligently seek** expresses great intensity. It implies more than mere searching or ordinary seeking. The primary Greek word translated *seek* is *zeteo (zay–teh'–o)*. It is used in the New Testament 119 times to express inquiry or endeavor, and is the normal word for "searching." In this verse the Greek word translated **diligently seek** is *ekzeteo (ek–zay–teh'–o)*. It is an intensified form of *zeteo* meaning "to seek with desire and determination." *The Amplified Bible* version of this verse reads: ...**For whoever would come near to God must (necessarily) believe that God exists and that He is the Rewarder of those who earnestly and diligently seek Him (out).**

Seeking out the Lord is a lifetime pursuit for the believer. As we continually seek wisdom, we find the wisdom needed for each situation. As we continuously seek knowledge, we find that knowledge increases. As we seek answers and solutions, we find the deliverance, guidance, direction, understanding, strength, and power necessary for each step of our daily Christian journey. We become living witnesses to the validity of Jesus' statement that it is in seeking that we find.

There are prayers, and there are intense prayers; intercessions, and strong intercessions; tears, and powerful tears. There is normal, routine seeking, and there are times of determined, forceful, diligent seeking. This is the kind that is greatly rewarded. In Jeremiah 29:13 God says:...**you will seek Me and find Me, when you search for Me with all your heart** (NKJ).

Thou shalt not see evil any more.
Zephaniah 3:15

Here the Lord assures us of total deliverance and complete freedom from whatever it is that is pressuring us. One translation of this verse reads:"...you shall see disaster no more." Another states: "...never again will you fear any harm." A third declares: "...you shall have no more trouble."

It has been an interesting experience as I have shared this verse and others similar to it with audiences around the country. Reactions have ranged from general hesitancy to outright disbelief. Many Christians have told me: "Yes, that verse is in the Bible and I believe it is true for many people. *But* my experience has proven otherwise! Despite what it says, my life is still filled with all kinds of problems. God has promised that we will not see evil any more, but in my case, that promise is simply not operative."

We must not judge God's Word by our experience. Rather, we must take the promises of God not as theoretical ideals beyond our grasp, but as living realities which are ours in Christ. We must appropriate them to our own case by quoting them as our declarations of faith: "Once I was in darkness, but now I walk in light. Once I was weak, but now I can do all things through Christ who strengthens me. Once I was in want, now God supplies all my needs. Once I was sick, now with His stripes I am healed. Once I was a victim, now I'm more than a conqueror."

This verse expresses a passing from death to life. It allows us to proclaim: "Because of what Jesus has done for me on Calvary, I shall not see evil any more!"

> **And having shod your feet with the
> preparation of the gospel of peace.**
> **Ephesians 6:15 NKJ**

The ability to remain on one's feet during battle requires good footing, strong ankle action, and proper footwear. This expression, "...having shod your feet with the *preparation* of the gospel of peace," says a lot. The original Greek word translated **preparation** in this verse is *hetoimasia (het–oy–mas–ee'–ah)*. It is defined as "being ready to take action at a moment's notice."

This is a word that is both defensive and offensive. In Roman times, the warrior's sandal was equipped with a cleat-like sole for sure traction and fast mobility. Taking the gospel to the ends of the earth stirs up opposition. The enemy's strategy is to aim his artillery at us to stop our forward progress. Being shod with the warrior's sandal of readiness will assure us of the steadfast footing and nimble agility necessary to dodge Satan's missiles.

We can also launch an offensive when shod with this footwear. The New Testament usage of the word *hetoimasia* implies a readiness for good works (Titus 3:1), a readiness for witnessing (1 Pet. 3:15), and a readiness for the Lord's return. (Matt. 24:44.) Such readiness imparts to us a distinctive character and nature because at any moment we expect a triumphant return of our Commander-in-Chief. Readiness also keeps us open to the demands of the action necessary to reach our goal of world dominion.

Shod with the right kind of combat sandal we are able to defend ourselves. We are also equipped to launch a worldwide invasion of the kingdom of darkness.

The Lord is my shepherd.
Nothing shall be lacking to me.
Psalm 23:1 (author's literal translation)

This is a security verse. Safe in the shepherd's fold we know no lack, no want, no deficiency, no shortage. Psalm 84:11 assures us:....**No good thing will He withhold from those who walk uprightly** (NKJ). In Psalm 34:9 we are told: **Oh, fear the Lord, you His saints! There is no want to those who fear Him** (NIV).

One way a shepherd tends his flock is by seeing that they have good nourishing food. As our Divine Shepherd, the Lord wants us to have a healthy diet. The Word of God is one source of Spiritual nourishment. Worship of the Lord is another. Inspired and anointed teaching and preaching is food for the soul. Our Shepherd will supply to us just the right nourishment, if we will let Him, if we will follow Him in obedience.

A shepherd also protects his flock. We can trust our keeping to our Chief Shepherd, Jesus, Who will not leave us open to the enemy's designs. Our protection, our safety, our preservation, our care, and our safekeeping are all His personal concerns. We believers are ever under His watchful eye. Jesus protects the flock from marauders. He has given to His undershepherds (pasters) an admonition to keep the wolves out of His sheepfold.

A shepherd continuously leads his flock to better pasture. Our Chief Shepherd is constantly looking out for our best interests. He only wants for us what is for our ultimate good.

Saying "The Lord is *my* Shepherd" personalizes this statement. To proclaim "*I* shall not lack or want" is to declare that, as one of the Lord's followers, each of us is supplied and contented in every way.

**And I will give you shepherds according to
My heart, who will feed you with knowledge
and understanding.
Jeremiah 3:15 NKJ**

I am grateful for all the sincere men and women of God who I know personally are in the ministry because of a "call" of God upon their individual lives. It is an awesome responsibility to be a pastor. It is also a glorious and high calling.

The word *shepherd* as Jeremiah used it here means "a guide for the people." According to the prophet, God's people are destroyed for lack of knowledge. (Hos. 4:6.) I believe that one of the main functions of future pastors will be the feeding, tending, and instructing of their respective flocks with knowledge and understanding.

If God has called you to be a pastor, then ask the Lord to fulfill this verse in your life. Pray that you will be a man or woman after God's own heart. Pray you will be able to feed the flock intrusted to you with knowledge and understanding. If you are a new convert and are looking for a church home, then pray that the Lord will lead you to a church with the kind of pastor who leads his people into the full truth of God's Word. If you are already in a church and functioning as an active member, then pray lovingly and charitably without a critical attitude or judging mind for your pastor to fulfill this verse.

I believe that drastic changes are coming soon to our planet. God is raising up shepherds to feed the flock and guide them through this uncertain world to the next. The pastor who understands his time and function will be able to relate to the flock on how to survive the perilous times which lie ahead.

Do not be conformed to this world, but be transformed by the renewing of your mind....
Romans 12:2 NKJ

A lady came home from a revival meeting and cheerfully announced to her agnostic husband, "I have been born again." In contempt he snarled these words at her: "You have lost your mind!" She lovingly responded, "You're right! Now I have the mind of Christ." She was sharing with him that her whole way of thinking had been changed as a result of her conversion.

One of the key words in this verse is **transformed**. In the original Greek text it is *metamorphoo (met–am–or–of'–o)*. The interesting thing about *metamorphoo* is that it is the same word used to describe the change Jesus underwent going up the mount of transfiguration. (Matt. 17:2.)

As Jesus ascended the mountain, His clothing became as white as light and His face shone with a dazzling glory as bright as the sun. He was transfigured *(metamorphoo)* or transformed. What happened to Jesus was a drastic and dramatic change from His former condition. Here in Romans, Paul is urging you and me to undergo the same process.

In 2 Corinthians 3:18 Paul writes: **But we all, with unveiled face, beholding as in a mirror the glory of the Lord, are being transformed** *(metamorphoo)* **into the same image from glory to glory, just as by the Spirit of the Lord** (NKJ).

The radiance Jesus demonstrated on the mount of transfiguration is resident within us by the indwelling Spirit of God. As our hearts and minds respond to His dealings, we, too, are being transfigured or transformed.

**Many are the afflictions of the righteous,
But the Lord delivers him out of them all.
Psalm 34:19 NKJ**

This verse is not declaring that you and I are going to suffer all our lives. There is no redemptive value in suffering; it entered the world as a result of sin not as a "cure" for it. Sin and suffering are two ominous figures that have dogged the footsteps of humanity ever since the fall of man. Jesus came to do away with sin and suffering.

Job's suffering was labeled a "captivity" from which he was released by God. (Job 42:10.) The woman with a crooked, deformed back was pronounced by Jesus as one "whom Satan hath bound." (Luke 13:16.) In Acts 10:38 we read **how God anointed Jesus of Nazareth with the Holy Ghost and with power: who went about doing good, and healing all that were oppressed of the devil.**...This word translated **oppressed** could also be rendered **tyrannized.** When the Bible describes afflictions as captivity, bondage, oppression, and tyranny, then we are safe in saying that suffering has no redemptive value.

In the Greek Old Testament (LXX), this word **afflictions** is *thlipsis (thlip'–sis)* which is defined as "pressure."

Many are the pressure of the righteous. We are on an uphill journey, an obstacle course. Every turn in the road is a pressure point. The Lord delivers us out of them all and we manage to keep going. Do not major on the pressure points of life; rather, major on deliverance. Negative people are always talking about their afflictions and pressures. Positive people of faith are always talking about their deliverances.

**The children of Issachar...had understanding
of the times, to know what Israel ought to do....
1 Chronicles 12:32 NKJ**

A person who reads his Bible consistently is soon attuned to world conditions. After you have read Jesus' description of the last days (Matt. 24,25), it does not surprise you to hear news reports of worldwide violence, global turmoil, or climatic disturbances. Students of the Word of God know that these things have been predicted. When they come to pass, inwardly we know that all this is a fulfillment of Bible prophecy.

The tribe of Issachar had the unusual ability to understand their times. They were cognizant of what was going on. They could relate to their contemporary world. They understood the past, the present, and the future. As last-day believers, we can have the same mindset, the same abilities, and the same understanding of our times.

In the Septuagint Greek Old Testament (LXX), the word translated **times** is *kairos (kahee–ros')* meaning "opportunities." The children of "Issachar" were aware of their chances, their opportunities. The Christian Church has great opportunities right now. Global evangelism, missionary thrust, and international soulwinning are readily available to all believers. I want to be an "Issachar" who fully understands his opportunities for the Lord.

These people knew what Israel ought to do. It is one thing to wake up and know it is 6 a.m. It is another thing to arise, get dressed, and go to work. Knowing your opportunities sets the stage for action. Action is a result of knowing what you are to do!

> **Shammah....stationed himself in the**
> **middle of the field, defended it....And the**
> **Lord brought about a great victory.**
> **2 Samuel 23:11,12 NKJ**

Shammah was one of David's heroic warriors. He came to a field that was a food supply for David's army. The Philistines had moved in and captured it. The people ran away in fear but Shammah stationed himself in the middle of the field, defended the acreage all alone, and the Lord intervened to help him. The outcome was a *great victory!*

Shammah took a stand and refused to be moved. This could be the origin of the expression "stand your ground." It is not easy to stand your ground when the rest of the crowd is running for their lives leaving you to face the massed and armed might of the enemy alone.

I once lost a job because I took a stand for a principle I knew in my heart to be right. Something was going on in the office that I felt was wrong, immoral, dishonest, and indecent. The office staff wanted me to participate in that activity. When I explained my position of conscience, my superior discharged me. The victory in that situation was locating a better job — one that was everything I could have ever asked for. It was great!

Standing your ground does not mean being stubborn when the Church is moving forward or trying to prove to your mate that he or she is wrong. It is not being belligerent, hardnosed, or uncooperative. It is simply taking a firm position based on personal integrity. It is saying to yourself: "I want to live by the principles of God's Word. I am standing for truth and trusting the Lord to defend me and bring me to victory."

I planted, Apollos watered, but God gave the increase.
1 Corinthians 3:6 NKJ

Assuming leadership as pastor of a church put me in position to "do it all." I picked up people in my car to bring them to church, then led the singing, made the announcement, performed the musical solos and specials, preached the message, prophesied over the congregation, laid hands on them, and blessed them. Then I took them home. At the end of the day, I fell into bed totally fatigued but contented. All this for a grand total of 30 to 40 people. This foolish heart had so much to learn. Church is for the cultivating and developing of gifts, talents, and ministries. It is not meant to be a "one-man show" in which one person puts on a performance while everyone else fills the role of spectator.

Paul points out that one person is called to plant a seed of faith. Another has the ministry of watering the seed to produce growing crops. The Lord gives the increase. This Greek word translated **increase** is *auxano (owx–an'–o)*, defined as "growth and enlargement." Our word *auxiliary* comes from *auxano*.

It was a painful lesson for me, but I had to learn it: If one person dominates a church (it could be a monied person, and influential board member, or the one who pioneered the church), its growth potential is practically nil. Teamwork is the word. Delegating authority is vital to church growth. Discovering talents and gifts in a congregation and then encouraging and developing those ministries is essential to church enlargement.

Lord, deliver us from the "do-it-yourself" syndrome and give us a teamwork mentality.

Let each be fully convinced in his own mind.
Romans 14:5 NKJ

Out of the Reformation there emerged a manifesto, a new idea that each believer could read the Bible for himself. He could trust the Holy Spirit to interpret what he read and illuminate it to him personally. Then he could determine the will of God for his own life and act accordingly. Having the Word of God for a guide and the inner witness of the Holy Spirit for confirmation allows each individual to be a priest to the Lord. The priesthood of the believer is thus a Reformation concept.

Frequently people approach me to ask me to make some decision for them that they should make for themselves. Some ask if I think they should get married. Others ask if they should sell their house, or quit their job, or get a divorce. According to this verse in Romans, each person is capable of finding God's will for himself. Each is capable of making his own decisions. James 1:5 encourages us to ask God for the wisdom and direction we need, fully expecting to receive it.

There is safety in a multitude of counselors, but after all the suggestions, input and advice are accumulated and analyzed, each of us must make the final decision for himself. Earlier in life I went to others and relied upon their knowledge and ability. Slowly and graciously the Lord brought me to the place where I could be persuaded in my own mind. It took a long time to reach that place, and it was not without mistakes along the way, but the trip was worth it. In John 7:17 the Lord Jesus says of God, **"If anyone wants to do His will, he shall know...."** (NKJ). This verse says that you and I can be *fully* convinced in our *own* mind!

To another the working of miracles....
1 Corinthians 12:10 NKJ

There are four types of miracles described in the New
Testament. This list could be the manual or guideline for
your place of worship:

Notable miracles (Acts 4:16). A *notable* miracle is one
that comes to the attention of those outside the local
congregation. It makes the newspaper and the television
evening news. The healing of the lame man in Acts 3:6-10
attracted such a community interest that it became a media
event and a conversation piece. Two chapters in Acts (3 and
4) detailed this happening.

Great miracles (Acts 6:8). In Acts 8:13 Luke uses the
Greek words *mega dumamis* or "great miracles." This is not a
reference to a "one-incident-only" event. It refers to a
steady stream of signs, wonders, and miracles. God moves
in a lavish way so that the list of miracles is great in quantity
as well as quality.

Special miracles (Acts 19:11). The thing stressed here is
the geographical location involved. The disciples were in
Ephesus, center of the worship of the Greek goddess Diana,
a practice which led to depravity, degeneracy, and
immorality. It took something special to free people from
such a sensual trap.

Divers(e) miracles (Heb. 2:4). This verse points to
miracles of a manifold nature. There are special spiritual
miracles for any church, special physical miracles for
people with all kinds of ailments, special financial miracles
for everyone in need. Claim all four types of miracles for
yourself and your groups: notable, great, special, and
diverse.

> In righteousness you shall be established:
> you will be far from oppression; fear
> and terror will not come near you.
> Isaiah 54:14 KJV (Paraphrased)

Far from fear and oppression, what a wonderful and reassuring word. This promise guarantees us peace of mind. No mental hassle. No mental fatigue. No mental oppression or depression. But we must appropriate that peace to ourselves

Active within the Christian is a real battle for the mind. Thoughts can originate from the Holy Spirit, the evil spirit, or the human spirit. One of the ministries of the Holy Spirit is that of the discerning of spirits. This discernment is the ability to isolate each thought to determine its origin or source and the proper response to it: The Holy Spirit always exalts Jesus; the evil spirit discredits Jesus; the human spirit attempts to exalt man and his cleverness, knowledge, ability and achievements.

This verse tells us that our thoughts do not have to annoy us. Stabilized by the righteousness of God, we need not be plagued by oppressive mental impulses. No longer must we be victimized or dominated by fearful, terrifying or traumatic suggestions, memories or imaginings. Now that we are in Christ, we have His mind. We can literally dismiss from our thinking any oppressive or depressive thoughts, replacing them with positive affirmations and images. Whenever any wrong thought comes to your mind, you need to verbally speak a word of refusal to it. Say: "I do not accept that thought. Jesus does not think that way, and neither do I." If you will do that, you will soon be far from oppression.

Whosoever is born of God doth not commit sin....
1 John 3:9

Because of a misunderstanding of this verse, some sincere Christians have struggled to arrive at a place of absolute perfection where they will never make another mistake for the rest of their lives.

This struggle to avoid sin by self-effort is doomed to failure. It creates a tension within the believer which eventually traps him into committing the very sin he is trying to overcome. Demoralized, he tries again and again to reach the top of Mount Perfection only to realize that he will never be able to make it on his own.

Using this verse as a guide, Christians can spend a lifetime sliding up and down the mountain — which can be very frustrating, to say the least.

Others live on the cutting edge of guilt because of this verse. Every time they make a mistake, the old spirit of condemnation comes back to taunt them: "How can you call yourself a born-again Christian when you still commit sin?"

In the original Greek text the work translated **commit** has to do with a behavior pattern, a mode of conduct, and a way of life rather than a single action. Literally the Greek reads "He that is begotten of God does not make a *practice* of sin." In other words, it is not in the nature of a Christian to sin. He has a new inclination, a new desire, and a new tendency.

Be encouraged, then, to know that this verse simply means that the Christian does not make a *habit* of sin. Sinning is not in his makeup; it is foreign and repugnant to him. He does not make a practice of sinning, rather he practices righteousness because of a renewed nature!

> **You will keep him in perfect peace,**
> **Whose mind is stayed on You,**
> **Because he trusts in You.**
> **Isaiah 26:3** NKJ

Part One

Perfect peace is a good translation of this phrase from the Hebrew Old Testament. In the original text the words read *shalom shalom*. This double word indicates a dual peace internally and externally.

This verse promises us an inner peace that stays with us 24 hours a day. According to Romans 14:17 the kingdom of God within us is righteousness, peace and joy in the Holy Ghost. Isaiah 32:17 promises us a work of inner peace that will also bring us calm confidence, settled assurance, and abiding trust. This inner peace is the one quality that can hold us together when everything in the world about us is falling apart. When you read the newspaper and find Bible prophecies being fulfilled, you may wonder how God's people are going to survive all the violence and turmoil ahead. Inner peace is the sustainer which will assure our holding steady in a turbulent world.

This verse also promises an external peace. Inner-city Christians have discovered this peace. Soldiers on the battlefield and workers in hectic offices and noisy factories have learned to draw from it. Once, where I worked there was a fellow employee who enjoyed heckling me. I called on God in prayer and He gave me this verse: **When a man's ways please the Lord, He makes even his enemies to be at peace with him** (Prov. 16:7 NKJ). As a result, an external peace came into a work place where turmoil and confusion had reigned before. I discovered and enjoyed both inner and outer peace in that situation.

You will keep him in perfect peace,
Whose mind is stayed on You,
Because he trusts in You.
Isaiah 26:3 NKJ

Part Two

A mind *stayed* on the Lord. Have you ever wondered what that means? In the original Hebrew text the word translated **stayed** is *camak (saw–mak')* which is defined in its reflexive form as "to lean upon." One older grammarian consulted described the action expressed by *camak* as "to place or lay something upon an object so that it rests upon and is totally supported by that object." The word thus contains the idea of something's being undergirded, upheld or sustained so that it remains firm and unmoved.

When a person's mind is "leaning on" the Lord, the peace promised him is sure and perpetual. You and I can lean on the Almighty continually and His peace will be ours continually. This "leaning" is an attitude of mind which gives God the benefit of every doubt and question; it trusts Him unequivocally and believes implicitly that all things work together for good to those who love Him.

When the Bible says that David was a man after God's own heart, it is speaking of direction. It is saying that David's inclinations (his leanings) were toward the Lord. David sought after God. He even pursued Him. David was always headed in God's direction. We can display this same kind of continual pursuit of the Lord by having a heart which is always hungry for Him.

One way to transform Isaiah 26:3 into a personal confession is to state: "The Lord will watch over me and guard me with an internal and an external peace because my mind and its thought are ever leaning in His direction."

So likewise you, when you have done all those things which you are commanded, say, 'We are unprofitable servants. We have done what was our duty to do.
Luke 17:10 NKJ

Can you visualize yourself bringing salvation to a billion people? Imagine yourself laying hands on millions of people and bringing healing to them. Picture yourself leading thousands of people to the baptism of the Holy Spirit. How would all this affect you? If God raised you up to do something great in His kingdom, what would your reaction be?

This statement from our Lord is a great equalizer. It helps to balance out ministries, to reduce them all to the same plane. Those with tremendous results have no more right to boast than those which produce much less.

When all the results of our efforts for the kingdom of God are in, we should say to ourselves, "All the glory should go to God. I'm just one of His submissive servants. I only did what I was told to do."

This is not to suggest a phony modesty or a false humility. But I really believe the Lord does have to condition us for success, to groom us for results. Someone has remarked that a codfish lays 1,000 eggs and doesn't say a word, while a hen lays one egg and cackles about it all day. Let us be such humble servants that we can experience great results in God's kingdom and still remain unassuming.

Notice: it is not the Lord but the disciples who make the statement, "We are unprofitable servants." The Lord says of them: "You are my precious jewels." (Mal. 3:17.) Keep things in proper perspective. Do not overrate yourself and the Lord will exalt you.

But where sin abounded,
grace did much more abound.
Romans 5:20

The Apostle Paul had a way with words that made their truth loom up clearly and powerfully. One habit he had was that of adding intensifiers to words to sharpen their impact.

For example, when speaking of sin in this verse, Paul used the Greek word *pleonazo (pleh–on–ad'–zo)* which refers to "increase" or "more." Yet when he spoke of God's grace, he added the intensifier *huper* to the verb to create a compound Greek word *huperperisseuo (hoop-er–per-is–syoo'–o)* which literally means "beyond surplus."

The Bible assures us that as we draw near the end of the age, sin will multiply. We know that with the world's population doubling every generation or less, there is bound to be tremendous increase in wrongdoing, crime, lust, hatred, and sin in all its malignant and hideous forms. Yet as true as that is, Paul would remind us that where sin abounded in times past, God's grace "did much more abound." In other words, he is saying to us: "Wherever sin is in 'surplus', grace is in 'super-surplus'."

This verse tells us that although sin is multiplying fast, the grace of God is multiplying even faster. Sin is an outrage that reaches the boundaries of the highest heaven. But above all sin, the grace of God is enthroned higher than any evil or wrong can ever reach.

In relating this verse to himself, one man said: "I was not running towards God, I was running from Him. I did not go looking for Him, He came looking for me." Such is God's "super-abounding" grace toward us.

**Awake, O north wind; and come, you south
wind, both you blow upon my garden, that
its fragrance may be wafted abroad....
Song of Solomon 4:16** MLB

According to *Hastings Bible Dictionary*, in the ancient
Israel of Solomon's day, the north wind was cold and
cutting. The south wind was warm and balmy. Thus these
words have spiritual significance to us today.

The cold and penetrating north wind comes to clear
away the mists of gloom, error, unbelief, and sin. It goes
right through to the bone and reveals to us our heart's
condition so we can turn from our sins and be saved. Smug,
complacent, apathetic, and listless individuals will remain
in their sins until the north wind of God's Holy Spirit
awakens them to their need of forgiveness and salvation.

Think back to your own conversion and what it was
that awakened you to your spiritual need. God is not cruel.
He does not send chilling winds to make people miserable,
only to awaken them out of their death-sleep.

The south wind was a balmy breeze like the one which
wafted through the fragrant Garden of Eden. This wind has
many pleasant associations with the mild and gentle graces
of the Holy Spirit. After our conversion, the Lord invites us
to follow Him on the road as committed disciples. His yoke
is easy and His burden is light. His commandments are not
grievous.

Cold north winds awaken us to serve the Lord. Warm
south winds refresh us in our task. The north wind of the
Holy Spirit convicts us of our sin. The south wind comforts
us in our need. Both winds are vital to eternal salvation.

Behold, it is Solomon's couch,
With sixty valiant men around it,
Of the valiant of Israel.
they all hold swords,
Being expert in war....
Song of Solomon 3:7 NKJ

This verse and the preceding one speak to us about journeying in the days of Solomon, King of Israel. At night the king's company would find a temporary resting place. There Solomon would sleep while sixty men armed with swords stood guard around his bed.

I find this image highly amusing. Just put yourself in Solomon's place: it has been a long, tedious tiresome trek. Finally you stop to rest for the night. All you want to do is sleep, but every time you open your eyes you see sixty armed men surrounding you and staring at you!

In the military I had to sleep in a crowded army barracks. Besides my own narrow cot there were twenty-three other beds stretched out side-by-side in the same long room. Men snored, talked in their sleep, got up in the night, tossed and turned, came and went—all night long. I literally had to learn to sleep right through the war. I don't know what I would have done if there had been sixty armed guards around my bed!

One writer in the 17th century observed that Solomon with his 60 armed guards was not as protected as we believers. Philippians 4:7 says, "The peace of God that passes all understanding will stand as a sentinel and a guard over your heart and mind through Christ Jesus." That is real protection.

**Ye were sealed with that holy Spirit of promise,
Which is the earnest of our inheritance until the
redemption of the purchased possession....
Ephesians 1:13,14**

Part One

As a youngster seeking the experience of being filled
with the Holy Spirit, I was preconditioned by the
terminology of finality which accompanied that event.
Whenever a seeker received the baptism of the Holy Spirit
and found a fulfilling release in the Lord, he was said to
have "prayed *through*." The one thing wrong with that
statement is the word *through*. The problem is that *through*
also means "finished, done, terminated, ended, all done."

Being baptized in God's Spirit is such a meaningful
and fulfilling experience that no one should ever stop there.
They should go on until they have been empowered by the
Lord for service and fully released in the power of the Holy
Spirit.

The overflowing or outflowing of the Holy Spirit is not
an end-of-the-line experience. It is not the last stop in a
Christian's spiritual journey. It is really the first step, the
beginning of a whole new life in Christ.

After being filled with the Spirit, my prayer life was
energized, my witness for the Lord became bolder, my love
for God's Word and His people intensified, my attendance
at church became more consistent. Do not ask a person if he
or she has "prayed through" for the Holy Spirit. That term
suggests arriving at a terminal position with the Lord. We
will always have the desire for more of God. Being filled
with His Spirit is just the beginning.

Ye were sealed with that holy Spirit of promise,
Which is the earnest of our inheritance until the
redemption of the purchased possession....
Ephesians 1:13,14

Part Two

Here Paul refers to the Holy Spirit as the "earnest" of
our inheritance. This word translated **earnest** is the Greek
word *arrhabon (ar–hrab–ohn')*. It was the word used in
business transactions to indicate a deposit or a down
payment. In Biblical days, the earnest was a pledge of
property or money as security to insure full payment of a
loan or debt. Paul is telling us here that the Holy Spirit is
God's pledge to us of full provision of everything He has
promised us. In effect, it is:

1) *A guarantee of His daily blessings* — God did not send
His Holy Spirit to us only to withdraw Him later and leave
us to face life alone. The daily presence of the Spirit in our
hearts is a guarantee of daily guidance, provision and
blessings, as well as of future bliss.

2) *A first installment of future reward* — Jesus comes into
our hearts by the agency of the Holy Spirit. At the time of
our death, this same Jesus is personally waiting to greet us
and welcome us into heavenly splendor. (Acts 7:56.) This
reception is the second installment of God's salvation
pledge to us; the third is introduction into the royal court of
the Ruler of the Universe in Whose presence we will spend
eternity.

3) *Security deposit* — The Holy Spirit in our lives is a
deposit given to assure us of all the good things God has in
store for us. We Christians have so much to look forward to.
Receiving the Holy Spirit stimulates us to press on to
perfection and to all the better things He has promised.

For the earnest expectation of the creation eagerly
waits for the revealing of the sons of God.
Romans 8:19 NKJ

John referred to Satan as **that** *old* **serpent, the Devil** (Rev. 12:7). Jesus indicates that our enemy has been a liar and a murderer **from the beginning** (John 8:44.) Paul called his lies **profane and** *old* **wive's tales** (1 Tim. 4:7.) Peter spoke of the unregenerated world system as **the** *old* **world** (2 Pet. 2:5) and said the present solar system is **of** *old* (2 Pet. 3:5), emphasizing that they are both **reserved unto fire against the day of judgement** (2 Pet. 3:7.)

John spoke prophetically of a *new* **heaven and a** *new* **earth** whose capital will be the city of God — **the holy city,** *new* **Jerusalem** (Rev. 21:1,2). In this verse Paul speaks of how eagerly creation awaits the appearance of this new creation at the time of the Second Coming of Christ, the "earnest expectation" of which he calls "the blessed hope" of the Church. (Tit. 2:13.)

In the original Greek text, the word translated **earnest expectation** is *apokaradokia (ap–ok–ar–ok–ee'–ah)*. It is a compound word made up of three words: *apo*, "away from"; *kara*, "the head"; and *dokeo*, "intense anticipation." Thus, this word has two connotations: *abstraction* (turning the head away from any distracting influence), and *absorption* (looking with intensity, concentration, and anticipation). One translation of this verse says: "All creation is yearning" (another says, "on tiptoe") "to see the wonderful sight of the sons of God coming into their own." As Christians, our "own" is totally *new* and perfect creation in which we will enjoy total fulfillment and complete joy forever and ever! What a prospect!

**Your enemies...shall come out against
you one way and flee before you seven ways.
Deuteronomy 28:7 NKJ**

This is God's promise to us that the forces of our evil
adversary will be scattered before us and their opposition
turned into fearful flight. When the Bible states that our
enemies will flee in *seven* directions, it is using symbolic
language to indicate a rout so complete there is no hope of
recovery or regrouping.

Seven is the Biblical number of completion, perfection,
and termination. When wisdom is said to build seven
pillars (Prov. 9:1), the picture presented is of an edifice so
complete that nothing further could be added to it without
being redundant or unnecessary.

An enemy fleeing in seven directions is the result of
combining the believer's faith with God's power. When
man stands forth courageously to fight the good fight of
faith, God unleashes His ability on his behalf. The
combination is unbeatable because it represents
completion. The number of man is four. God's number is
three. Whenever man's faith is combined with God's
power, the enemy is always put on the run.

In Revelation 3:1, the Bible speaks of the seven spirits
of the Lord. Some scholars believe these are the same as the
seven eyes of Zechariah 3:8 and the seven lamps in
Revelation 4:5. The names of these spirits are listed in Isaiah
11:2. However, these are not seven different spirits of God,
only the sevenfold ministry of the one Holy Spirit. Our foes
may seem to come at us as a united front, but God has
promised that His sevenfold Spirit will send them retreating
in seven directions. What a promise of victory!

**I exhort first of all that supplications,
prayers, intercessions, and giving of thanks
be made for all men.
1 Timothy 2:1 NKJ**

In this verse Paul lists four kinds of prayer. Each word used is individually descriptive of one form of prayer:

Supplications: This word indicates petition for a specific object. It focuses on personal needs and freely acknowledges insufficiency to provide the solution. It is a good word to begin the list because its basis is humility in approaching God. An old song best captures the sense of this word: "It's me! It's me, oh Lord. Standing in the need of prayer."

Prayers: In the New Testament, this word is restricted to requests made of God. Whereas supplications are specific requests, prayers are more general. This term includes wishing, desiring, asking, and petitioning. Its significance is indicated by the saying, "More things are wrought by prayer than this world ever dreamed of."

Intercessions: This word describes the action of standing in the gap for another. Abraham interceded for Lot and Sodom. Jesus interceded for Jerusalem. At present He is interceding with the Father for all of us. The original Greek word means to have an audience with a dignitary — to meet with him, spend time in his presence, and then to make requests of him on behalf of another.

Thanksgiving: The giving of thanks should precede all our prayers. It should go on all during our prayer time. It should continue after our formal prayer has ended. True thanksgiving is a continuous expression of gratitude to God for His constant blessing on our lives!

**Wherefore gird up the loins of
your mind, be sober....
1 Peter 1:13**

Part One

In Biblical days in the orient, a man would normally wear a long flowing gown. This style of dress was appropriate when in a relaxed mood and position. However, if he had to move fast or engage in any strenuous activity such as manual labor, he would tie his robe around his waist with a belt for more freedom of movement.

Here Peter is telling us to do this same thing with our minds. One translator has rendered this phrase "brace up your minds." Another interprets it "have your minds ready for action." In Exodus 12:11 we read God's instruction to Israel about how they were to partake of the Passover meal: **"'And thus you shall eat it: with a belt on your waist, your sandals on your feet, and your staff in your hand....'"** NKJ. The children of Israel were told to eat in preparation for the march ahead.

We believers should be as ready to move fast and to endure long as those who prepared for battle, for labor or for a race. As one source puts it: "Christians must bring all loose thoughts and feelings under restraint. We need to brace all the powers of the thinking faculty in order to keep going on our pilgrimage towards heaven."

We believers are engaged in spiritual warfare. If we are to win the battle for the souls of men, we must first win the battle for our own minds. We can be capable of energetic mental action and unfettered practical intelligence. We can fortify our minds with the mind of Christ in Whom there is no fatigue, no fantasy, no overworked imagination. With our minds harnessed for the long and arduous trek which lies ahead. Let's get going!

Wherefore gird up the loins of your mind, be sober....
1 Peter 1:13

Part Two

In the original Greek text this word translated **sober** is *nepho (nay'–fo)*. It is usually interpreted as meaning "to abstain from alcoholic beverages." So this phrase could be translated *"stay* sober." *Nepho* also has a connotation of watchfulness. Just as sleep is the usual companion of drunkenness, so vigilance is one evidence of sobriety. To tell a person to stay sober is the same as telling him to remain wide awake and on the alert.

Christians need to preserve a healthy balance between physical, mental and spiritual activity. Just as it is possible to become drunk from overindulgence in what goes into the stomach, so it is also possible to become drunk from overindulgence in what is allowed into the mind and spirit. It is very easy to become intoxicated and carried away by the latest psychological, philosophical or theological fad, fashion, or craze.

I like one writer's version of this verse: "Brace up your minds, then keep cool." Another renders this last phrase: "Keep full mastery of your senses." A third defines sobriety as: "A complete clarity of mind and its resulting good judgement."

In day-to-day life I see a contrast between believers and non-believers—so many of whom seem frivolous, superficial, and shallow. Those caught up in the world system seem to be always giddy and partying. The Christian marches to a different drumbeat. He knows he is a soldier with a job to do. His joy is eternal; his song internal. His happiness comes from winning battles, not emptying bottles. Most of all he is wide awake and obedient to his marching orders: "Take the high ground!"

Know this, that in the last
days perilous times will come.
2 Timothy 3:1 NKJ

Sometimes it is easier to understand a word when we see how it is used elsewhere in scripture. This is the case with the word translated here as **perilous**. In the Greek it is *chalepos (khal–ep–os')* which has to do with the idea of reduced strength, difficulty, danger, stress, and hardship. The only other time *chalepos* is used in the New Testament is in describing the condition of the two Gadarean demoniacs. In Matthew 8:28 they are said to be **exceeding fierce**. Other translations render this phrase "violent," "dangerous," "furious," and "hard to deal with."

To be forewarned is to be forearmed. This verse actually tells us how to prepare for the last days. It is not a word meant to discourage or unnerve us, nor to give us the idea that we are going to be run over by a demonized world. On the contrary, the Bible deals with principles of practical, victorious Christian living.

Here Paul is simply saying that in the last days believers will have to face a *"chalepos"* time. The same spirit will be running amok in the world that was controlling the two Gadarean men. But the good news is that Jesus met those men and took authority over the evil within them. He cast out the violent and furious spirit and then went on with His ministry of peace and reconciliation.

We Christians are not told that we will never have to face demonic opposition. We are told to "get tough," to put on our spiritual armor, to fight the good fight of faith, and to win battles in the name of the Lord!

I sleep, but my heart is awake....
Song of Solomon 5:2 NKJ

Part One

This verse indicates a restless state. The spiritual man wants to stay awake and alert to the Lord's visitation, but the fleshly man wants to sleep.

There is a New Testament parallel in this verse in the parable of the ten virgins who had all grown weary waiting for the bridegroom to appear. (Matt. 25:1–13.) In their spirits they were in a state of anticipation and expectancy. But in the flesh, they were exhausted. They were waiting, yet sleeping at the same time.

Several factors contribute to the same state of drowsiness which grips the modern-day Christian Church: 1) the delay of the Second Coming causes some believers to grow weary and lose patience, 2) the increase of violence and ungodliness in the universe makes it easier to stay locked away in one's own little world, 3) a general disinterest in spiritual matters by the world makes it seem less and less worthwhile to continue to confront the increasing cynicism, pessimism, and unbelief, and 4) continuous opposition from demonic forces takes its toll on the human frame.

We are all subject to becoming fatigued and tempted to just give up the struggle and "take it easy." The antidote to this apathy is a fresh outpouring of the Holy Spirit. In the past, revivals were called "great awakenings." The Lord has the answer for us. He knows how to wake us up. The good news is we are not going to sleep through the war. God is sounding the trumpet, alerting His troops, calling out the garrison. We are waking up to our great calling and commission as soldiers of the cross. The spirit is winning over the flesh!

I sleep, but my heart is awake;
It is the voice of my beloved!
He knocks, saying,
"Open for me...."
Song of Solomon 5:2 NKJ

Part Two

This verse is good news. The voice of the beloved who knocks is that of Christ, Who neither slumbers nor sleeps. He is waking up His drowsy, indolent Church. His tender language to the sleeping Church of Laodicea was: **"Behold, I stand at the door and knock...."** (Rev. 3:20 NKJ). Although His disciples fell asleep in the Garden of Gethsemane, Jesus did not sleep. He was so intensely engaged in prayer that He sweat great drops of blood. It was for them, the ones who slept, that He was awake and interceding.

I once went through a really dry period in my life. I tried reading the Bible, but was too apathetic to concentrate on what I was reading. I tried praying, but soon became drowsy and could not stay awake. I went to church, but my mind was on other things. I was there physically, but not mentally or spiritually. In relationships, I made all the right sounds and gestures, but my spiritual condition was one of numbness, dullness, and stupor.

God graciously woke me from my lethargic condition. He did not censure me, reprove me, or treat me harshly. Rather, He lovingly touched the strings of my heart and tuned it to respond to His love. The promise of the Lord is that nothing will be able to separate us from His love. (Rom. 8:39.) In Hebrews 7:25 we read that Jesus ever lives to make intercession for us. Jesus is praying for us and our spiritual condition right now! What a comforting thought!

**In the year that King Uzziah died,
I saw the Lord sitting on a throne....
Isaiah 6:1 NKJ**

In the sixth chapter of Isaiah, we see that the prophet received three distinct visions. As a result, his whole perspective and purpose was dramatically changed:

Vision One: Isaiah saw *the Lord.* (v.1.) Life begins with a look. Looking precedes action. We look and see. Then we respond and go. Just as Isaiah saw the Lord, we, too, can look to Calvary and see Jesus as our substitute.

A lady expressed disinterest in a best-selling book. Later she met and married the author. She reread the book, enjoyed it, and told her best friend, "It means so much more to me, knowing the author." Christianity allows us to meet the Author of Life. Isaiah saw the Lord and it gave him a new beginning, a whole reason for being.

Vision Two: Isaiah saw *himself.* **"Woe is me,"** he exclaimed, **"for I am undone!"** (v.5). God is so pure, so holy, so clean, and so good, that when we catch the slightest glimpse of His holiness, by contrast, we seem terribly defective. This happened to Job. (Job 42:5,6.) He had heard about the Lord, but when he met Him face to face, he could not stand himself.

Vision Three: Isaiah saw a *needy world.* **"Whom shall I send, and who will go for Us?"** (v. 8a) asked the Lord. Isaiah responds by saying, **"Here am I! Send me."** (v. 8b).

Isaiah had three visions. He saw the Lord in His majesty, himself in his misery, and the world in its malady. Then he saw the answer: ministry.

Love not the world, neither the
things that are in the world....
1 John 2:15

THREE "D'S" AND THREE LOVES

Demas, Diotrephes, and Demetrius each had a love,
but each loved a different thing.

DEMAS: ...**Demas has forsaken me, and has departed
for Thessalonica....** (2 Tim. 4:9,10 NKJ). Paul was facing trial
in Rome. Realizing it was dangerous to be connected with
one who was certain to be condemned by Nero, Demas
forsook Paul. His love of money and desire for self-
preservation led Demas to abandon the hardships and
dangers of the life of an apostle. In the next century,
Chrysostom wrote of Demas: "He chose to live in luxury at
home." Demas loved *the world.*

DIOTREPHES: **I wrote to the church, but Diotrephes,
who loves to have the preeminence among them, does not
receive us** (3 John 9 NKJ). Demas is gone, but Diotrephes is
still in the Church. He is ambitious, aggressive, and self-
assertive. He is a brother, but his primary motivation is not
love of the brethren, but his ego-drive. Diotrephes loved *the
preeminence.*

DEMETRIUS: **Demetrius has a good testimony from
all and from the truth itself....**(3 John 12 NKJ). Some Bible
scholars believe that this Demetrius was the silversmith in
Acts 19:24 whose business was threatened by Paul's
preaching of the gospel. Upon his conversion, Demetrius
had great credibility: 1) with the Christian community, 2) of
the truth itself, and 3) with John. Demetrius loved *the truth.*

Three loves: the world, the preeminence, and the truth.
Take your choice!

The chiefest among ten thousand.
Song of Solomon 5:10

Part One

How could anyone ever exhaust the list of titles given to Jesus Christ? It is so easy to use words from the Bible that describe Him.

One time I was struck with an affliction that had all the earmarks of polio. Five symptoms surfaced in me calling for immediate action. My wife called the hospital to find out how to get me into a portable iron lung. At the same time Jesus appeared to me for a brief moment. He looked right at me, and with an understanding and knowing glance transmitted healing virtue to me. I was immediately set free from whatever it was that had struck me down.

That appearance of Jesus has given me a great sense of respect, appreciation, and admiration for Him. As a man, I unashamedly want to tell the whole world that I love my Lord with all my heart, soul, mind, and strength. Someone has enumerated from the Bible 365 names that can be used to describe Jesus (rock, door, sword, shepherd, etc.). This means that every single day of the year we can employ a new name to recall the beauty, the greatness, the majestic splendor of the Son of man.

Nowhere in scripture are we instructed to love the Lord with any kind of emotion or feeling. We are commanded to love Him with *agape* love — the kind of selfless love that is not based on emotion or sentiment. Those who love the Lord can choose to do so by an act of the will.

No one ever needs to feel awkward or uncomfortable worshipping, praising, and loving Jesus — the chiefest among ten thousand!

The chiefest among ten thousand.
Song of Solomon 5:10

Part Two

The root definition of this word **chiefest** gives us a three-dimensional view of Jesus Christ not evident from its surface usage. In the original Hebrew version of this text, the word is *dagal* (*daw–gal'*). One of the definitions is "a standard bearer" or "one who sets up an ensign or banner." In military skirmishes when the battle was often spread out over acres of terrain, a standard would be lifted up as a rallying point for the scattered troops who would converge on it.

The fragmented Church of Jesus Christ is being united by the Head of the Church Himself. It is He Who is the standard bearer. True worshippers are being drawn by the Spirit of God to rally around the person of Jesus Christ. Doctrines have kept us divided. Denominations, sects, and splinter groups have fragmented the Body of Christ. Modes of water baptism have caused dissension and separation.

All these things that have kept us apart in the past are now being replaced by the new thing the Lord is doing in these last days. By His Spirit He is rallying His people around His Son. As all true worshippers gather to Him, we will automatically be drawn closer to each other.

The Lord's banner over us is love. (Song of Sol. 2:4.) In a world filled with hate, it is easy to respond to real love. Even if people have been hurt and offended by negative church experiences, the love of Christ can cause them to surrender to Him — the chiefest among ten thousand, the standard bearer. He draws us to Himself with cords of love. (Hos. 11:4.) Don't resist, respond!

The chiefest among ten thousand.
Song of Solomon 5:10

Part Three

The old gospel song, "The Lily of the Valley," refers to Jesus as "the fairest of ten thousand to my soul." This verse is the source of that expression.

There are other definitions of the Hebrew word *dagal* (*daw–gal'*) we want to consider. They show us another side of our precious Lord. Besides its relation to a banner or standard, *dagal* is also defined as "conspicuous and distinguished." Jesus always stood out in a crowd. Even in His humanity, He always attracted people to Himself. Mark tells us that **...the common people heard him gladly** (Mark 12:37). The needy sought Him out eagerly. Multitudes followed Him to hear His life-bringing words. As "chiefest (*dagal*) among ten thousand," Jesus was quite conspicuous and distinguished.

The New International Version translates this phrase **outstanding among ten thousand.** Jesus stands out visibly as the very heart and center of our worship. Reading other translations gives us an even better picture of Him Who is "conspicuous above a myriad," "choicest," "distinguished," and "the pick of ten thousand." It is easy to worship the One Who leads us so conspicuously and so capably.

Dagal also carries the idea of exulting or glorifying, as in Psalm 20:5: **We will rejoice in thy salvation, and in the name of our God we will set up our banners** (*dagal*). Our flags are flying with praise to our Lord — the chiefest, our standard bearer. When He raises His banner of love as our rallying point, we will gather together joyful and triumphant. The Captain of our salvation is leading us on to final victory!

**Looking for that blessed hope, and
the glorious appearing of the great
God and our Saviour Jesus Christ.
Titus 2:13**

For nearly 2000 years now the Church of Jesus Christ
has waited for the return of her Lord. Since Jesus has
promised to come back again, and since we are drawing
closer to that time, what kind of plans should we be
making? Are we to invest in buying property and building
new churches if Jesus is coming so soon? These are valid
questions that must be dealt with scripturally.

Jesus did not say when He would return. When He told
His disciples, ...**Occupy till I come** (Luke 19:13), He was
putting an emphasis on activity with expectancy. Can you
imagine how non-aggressive the Christian Church would
have been if Jesus had said, "I am going away, but I will
return in 2000 A.D."?

The blessed hope has actually been the motivator for
all Church growth and expansion. It keeps all believers on
the stretch for the Lord. It keeps us active, alert, and awake.
It prevents apathy, drowsiness, lukewarmness and
indifference. The blessed hope keeps our interests up. We
can sing of His glorious return, "What if it were today?"

In 1922 when Angelus Temple was being built by the
followers of Aimee Semple McPherson, someone told
them, "Don't invest in concrete; it's too expensive. Since
Jesus is coming so soon, you could save money by building
a wooden tabernacle." The advice was disregarded and a
nice sturdy concrete temple was erected that is still
functional today, over 60 years later.

Someone has said: "*Live* as though Jesus is coming any
moment, but *plan* as though you have 100 years!"

I will make the place of My feet glorious.
Isaiah 60:13 NKJ

I had been fasting and praying for a miracle ministry of signs and wonders. My request was for the life and ministry of Jesus to be duplicated in me. After the fast was over, a godly person gave me this encouraging word: "Jesus is going to manifest Himself to you real soon. It will be according to His timetable and on His terms."

Shortly afterwards, I was leading in worship when the Lord spoke to me and said, "Have the people come down to the front of the church and kneel in a state of expectant waiting."

I positioned myself at the altar between two elderly sisters who had a great prayer life. I was young at the time and felt that if I were near them, some of their saintly qualities might rub off on me.

Suddenly I had a vision of Jesus coming down in our midst. The thing I noticed most about Him was His feet. It looked as though they were made of dazzling fine brass, highly refined. (Rev. 1:15). The Lord spoke to me and gave me this verse from Isaiah. Then He gave me this word of admonition:

"Men seek for earthly honors, worldly gain, promotion, advancement, and high position. Their quest is to 'make it to the top.' I am looking for people who will go the other way and sit at My feet as Mary did. I am looking for those who are willing to be lowly that I might be exalted, empty of self that I might fill them, and foolish in the eyes of the world that I might be their wisdom. *I will make the place of My feet glorious.* Before I ascended, I first descended. You are to do the same!"

Looking unto Jesus, the author
and finisher of our faith....
Hebrews 12:2 NKJ

The word translated **looking** in this verse is very interesting. In the original Greek text it is *aphorao* (*af–or–ah'–o*) and has to do with attentive and concentrated vision. One translation of this phrase reads: "...simply fixing your gaze upon Jesus...." Another renders it: "...having eyes for no one but Jesus...."

The use of *aphorao* by the writer of Hebrews emphasizes that we Christians are to turn our attention away from all the distractions of this world and to focus our eyes on the most important thing in our life. This indicates more than loyalty. More than respect. More than devotion. It means looking to our sole source of supply because nothing else on earth is more deserving of our full attention.

An Olympic runner keeps his eyes glued on the finish line. A soldier in the field constantly looks to his commanding officer for direction. A musician keeps his attention trained on the conductor. A motorist carefully watches the gestures of the traffic policeman. Two lovers may be in a crowd of people, but they only have eyes for each other.

This verse tells us that we believers are to concentrate our gaze upon the Lord. We are to look unto Him as the only One Who can direct our lives. He is our fulfillment, our source of satisfaction. He leads us, directs us, and — most of all — sees us through every situation of life. He is the author and finisher of our faith. He is with us from start to finish.

In Your presence is fullness of joy....
Psalm 16:11 NKJ

The Hebrew word translated **presence** in this verse is *paneh* (*paw–neh'*) which has several interesting meanings. One of these is "to turn one's face in a certain direction." The image is that determination expressed in Luke 9:53 in which Jesus is said to have had His face set to go to Jerusalem.

"One of my joys," David is saying to his God, "is knowing that You are facing me. You have set Your sights on my victory and triumph. As I follow You and go Your way, I am assured that my life will be a happy and successful one. You lead and I will joyfully follow."

Another meaning of *paneh* is "to turn *from* something *to* something." The Lord has promised that if we will repent (turn from our sins) and return (turn) to Him, He will remove our sins and remember them against us no more. Like Paul, we can then forget those things which are behind and press on toward those which lie ahead. (Phil. 3:13.) It is a comforting thought to know that God's face is turned away from our past sins and turned toward our future life and triumph. That kind of knowledge produces joy.

Another meaning of *paneh* is "personal presence." In Exodus 33:14 the Lord states, **"My Presence will go with you, and I will give you rest"** (NKJ). Bible grammarians such as Gesenius render this phrase, "I Myself, I in person, My person, will go with you." This is another reason for full joy: our God is with us!

Finally, *paneh* means "to look upon with personal approval or with favorable regard." No longer alienated, we can now have God's presence, His look of acceptance. We can all be happy knowing that God is pleased with us.

Blessed is the man who listens to me,
Watching daily at my gates,
Waiting at the posts of my doors.
Proverbs 8:34 NKJ

Life is a learning process. Every day that goes by can add enrichment to it. One of the requisites for the adding of spiritual knowledge is a teachable spirit. This verse encourages that kind of attitude.

Here wisdom is speaking to us. It is to our best advantage to be alert to hear what she has to say and to be receptive to her message. We can find happiness by listening to wisdom's pronouncements. We can also be blessed by being constantly on the lookout, watching daily for her. This verse suggests an attentiveness that comes from total concentration on wisdom and her words.

In His multi-faceted wisdom (Eph. 3:10), God has so many things to reveal, unveil and unfold to those who wait upon Him faithfully and attentively. It is as we seek Him, serve Him, and wait upon Him in daily prayer and meditation that He discloses to us ever new facets and perspectives of His limitless wisdom and knowledge.

Eternity will be a marvel to us. In the other world to which we are bound, you and I will be witnesses to a continuous display of God's attributes, purposes and nature. Instead of waiting till we all get to heaven to behold the majestic greatness of our God, we are invited to begin now. A quest for knowledge is all we need to get started. A teachable spirit will keep us going. A daily discipline of Bible reading and prayer communication sets us right at the portals of wisdom. All this takes time, but the advantages of receiving God's wisdom makes it all well worth the sacrifice.

The lines have fallen to me in pleasant places;
Yes, I have a good inheritance.
Psalm 16:6 NKJ

How many truly contented people do you know? How many of your friends or acquaintances seem to be satisfied with their lot in life? Listen to the man David as he begins to write the Sixteenth Psalm:

The lines have fallen to me in pleasant places... This statement has all the indications of an expression of great contentment. It evokes an image of surveying boundary lines and measuring off a person's inheritance. David seems to be saying that his allotted territory is a source of satisfaction to him.

This poem is called a *michtam* psalm, a title given to six of the psalms of David. In Hebrew the word *michtam* has to do with etching, engraving, and inscribing. Having a familiarity with gold and etching, Bible scholars saw this as a "golden text." The *King James Version* labels it "a michtam of David." James Moffatt describes it as "a golden ode of David." This could mean that this psalm needs to be etched in the mind and recorded there as a message worth remembering.

...Yes, I have a good inheritance. "Life has been good to me," David seems to be saying. "My father left me this property and I am quite contented with it. The view is good. The brooks are clean and cool, and the meadows are green and lush. The land is well situated. My heritage is truly pleasing, indeed!"

Can you say this about your heritage — your home, job, neighborhood, church, town, station in life? David could! So can we, when our heart is at peace with God.

In Your presence is fullness of joy....
Psalm 16:11 NKJ

This verse is a continuation of yesterday's lesson in which we considered David's record of his enjoyment and satisfaction with his allotted inheritance. Now in this passage he indicates the source of happiness. Note that it is *not* a product of:

1) *Environmental location:* Happiness does not depend upon physical surroundings. I have met some people who are capable of being happy no matter where they are. They take their happiness with them wherever they go. If they were to be transported to the North Pole, and left there all alone with no one around for a thousand miles in any direction, they could still be happy. On the other hand, there are those who cannot be happy no matter where they are.

2) *Wealth and riches:* Neither is happiness found in material possessions. I know people who are quite happy without wealth. I also know people who are fabulously rich, and totally miserable.

Happiness is a state of being which has nothing to do with age, education, location, accumulation, possessions, honors, titles, pedigrees, gender, height, color, or religious affiliation.

David tells us the source of all true happiness — the presence of God. The Hebrew word translated **presence** here is *paniym (paw–neem')*. It is derived from the word *paneh (paw–neh')* referring to the face. Being in the presence of God is the same as basking in the smile of His acceptance and approval. If you and I could see the face of our Lord smiling at us, we would be very happy indeed — regardless of our location or circumstance.

**He has delivered us from the power of darkness and
translated us into the kingdom of the Son of His love.**
Colossians 1:13 NKJ

In the Greek, this word **translated** is *methistemi*
(*meth–is'– tay–mee*) meaning "to transpose, transfer, remove
from one place to another." Our conversion literally lifted
us out of the quicksand of sin and placed us on the solid
rock of truth.

One of the most impressive features of this translation
from darkness to light is the suddenness of it all. I remember
a testimony I heard in a Christian drug recovery unit. The
young man was 26 years old. For 13 of those years, or half
his life, he had been a heroin addict. Now he was an
outstanding leader in the drug program. He was giving his
testimony to a narcotics agent who seemingly could not
comprehend the translation from addiction to deliverance.
The officer asked him, "How long did all this take?" The
answer came back, "It only took about two minutes. When
Jesus came in, the drugs went out."

We cannot argue a person into change. We cannot nag,
harangue, pressure, or even manipulate anybody into a
transformation of his whole life. The good news is that
Jesus is still translating thousands of lives every day. Every
time a new convert comes into the kingdom of God, a
genuine translation takes place.

Another word for *translate* is *transpose*. In music to
transpose is "to change to another key." Before salvation we
were in a minor key and our life's song was a sad one. Now
we are in a major key and our song is one of joy. The
transposing of our life gives us a different tune to sing! The
Bible calls it a new song! (Rev. 5:9.)

> So I will restore to you the years
> that the swarming locust has eaten,
> The crawling locust,
> The consuming locust,
> And the chewing locust....
> Joel 2:25 NKJ

Part One

The word *restore* is vital to our spiritual walk. It refers to more than bringing something back that is missing or has been taken away. When the Lord speaks of restoration He means bringing back the missing or lost ingredients so that a person can complete and finalize the very things he started out to do in life.

Our original vision can only be realized when all the spiritual components of our original call are brought back together. That is why restoration is so important to us. In order for God's will to be done on earth as it is in heaven, the end-time Church of Jesus Christ must have restored to it all the pristine qualities of the first-century Church.

Sometimes some believers lose things in the spiritual journey and in the conflict with the powers of darkness. In this verse, the Lord promises to restore whatever has been consumed.

The natural world has no such program for rejuvenation, restoration, and renewed vision and strength. It is so absorbed with the aging process that restoration does not fit in with its way of thinking.

In our next lesson we will examine some of the things God has promised to restore to His people. Praise the Lord that we are coming back to full strength. Everything consumed by time, trial, and tribulation is being restored to us!

So I will restore to you the years....
Joel 2:25 NKJ

Part Two

In our last lesson we defined the word *restore* as "bringing back that which had been missing in order to complete an original purpose and calling." Our God promises us restoration in many areas of our lives:

1) *Restored physical soundness* (Jer. 30:17.): We are told by doctors that some ailments leave people with no hope of recovery. This word from the Lord says that lost health can be regained.

2) *Restored happiness* (Ps. 51:12.): Upon confession of wrongdoing and receipt of God's forgiveness, joy returns to the soul. If you have lost your joy, search your heart to see if there is something you need to confess and repent of.

3) *Restored paths* (Is. 58:12.): During times of spiritual declension, the path of service is not always easily discerned. When revival comes, the path leading home to the Father's house is always clear.

4) *Restored life* (Ruth 4:15.): Here is a promise of rejuvenation despite the aging process. The Lord promises us that our youth shall be renewed like the eagle's. (Ps. 103:5.)

We begin our journey of faith with a fresh vision, a great deal of courage, a burning desire, and a devoted willingness to go the distance. As time passes, a devourer comes along to consume these blessings of God. If we do not know the principles of spiritual warfare, we may give ground and lose some of these precious gifts. This verse is a promise of compensation and reward. Whatever has been lost is going to be restored — to our church, our family, and our individual lives!

Lift up your hands in the sanctuary, And bless the Lord.
Psalm 134:2 NKJ

Part One

Photographers claim that hands are the hardest things to deal with when posing people for pictures. It seems that no one knows quite what to do with them once they become conscious of them.

The photographer taking the family portrait of Abraham Lincoln and his household is reported to have spent close to an hour arranging and rearranging the president's hands.

If you seem nervous and ill-at-ease in a crowd of people or in front of an audience, invariably your hands will register your nervousness. I believe some of the awkwardness we have with our hands is due to a lack of knowledge. We can discover from the Word of God how our hands can be used for spiritual blessing.

Our hands were not given to us merely to improve our manual dexterity; nor are they simply useless appendages to hang awkwardly at our side like two ham hocks. They were designed by our Creator to be instruments of worship and channels of blessing; they are divinely chosen means for extending the ministry of Jesus Christ.

The psalmist tells us to lift up our hands in the sanctuary and bless the Lord. Raised hands can actually be a means of blessing our heavenly Father. We usually think of blessing the Lord as part of our vocal expression. We worship Him with praise and thanksgiving. But we can also worship Him with our uplifted hands. Job says our hands are clean from sin. (Job 17:9.) The Apostle Paul exhorts us to lift up holy hands. (1 Tim. 2:8). With our hearts we adore the Lord, and with our hands we bless the Lord.

Lift up your hands in the sanctuary, And bless the Lord.
Psalm 134:2 NKJ

Part Two

Yesterday we saw how the hands can be used as instruments of worship. Today we will point out from scriptures other uses of the hands for spiritual ministry:

1) *Prayer* (Job 11:13.): Stretch out your hand toward God. This is a prayer posture engaging the hands.

2) *Blessing Children* (Gen. 48:13; Matt. 19:13-15.): Both Jacob and Jesus reached out their hands to bless children. We can impart something special to youngsters by this kind of touch.

3) *Intercession* (Lam. 3:41.): As intercessors we can lift up our hands and stand in the gap for God's intervention in the lives of others.

4) *Healing* (Mark 16:15-17.): The power of God in us who believe is greater than any sickness or disease. By the laying on of our hands in accordance with the Lord's command, this greater force is released to remove the ailment from the body of the sick and afflicted.

5) *Miracles* (Acts 5:12; Acts 19:11): These verses tell us that signs, wonders and special miracles were done by the hands of the apostles. We have the same apostolic power residing in us that was in them. We are not claiming apostolic succession, but apostolic success.

6) *Holy Spirit Baptism* (Acts 8:17.): One translation of this verse reads: "They laid hands on them one by one, and one by one they received the Holy Spirit." Your hands can be used to bless seekers of this experience.

Don't let your hands be idle or awkward. Put them to work in the Lord's service.

Seek the Lord while He may be found,
Call upon Him while He is near.
Isaiah 55:6 NKJ

The key words in this verse are **seek**, **found**, and **near**. Let's consider each of them separately:

Seek: In Hebrew this is an interesting word, one which expresses special intensity. It literally means "to beat a path or to go over an area so often as to rub or wear away a recognizable path." It carries with it the idea of inquiry, search and request. To seek is to tread a path as a pursuit. Seeking the Lord can — and should — become a life-long endeavor.

Found: This word in Hebrew is the word for discover or locate. It is one thing to search for gold. Many people are doing that. It is quite another thing to find gold. This verse tells us to search for the Lord while He may be located, discovered, found. This word also implies attainment or "meeting." Any effort put forth to "meet" the Lord will be well rewarded with success.

Near: This word in Hebrew means "akin to, nearby or in the neighborhood." We are urged by the prophet to call upon the Lord while He is in our vicinity. There are times and seasons in which the Lord's presence is especially felt. That is the moment when we are encouraged to open up to Him. Call upon Him while He is that close to us.

This word is also defined as "dignity." We are made aware of our own dignity by God's presence in our life. It also means "intimate." God's nearness to us makes it possible for us to have a "close encounter" with Him.

My beloved is white and ruddy....
Song of Solomon 5:10 NKJ

The word **white** in this verse has to do with radiance like clear light. It is an allusion to rays of morning sunshine, scattering the somber effects of the night.

White is also a symbol of purity. Jesus is the **lamb without blemish and without spot** (1 Pet. 1:19 NKJ). When Daniel saw Him as the ancient of days, **His garment was white as snow, and the hair of His head like the pure wool** (Dan. 7:9). When John saw Him, **His head and His hairs were white like wool, as white as snow** (Rev. 1:14). When the disciples saw Him on the Mount of Transfiguration, **His face did shine as the sun, and His raiment was white as the light** (Matt. 17:2).

No one was ever pure and white like Jesus. The color white as applied to our Lord is not an indication of race or nationality, it is a reference to the glorious radiance and dazzling splendor that caused Malachi to call Him **the *Sun* of righteousness** (Mal. 4:2).

Ruddy is the word used to describe the blood of Jesus. It reminds us of the sacrificial death of our precious Savior, the **lamb slain from the foundation of the world** (Rev. 13:8). In eternity, in the midst of the throne, He is still seen as a **Lamb as it had been slain** (Rev. 5:6). In days coming, He shall appear clothed **with a vesture dipped in blood** (Rev. 19:13). Isaiah says of him: **...red is thine apparel, and thy garments like him that treadeth the winefat** (Is. 63:2).

The expression **white and ruddy** portrays radiant splendor clothed in blood-dyed garments, future glory wrapped in past remembrance of His crucifixion.

I awoke, for the Lord sustained me.
Psalm 3:5 NKJ

There are many things that can keep a person from sleeping soundly. Guilt, fear, a troubled conscience, improper eating habits, even anxiety about the economy can make sleep impossible. Spiritual burdens and calls to intercede for others can awake the sleeper and remove his drowsiness from him.

Here the psalmist rejoices in the gift of sleep. His conscience was not bothering him. He had nothing on his mind that would rob him of peaceful slumber. The sleep he speaks of is God's gift of re-creation and recuperation to His children to allow their bodies the opportunity to rebuild and restore themselves after a normal day's work.

The key word in this verse for all of us is **sustained**. It is a translation of the Hebrew word *camak* (*saw–mak'*) which refers to the act of supporting, upholding or undergirding. We learned this word when we studied Isaiah 26:3 which could be paraphrased: "You will keep that one in perfect peace, who has his mind stayed (*camak*) on You (or inclined in Your direction)."

This verse also suggests the idea of liberal provision for needs. **He gives His beloved sleep** and **He gives to His beloved in their sleep** are both valid translations of Psalm 127:2. David could be saying, "I lay down and slept soundly; then I awoke to find that the Lord had taken good care of me." When you know you are in good hands — that the Lord is supporting, upholding, and undergirding you — then you will not be sleeplessly tossing and turning all night because of fear and anxiety.

For You, O Lord, will bless the righteous.
With favor You will surround him as with a shield.
Psalm 5:12 NKJ

Favor is the word that speaks to us in this verse. We meet the combined promise of blessing and favor in Deuteronomy 33:23 in which God assures one of the tribes of Israel that they will be satisfied with favor and full of the blessing of the Lord. Here in this verse from Psalms, the order is reversed. The psalmist says that the righteous will be blessed by the Lord and shielded with favor.

Sometimes we feel we know what a word means until we examine it a bit closer. All my life I had an instinctive feel for the word *favor*. It is a word we like to use. It fits into our prayer vocabulary nicely and slips easily into our speech. With all the linguistic tools available to us today, it is possible to expand the possibilities of this word and give it real depth and dimension.

In this Old Testament verse, the Hebrew word translated **favor** is *ratson (raw–tsone')*. It refers to acceptance, good pleasure, delight, approval, satisfaction. To have God's favor is to bask in the sunshine of His smile of approval. It means having the Lord single you out for special attention: "This is My beloved son (or daughter) in whom I am well pleased!" (Matt. 3:17.) Having God's favor is having His goodwill and being in a position to receive His benefits.

Three translations consulted read: "You protect him with Your shield of love," "You surround him with the shield of Your good will," and "You do throw Your loving-kindness about him like a shield." We need to pray for favor from God. It is worth asking for.

And so find favor and high esteem
in the sight of God and man.
Proverbs 3:4 NKJ

Coming from a legalistic church background, I can well remember the "either-or" decision that was put to us as believers. The idea seemed to be: "If God loves you, man will hate you. If man loves you, God will hate you." That is a tough choice for a teenage boy to have to make. Especially if that teenager is struggling with self-acceptance, as I was.

There are four verses that tell us we can win God's favor and man's goodwill simultaneously. They are: 1 Samuel 2:26, Proverbs 3:4, Luke 2:52, and Romans 14:18. John Calvin claimed a principle could be established as doctrine if three verses could be found to agree with it. With four verses in agreement that we can have favor with God and man, we are one over the required minimal limit for doctrinal substantiation.

The Hebrew word translated **favor** in this verse is *chen* (*khane*). It refers to a graciousness that will bend or stoop down to grant a kindness or show favor to anyone who petitions for help. God favors us by granting our petitions. Every time He answers a prayer for us, He shows us favor.

Having favor with men means they will trust us when by nature they usually trust no one. It means they will open up to us when by inclination they seldom confide in anybody. It means they will believe in us even though they find it almost impossible to have confidence in any other human being.

Favor with God and man means having God's approval *and* man's trust. That is a blessing to be desired!

**Behold how good and how pleasant it is
For brethren to dwell together in unity!
Psalm 133:1 NKJ**

Have you ever wondered about Jesus' prayer for unity: **...that they all may be one....even as we are one** (John 17:21,22)? Have you ever questioned how this unification could ever be realized? What is it going to take to see unity come to the fragmented and divided Body of Christ?

The good news is: it is going to happen! Every time we pray the Lord's Prayer, we speed the day of its fulfillment. "Thy kingdom come. Thy will be done in earth, as it is in heaven" is a request that is sure to be granted. Jesus never prayed a prayer that was not answered.

Some people feel it will take global persecution to unify the Church. "Just put the saints before a firing squad," they say, "and they will settle their differences in a hurry." Some even point out how persecution in Communist countries is bringing the saints together.

I feel God would get more glory from a unity based on internal love than one based on external coercion. We seem to be saying, "Lord, You can't unify us with the message of love and forgiveness, You'll have to do it with the threat of extermination." I don't really believe God's grace, mercy, and love are exalted by a unity which comes only through martyrdom.

One translation of this verse reads: "What a wonderful thing it is when brothers live together in harmony." Remember: the closer we get to the Lord, the closer we get to each other! Our Lord prayed that we would be one. **"...has He said, and will He not do it? Or has He spoken, and will He not make it good?"** (Num. 23:19 NKJ). Unity is coming!

**"Now I will rise," says the Lord;
"Now I will be exalted,
Now I will lift Myself up."
Isaiah 33:10 NKJ**

This is a positive verse in the midst of a negative setting.

Because of treachery and moral decay, the spiritual condition of the nation of Israel at this time was at a low ebb. In the midst of hypocrisy and double standards, the prophet requests the Lord to intervene. In verse 2, he asks the Lord to be gracious. In verse 3, he describes what will happen to the nations when the Lord lifts Himself up. In verse 5, he expresses hope by declaring that the Lord is exalted, listing all the benefits that go with His exalted state.

In response to Isaiah's confession of faith, the Lord answers: "I am everything you say I am and more. *Now* I will rise. *Now* I will be exalted. *Now* I will lift Myself up."

The key to victory is to magnify the Lord as Isaiah did. We cannot make the Lord any larger than He already is by our words. He already fills all of heaven and earth. (Jer. 23:24.) How can He be made any greater than omnipresent? We can't "increase" God by our words, but we can "decrease" Him.

When we magnify our situation and our problems, we minimize the Lord and His ability to help us. When we magnify the Lord with our praise, we actually minimize our circumstances. The key to our personal triumph is to recognize and declare that the Lord is bigger than any problem we are facing. We do this by praising Him, worshipping Him, and quoting His promises.

> We have been made a spectacle to the world,
> both to angels and to men.
> 1 Corinthians 4:9 NKJ

Paul's use of the word **spectacle** in this verse has a special message to all of us. In the original Greek text it is *theatron* (*theh'–at–ron*) from which we derive our English words *theater* and *theatrics*. Grammarians define *theatron* as "a place for public show" or "a general audience-room." One writer defined it as "the place where a man is exhibited and gazed at."

In his play, *As You Like It*, William Shakespeare has one of his characters speak these lines: "All the world's a stage, and all the men and women merely players: They have their exits and their entrances; and one man in his time plays many parts."

Paul states that there are three audiences to this universal drama called life: 1) the angels, 2) the unbelieving world, and 3) the Christian Church. (Eph. 3:10.) All three groups are watching as we believers play our role. Each audience judges our performance by its own set of criteria.

The ancient dramatists only had two types of plays from which to choose: comedy or tragedy. As Christians, we have a third type: godly fear and holy living. The world may want to categorize our performance as comedic relief or personal tragedy, but the Lord has called us to set an example of normality in an abnormal world. We are to be sober in an intoxicated society, pure in a world of sin and degradation. We are the *theatron*, the spectacle, living epistles. Our performance speaks louder than our script. We preach more with our lives than we do with our lips. May our actions speak well of us and our Lord!

Give, and it shall be given unto you; good measure, pressed down, and shaken together, and running over, shall men give into your bosom....
Luke 6:38

The story is told about Widow Brown who was praying for bread. Her next-door neighbor was an atheist named Thomas Green. Mr. Green heard the good widow praying and decided to play a trick on her. After buying two loaves of bread at the store, he climbed up on her house and dropped the bread down the chimney.

When she saw the bread, Widow Brown immediately began to thank the Lord for answering her prayer. Irritated, Mr. Green called down the chimney: "Widow Brown, this is your neighbor, Tom Green. Jesus didn't send you that bread, I did. I did it just to prove to you that there is no God." The widow's response was, "Jesus, I want to thank You for the bread...even if the devil himself had to bring it!"

One of the more interesting aspects of this verse from Luke is the absence in the original Greek of the word **men**. Instead of saying, "...shall *men* given into your bosom," the original text simply reads, "...shall give into your bosom." The *New King James Version* reflects this fact when it renders this phrase, **...will be put into your bosom**.

This reading takes the lid off the Lord and allows Him to meet our need in any one of an endless variety of ways. To confine the source of our receiving to men is too restrictive. Let's let God meet our need as He wills in His infinite wisdom and out of His unlimited supply.

Another translation distills the essence of this verse: "You give to men, and God will give to you."

> **Until I went into the sanctuary of God,**
> **Then I understood their end.**
> **Psalm 73:17** NKJ

This verse is an encouragement to attend the house of worship in order to receive answers about life. David had the same questions about good and evil that we do. In Psalm 73 he exposes his pondering thoughts and thus provides us insight into the truth of life and death.

In this psalm, David questions God about why sinners seem to prosper while the righteous are put to severe tests. He admits to having been envious of the boastful when he saw their prosperity as compared with his personal problems. (vv. 3,14.) In verse 13 he reveals his self-pity, wondering if he had made a mistake by following the Lord.

Reasoning carnally, David makes a foolish comparison between the ungodly and the righteous: "They have everything going for them, and we have everything going against us. Are we on the wrong side or the wrong team?"

It is at this point that he goes into the sanctuary. As he views the holy place in which children are dedicated to the Lord, couples are united in marriage, funerals and eulogies are conducted, truth is proclaimed, righteousness explained, holiness displayed, God magnified, His name praised, and His presence manifested, life and death come into proper focus for the psalmist.

In the house of God, David discovers the link between this world and the next. Here he gets the picture of the true believer whose destiny is eternal reward and the non-believer whose future prospect is only eternal condemnation and misery. In the sanctuary we learn so much about life that cannot be learned anywhere else.

They shall come back from the land of the enemy....
...your children shall come back to their own border.
Jeremiah 31:16,17 NKJ

One of the most encouraging words from the Lord we have been hearing throughout the length and breadth of this land is: "All the children are coming home; those who have been away in the land of the enemy are going to return to their own border." It is hard to describe the gladness, joy, and peace this God-breathed message of assurance brings to distraught parents.

When the ark was finally all in readiness, just before the great flood descended, the Lord spoke these words to Noah: ..."**Come into the ark, you and all your household...**" (Gen. 7:1 NKJ). We are hearing these same words today: "A flood of tribulation and persecution is coming. Get your family together and bring them in."

When Israel was alerted to get ready to move out of Egypt, each family was instructed to sacrifice a lamb to cover their household. Jesus is our sacrificial Lamb whose blood is sufficient to cover our entire family.

One of the features of the last-day move of the Spirit of God is family salvation, family restoration, and family unity. If your children are away from home, you can take comfort from this passage in Jeremiah 31:16,17 which assures you that they will return.

In the parable, the prodigal son came home. The modern-day prodigals are going to do the same. Just as chickens come home to roost and cows come back to the barn at the close of the day, so our children will return to us before the final darkness descends. We are hearing this word all over the world. Believe it and be encouraged!

**Now therefore, go, and I will be with your
mouth and teach you what you shall say.
Exodus 4:12 NKJ**

Do you have it easy with words? Or is it difficult for you to express yourself? In this verse we are given an assurance of divine assistance in articulation, enunciation, and oral expression.

One day I came across an interesting word: *logorrhea*. According to the dictionary, it is a term used in psychology and psychiatry to indicate excessive and incoherent talk. I have not met too many people who suffer from logorrhea. I have met, however, many people who are verbally bound and unable to express themselves.

I once saw the dramatic recovery of a man over 40 years of age who was unable to communicate. He was a hard-working man, a good provider, a faithful husband, and a kind and caring father. His only problem was his inability to express himself orally. Physically he was able to speak, but intellectually, emotionally, and spiritually he was verbally frozen.

It was in a public worship service that a divine revelation came to me that this man's speech problem was a result of a childhood trauma. A heartless first-grade school teacher had shamed him in front of the class for not being able to write his name on the blackboard. The public ridicule was so damaging to his self-concept he withdrew into a protective shell of silence.

I prayed with the man and helped him to see his need to forgive those who had hurt him. He forgave, and was liberated on the spot. It was as though someone had cut the cord that was binding his tongue, and released him for a new-found freedom of speech!

Leah was tender eyed....
Genesis 29:17

The New King James Version of this verse says that Leah had "delicate" eyes. Another translation says her eyes were "attractive." A third states that she had "lovely" eyes.

The *Torah* gives a different report. It says that Jacob's first wife had "weak" eyes. An older English translation goes even further and states: "Leah's eyes were clouded."

Our research has revealed that Leah's eyes were, indeed, different from the other Jewish girls of her day. This difference may have been the reason she was less well-esteemed by Jacob than was Rachel.

I once read an interesting story (whether true or not I don't know) about a young Christian woman in the western world who grew up with a burning missionary call to the far-off land of Tibet. She only had one complaint with her lot in life. She didn't like her eyes. She fasted, prayed, and sought the Lord diligently — all to no avail. Her eyes remained the same. Undaunted, she still persisted in answering her call to foreign missions.

The day finally came for her departure to the mission field. Upon arrival, she found a warm welcome by the dark-skinned, dark-haired nationals who had always been known to turn away foreigners. Revival broke out and many were won to Christ. Upon inquiring about her ready acceptance, she was told that a prophecy had been given 100 years before that one day a young woman from the West would come with a message of salvation to the nation. This young woman would be easily recognizable, the prophecy stated; her eyes would be *blue*! Like Leah's!

**Please let my lord go on ahead before his servant.
I will lead on *slowly* at a pace which the livestock
that go before me, and the children, are able to
endure, until I meet my lord in Seir.**
Genesis 33:14 NKJ

Here is a verse which shows us how to deal with super-aggressive people. Every religious group has at least one person in it who is pushy, opinionated, strong-willed, vocal, and determined to "get this show on the road." How do you defuse such "hyper" people who "come on like gangbusters" to get things moving?

We can take a lesson from Jacob here. When he finally meets up with his long-lost brother and they turn toward home, he tells Esau to go on ahead and he will follow at a slower pace and meet him there later. Jacob and Esau may have been over that road many times before. It's likely that the two of them could have pressed on and reached their destination in record time. But Jacob held back from hurrying.

In verse 13 we see that he is concerned lest the flock and the children be overdriven. In verse 14 he expresses this concern by his suggestion that his brother go on ahead and allow him to follow along at a pace more suited to the animals and the young.

This is the way to handle aggressors. Tell them: "You go on ahead by yourself and set a pace that suits you. I am responsible for the young, tender, inexperienced travelers who move a lot slower than you. I will bring them along as quickly as they are able. We'll catch up with you later. It may take us a while longer to reach our destination, but we'll all make it. You go on; we'll meet you there."

Freely you have received, freely give.
Matthew 10:8 NKJ

I once knew of a father whose children craved attention from him. He seemingly was not able to give them the love they wanted from him. He went to the Lord in prayer and asked why he could not give the affection his offspring desired.

The Lord relayed this thought to his mind: "How can you give something to someone else that you have never received yourself?" The man realized that since he had never received parental affection himself, he had none to offer his own children.

The Lord did bless this father with an understanding of His love for us. Through Romans 5:5, the Lord showed him that unselfish, caring, giving, *agape* love is poured into our hearts by the Father, resides in us by the Son, and flows out of us by the Holy Spirit.

In life there are many things that we do not have. Consequently, we cannot give them to others. But there are many things we do have and can give. What you have freely received, that freely give.

We have received forgiveness. We are capable of forgiving.

We have received peace. We can give peace.

We have received light. We have light to share with others.

We have received joy. Let's pass it on.

At our conversion God poured His *agape* love into us. We have that love to give. As the Armed Forces advertisement says, "It's a great place to start!"

For unto us a Child is born....
Isaiah 9:6 NKJ

December 25 has been resisted by some as Christmas Day because of: 1) the improbability of shepherds being in the field during such a cold time as December (winter); 2) the pagan celebration of Saturnalia which falls on the same day (some believers fear that a pagan holiday was "borrowed" by the early Christians and given the "new dress" of Christian respectability; 3) the fact that the Eastern and Orthodox segments of the Church all celebrate the nativity on January 6. Some scholars seem to feel that the closer religious groups are to the original geographical sites of Bible events, the more accurate they are as to details. This would mean that the present-day groups closest to the Holy Land who celebrate Christmas on January 6 may know something the rest of us farther away have missed.

I am not trying either to defend or to question the authenticity of December 25 as the birthdate of Jesus. It really does not matter. However, an interesting quote has surfaced that does point to December 25 as the correct date of our Lord's birth. Justin Marty, Tertullian and Chrysostrom all state that in the public archives at Rome a registry existed of the census under August Caesar by which the Lord's birthday was conclusively established. Tertullian gives the words as he found them in the Roman archives, "Mary, the mother of Jesus." Chrysostrom asserts that through the public records of taxing preserved at Rome the date December 25 had long been known to the Christians of that city.

Whatever the case, today (as on any day) we can say with the prophet: **...unto us a Child is born....!**

Forever, O Lord,
Your word is settled in heaven.
Psalm 119:89 NKJ

Have you ever thought of a Scripture Hall of Fame? In eternity the possibility exists that each verse of scripture has a pavilion to give all the redeemed a historical overview of the verse and its history.

Can you imagine a building marked Genesis 1:1? In it would be the entire history of that verse, including all the mementos of how it came to be written. All the songs based on it. All the poems, pictures, articles, and stories derived from it. Even case histories of personages helped by it. I can visualize a replay room where we will be able to get a rerun of all the sermons preached throughout the ages on the subject of Genesis 1:1. After we have spent our time in the Genesis 1:1 Hall of Fame, we will then be able to move on to the next pavilion, Genesis 1:2.

"Your word is forever settled in heaven, O Lord." The Hebrew word translated **settled** in this verse means "to be stationed." "Your word is stationed permanently in heaven, O Lord."

One translation reads: "Your word stands firm in the heavens." Another states: "Your word is firmly fixed in the heavens." The Word of God will never become extinct, antiquated, passé, obsolete, archaic, outdated, or no longer functional. It will always remain fresh, new, lively, potent, illuminating, stimulating, challenging, and inspiring.

God's Word will last as long as heaven lasts — forever!

When my father and my mother forsake me,
Then the Lord will take care of me.
Psalm 27:10 NKJ

This verse has a wide range of possibilities. The word **forsake** stands at the farthest end of the word scale. It implies complete desertion, absolute rejection, total abandonment.

"Even if my own parents totally reject and desert me," the psalmist declares, "I can still make it in life because the Lord will take care of me." As tragic and regrettable as it is, parental neglect does not have to spell the end for a person. No one is destined to failure just because his parents failed in their duty to love and provide for him as they should have. Despite an unhappy past, the Lord still has a great future planned for that individual, an even greater one than his parents could ever have devised or provided.

But how do you share this verse with a person if his parents are present? How can you minister healing to the offspring without offending or hurting the parents? In order to minister to such people, the Lord allows me to share with them this modified version of this verse: "If my parents wanted to do things for me and were not able to, the Lord will take care of it. If there were things I needed that they could not provide, my God will meet that need. If they were not able to give me everything they would have liked to, my Father will make up those things to me in later life." This interpretation gives assurance to the person that all voids in his life will be filled, without seeming to judge or condemn either his past life or his parental upbringing. It comforts him, yet allows him and his parents to keep their dignity.

I humbled myself with fasting....
Psalm 35:13 NKJ

Fasting is a form of self-denial. It is a cure for unbelief. It is a pride-deflator, because no one can be proud on an empty stomach. Fasting is part of the Christian discipline. It demonstrates that no appetite masters the Christian, no hunger dominates him. It reminds him, "I do not live to eat, I eat to live."

The primary definition of fasting is "abstaining from food." It also includes the denial of pleasure, leisure, recreation, and hobbies. It is self-imposed discipline so a person can concentrate on seeking the Lord.

There are partial fasts. In Daniel 1, we find the Hebrew children eating only pulse (vegetables) and water for ten days. Yet at the end of that time they looked better than those who had dined on the king's fare. God blessed their self-denial openly and visibly.

Fasting is more conspicuous in the Old Testament than in the New. The Hebrews fasted on four different occasions: 1) times of grief and mourning (1 Sam. 31:13.), 2) times of personal and national need (2 Chron. 20:3), 3) times of honest repentance of sin or failure (1 Kings 21:27), and 4) commemorative days such as the day of atonement (Lev. 23:27).

In Jesus' day, religious people expressed their zeal by fasting each Monday and Thursday. (Luke 18:12.) Jesus warned against the common practice of marking the face so others could see that one was fasting. (Matt. 6:16–18.) It is not the denial of food or pleasure that makes fasting acceptable to God or helpful to the believer; rather, it is the attitude of the heart and the focus of attention upon the Lord that both pleases and prospers.

> Is this not the fast that I have chosen:
> To loose the bonds of wickedness,
> To undo the heavy burdens,
> To let the oppressed go free,
> And that you break every yoke?
> Isaiah 58:6 NKJ

When the disciples proved powerless to cast out the demon in a child, they asked the Lord why they had failed. (Mark 9:14–28.) His answer is enlightening: **"This kind can come out by nothing but prayer and fasting"** (v. 29 NKJ).

These words reveal the power base for moving in the realm of the supernatural. The prophet Isaiah says here that the fast of the Lord will radically change lives.

Fasting for aesthetic or health reasons produces physical benefits. Likewise, fasting for spiritual reasons produces spiritual benefits. Fasting can also demonstrate mastery over the appetite. Because it was the temptation of physical food (self-gratification) that caused man's downfall in the Garden of Eden, the Lord gave fasting (self-denial) as the way to spiritual power.

Through the ages those who have been great in faith and prayer have also fasted much. Faith needs prayer for its development and full growth. Prayer needs fasting for its completion. Fasting activates the believer's power and authority over the powers of darkness.

This verse implies that fasting will release the power of God in ways not otherwise possible. Fasting makes possible great deliverances. It breaks yokes, delivers captives, frees prisoners, and releases God's power in lives. Since God has chosen it, is this not the fast that you and I should also choose?

In fastings often....
2 Corinthians 11:27 NKJ

The week between Christmas day and New Year's day is an ideal time for fasting and prayer. All the Christmas activities are over and we find ourselves looking right into a brand new year. For those who are able to do so, this last week on the calendar is the best time of the year for soul searching.

In this verse Paul states that he fasted often. Here he is speaking of a voluntary denial of food. Earlier in the verse he mentions the hunger and thirst he had suffered as a result of his apostleship. Fasting and hunger are not the same. Hunger is an involuntary denial of food imposed by circumstances. In a fast, food is available but the person chooses not to eat it in order to better hear from the Lord.

Psychologists tell us that man has two basic appetites: food and sex. They relate these two drives to man's primal instincts for self-preservation and reproduction of his own kind. Man eats food, they say, for his own survival; he engages in sex to satisfy a deep-seated desire to assure the survival of the species.

The Christian does not deny that these two drives exist in man. He acknowledges these appetites. But he admits to a greater desire: hunger and thirst after righteousness. To the believer, his quest for God is even greater than his quest for sustenance and succession.

"In fastings often...." is an indication of the place the Lord occupied in the life of the great Apostle Paul. Seeking after God should also be Number One on our list of priorities.

**A land for which the Lord your God cares; the eyes
of the Lord your God are always on it, from the
beginning of the year to the very end of the year.
Deuteronomy 11:12 NKJ**

As we come to the end of this year and look back over
these past twelve months, we see so many times where the
Lord brought us through. His eyes were ever upon us and
His hand was always near to lift and sustain us.

Our having come through it all to this last day is a
tribute to the Lord's keeping power. It testifies to us and to
the world that, come what may, our God is faithful. We are
grateful to Him for His faithfulness in preserving us,
providing for us, and protecting us.

From the beginning of this year to this last day, His
eyes have been firmly set upon us in our progress. This
scripture lesson links past and future in one verse: "The
eyes of the Lord are always on *us*, from the beginning of the
year to the very end." It indicates past, present, and future
security: "He *has* delivered us (January 1 to December 30);
He *does* deliver us (today, December 31); and He *will yet*
deliver us (tomorrow, January 1 and throughout the new
year to follow)."

It might be good to pause to enumerate and reflect
upon all the good things the Lord has done for you this past
year. Use them as a basis for future blessings. The Lord of
the past is also the Lord of things to come. His eye is on
your daily and yearly progress. Like Paul, I am ...**confident
of this very thing, that He who has begun a good work in
you will complete it until the day of Jesus Christ** (Phil. 1:6
NKJ). God bless you!

References

Good News Bible, Today's English Version (GNB). Copyright © American Bible Society, 1966, 1971, 1976. Used by permission.

Interlinear Greek-English New Testament (INGENT) by George Ricker Berry. Copyright © 1897 by Hines & Noble. Reprinted by Baker Book House, Grand Rapids, Michigan.

New American Standard Bible (NASB). Copyright © The Lockman Foundation 1960, 1962, 1963, 1968, 1971, 1972, 1973, 1975, 1977.

The Amplified Bible, New Testament (AMP). Copyright © 1958, 1987 by The Lockman Foundation, La Habra, California. Used by permission.

The Amplified Bible, Old Testament (AMP). Copyright © 1965, 1987 by Zondervan Publishing House, Grand Rapids, Michigan. Used by permission.

The Bible: A New Translation (MOF). Copyright © 1950, 1952, 1953, 1954 by James A. R. Moffatt. Harper & Row, Publishers, Inc., New York, NY.

The Holy Bible: New International Version (NIV). Copyright © 1973, 1978, 1984 by the International Bible Society. Used by permission of Zondervan Bible Publishers.

The Holy Bible: Revised Standard Version (RSV). Copyright © 1946, 1952 by Division of Christian Education of the National Council of the Churches of Christ in the United States of American.

The Living Bible (TLB) Copyright © 1971. Used by permission of Tyndale House Publisher, Inc., Wheaton, IL 60189. All rights reserved.

The Modern Language Bible, The New Berkeley Version In Modern English (MLB). Copyright © 1945, 1959, 1969 by Zondervan Publishing House.

About The Author

Dick Mills is intensely involved in the Scriptural renewal and personal upbuilding of the Body of Christ. He shares the "hidden riches of secret places" with sensitivity and compassion. Many have been touched by the hand of God through this man's dynamic ministry.

Pat Robertson, founder of Christian Broadcasting Network and Regent University, says: "Dick Mills has one of the most unique ministries of any man of God I know. God has gifted him with what amounts to a photographic memory containing thousands of scriptures. Under the anointing of the Holy Spirit and at an appropriate time, these words are brought forth to minister to the needs of individuals. Dick has been used of God to bring deep spiritual blessings at crucial times in my own life, and I'm sure this is true of tens of thousands of others around the country."

Dick and his wife Betty live in Hemet, California. This veteran of more than thirty years has ministered to more than twenty denominations in countries throughout the world, including Israel, England, Australia, Singapore, Canada, and Latin America.

For a complete list of tapes and books
by Dick Mills, or to receive his
newsletter, *The Good Word Just For You*, write:

Dick Mills
P. O. Box 520
San Jacinto, CA 92383

Please include your prayer requests and comments
when you write.

For additional copies
of this book
in Canada contact:

Word Alive
P.O. Box 670
Niverville, Manitoba
CANADA R0A 1E0

The Harrison House Vision

Proclaiming the truth and the power
Of the Gospel of Jesus Christ
With excellence;

Challenging Christians to
Live victoriously,
Grow spiritually,
Know God intimately

Harrison House • P. O. Box 35035 • Tulsa, OK 74153